Air Power and the Ground War in Vietnam

Ideas and Actions

by

Donald J. Mrozek
Senior Research Fellow
Airpower Research Institute

Air University Press
Maxwell Air Force Base, Alabama 36112-5532

January 1988

Library of Congress Cataloging in Publication Data
Mrozek, Donald J.
    Air Power and the Ground War in Vietnam.

    Includes bibliographies and index.
    1. Vietnamese Conflict, 1961–1975—Aerial Operations, American. I.
Title.
DS558.8.M79   1988   959.704'348   87–31931

DISCLAIMER

For sale by the Superintendent of Documents
US Government Printing Office
Washington, D.C. 20402

In Memory of Joseph J. Malone

Contents

PART ONE
EVERYBODY'S WAR, NOBODY'S WAR

PART TWO
"TWO, THREE . . . MANY VIETNAMS"

PART THREE
REFLECTIONS AND CONCLUSIONS

LIST OF ILLUSTRATIONS

Foreword

Dr Donald J. Mrozek's research sheds considerable light on how the use of air power evolved in the Vietnam War. Much more than simply retelling events, Mrozek analyzes how history, politics, technology, and the complexity of the war drove the application of air power in a long and divisive struggle.

Mrozek delves into a wealth of original documentation, and his scholarship is impeccable. His analysis is thorough and balanced. His conclusions are well reasoned but will trouble those who have never seriously considered how the application of air power is influenced by factors far beyond the battlefield. Whether or not the reader agrees with Mrozek, the quality of his research and analysis makes his conclusions impossible to ignore.

JOHN C. FRYER, JR.
Brigadier General, USAF
Commander
Center for Aerospace Doctrine,
    Research, and Education

ABOUT THE AUTHOR

Dr Donald J. Mrozek

Donald J. Mrozek is Professor of History at Kansas State University, where he has taught since 1972. He earned both his MA and PhD degrees at Rutgers University, and his dissertation study on defense policy during the presidency of Harry Truman yielded articles in publications such as *Military Affairs* and *The Business History Review*. Later research in wartime and postwar defense issues resulted in articles in such journals as the *Annals of Iowa* and *Missouri Historical Review*. In 1980, his article "The *Croatan* Incident: The US Navy and the Problem of Racial Discrimination after World War II" appeared in *Military Affairs*. Also in 1980, he co-edited *The Martin Marauder and the Franklin Allens: A Wartime Love Story,* with Robin Higham and Jeanne Louise Allen Newell. With his colleague Robin Higham, he has also co-edited *A Guide to the Sources of U.S. Military History,* including the 1981 and 1986 supplementary volumes.

Dr Mrozek has also engaged in research, published, and taught American culture. Some of his publications have fused the areas of military and cultural history. In 1980, his essay "The Cult and Ritual of Toughness in Cold War America" appeared in Ray Browne, ed., *Rituals and Ceremonies in Popular Culture*. In 1984, "The Interplay of Metaphor and Practice in the US Defense Department's Use of Sport" was published in the *Journal of American Culture,* and in 1985, "Sport and the American Military: Diversion and Duty" appeared in the centennial issue of the *Research Quarterly for Exercise and Sport*.

One of his more recent sole-authored military history publications entitled "The Limits of Innovation: Aspects of Air Power in Vietnam" appeared in the January–February 1985 issue of *Air University Review*. In 1986, *Air University Review* also published his essay "In Search of the Unicorn," a discussion of the broad development of military reform movements since the Federalist era. Having completed recent studies focused on the era of the Vietnam War, Dr Mrozek plans a book-length essay on US defense policy after World War II.

Acknowledgments

Only those who have had great help can fully appreciate how important it is in developing a difficult argument on a contentious issue. Perhaps only those persons will sense the depth of my gratitude to Col Kenneth J. Alnwick, former director of the Airpower Research Institute, for his early and continuing interest in this project, and to Col Donald D. Stevens, then director of the Airpower Research Institute and commander of the Air University Center for Aerospace Doctrine, Research, and Education (AUCADRE). I have benefited from the thoughtful suggestions and insights of Lt Col Donald R. Baucom and Col Dennis M. Drew, who have guided research in the Airpower Research Institute. Their friendship I value as much as their advice.

In the revision and stabilization of this study, few persons labored as hard—and had as much to labor over—as Mr Thomas Lobenstein and Mr Preston Bryant of the Air University Press in AUCADRE. Their diligent efforts, close attention to wording, and ability to catch the thrust of my intended arguments have made this work much better than would otherwise have been the case. The skilled and highly responsive staff of the Air University Library made many of the tasks associated with developing the arguments in this work much easier than is usually the case in any long project. In addition, I owe a great debt to AUCADRE's highly professional and capable Document Processing Center—to all who worked on this project but especially to Jo Ann Perdue and Marcia Williams, successive directors in document processing. Also, Dorothy McCluskie oversaw skillfully the transformation of this work from a manuscript into a book.

The atmosphere of serious inquiry and the genuine desire to avoid merely convenient answers to nagging questions made my two years as a Visiting Research Fellow at AUCADRE's Airpower Research Institute a personal and professional pleasure of a most high order. The last thing a civilian working on temporary assignment in a military agency wishes to be is a court historian. So it was especially reassuring to find that this was the last thing AUCADRE wanted us to be. Beyond that, I must note my profound respect for the diverse talents I saw in the Air Force personnel with whom I worked, both military and civilian, and for the modesty with which they carry their ability. Informal conversations with a number of persons helped me to gain some added feel for the Air Force as a service. Without slighting the informal instruction I received from all of my military and civilian colleagues in research, I am especially grateful to Lt Col David J. Dean and Lt Col William B. Mack.

The personal aspects of living and working in Montgomery proved to be an unexpectedly rich benefit of my taking a temporary assignment at Maxwell Air Force Base. I shall always remember the friendliness and courtesy of the people I met during these past two years. Special fondness is reserved for the Montgomery Track and Running Club, however, and for the welcoming and engaging people I met on the run. It was also a pleasure to share my time in the South with my family, especially my parents, sometimes in person but more frequently in letters. Words can only suggest what their continuing support means.

This work is dedicated to the memory of Joseph J. Malone, a fine historian and genuine expert in Middle Eastern affairs, whose passing made me realize how much he meant—and continues to mean—to me. I used to kid that Joe Malone was the man who, as chairman of the Department of History at Kansas State University in 1972, "had the good taste to hire me." Actually, though, he was a man who took the risk of doing so. His support of my professional efforts did much to sustain my belief that something might come of it all in the end. I came to value Joe Malone all the more in the context of my closer studies of the frustrations and pain of the American experience in Vietnam. Only then did I appreciate Joe's service to our country in World War II and his sense of how life outside the military or the government might also be a real service to the nation's decency as well as to its security and prosperity. For that, I am grateful to him; and for that, I could not forget him even if I tried.

DONALD J. MROZEK
Visiting Research Fellow
Airpower Research Institute

Introduction

Ultimately, this study is about a smaller Vietnam War than that which is commonly recalled. It focuses on expectations concerning the impact of air power on the ground war and on some of its actual effects, but it avoids major treatment of some of the most dramatic air actions of the war, such as the bombing of Hanoi. To many who fought the war and believe it ought to have been conducted on a still larger scale or with fewer restraints, this study may seem almost perverse, emphasizing as it does the utility of air power in conducting the conflict as a ground war and without total exploitation of our most awe-inspiring technology.

Justifications for such a study may take many forms. The simplest is that air power contributed much to lower level conflict. Allowing for the great importance of strategic deterrence, the United States will still face challenges to its own and its allies' interests at far lower levels of conflict. In the context of these likely problems, the Vietnam experience assumes considerable interest.

Although the chapters in this study are intended to form a coherent and unified argument, each also offers discrete messages. The chapters are not meant to be definitive. They do not exhaust available documentary material, and they often rely heavily on published accounts. Nor do they provide a complete chronological picture of the uses of air power, even with respect to the ground war. Nor is coverage of areas in which air power was employed—South Vietnam, Laos, Cambodia, and North Vietnam—evenly distributed nor necessarily proportionate to the effort expended in each place during the war. Lastly, some may find one or another form of air power either slightly or insufficiently treated. Such criticisms are beside the point, for the objectives of this study are to explore a comparatively neglected theme—the impact of air power on the ground—and to encourage further utilization of lessons drawn from the Vietnam experience.

Part one examines the way in which ideas about air power affected the thinking of many Air Force personnel about how to fight both before and during the Vietnam War, some relevant conflicts within the Air Force, the relationship between interservice differences and the arrangements made for command and control, and the tendency among both civilians and the military to fail to differentiate between war as combat and war as politics. The three chapters do more than provide historical background. They argue that the Air Force was neither neutral nor passive with respect to the conflict in Southeast Asia. These chapters also argue that Air Force ideas produced only one set of strongly advocated options for managing the war. The centers of civilian authority themselves became important actors in the war in Southeast Asia far beyond mere reaction. Problems do not exist in a vacuum, nor are their dimensions understandable in isolation. They take on meaning when they pass through the lens of a beholder; and the character of the war in Southeast Asia could never be established to the general agreement of all parties on the allied side because they were using different lenses. Further, this frustrating divergence in the perception of the conflict severely complicated the development of a universally satisfactory command and control system. These and other factors show how problems originating largely in the United States added to the troubling complexity of an apparently Southeast Asian problem.

The succeeding three chapters deal more directly with the conduct of the war in Southeast Asia, although they are far from being conventional operational histories. While this study does not claim that air power in any simple sense revolutionized ground warfare, nor that it displaced traditional principles of war with some new set of principles, it does claim that air power inclined many military leaders and some civilians to alter their understandings of what the principles meant in the context of contemporary operations. Chapters 4, 5, and 6 deal with these altered understandings, their achievements and limits, and some of their implications. Traditional terms such as *interdiction, firepower, mobility,* and *surprise* make their appearance in these chapters, but the principal focus is to follow the extent to which they received a novel twist in the context of the Vietnam and Southeast Asian experiences.

The concluding chapter provides an opportunity for synthesis, for stating conclusions both general and specific in nature, and for enumerating recommendations based on the lessons offered by the Vietnam conflict. An assessment of what various parties have concluded about the Vietnam War becomes pertinent.

PART ONE

EVERYBODY'S WAR, NOBODY'S WAR

Many readily accept as a truism that US commitment to the war in Vietnam lacked unity, clarity, and coherence. But few ever state, much less accept, the corollary—that the commitment of the various parties to the war was similarly mooted. Fixed points of reference were lacking; and, without criteria for performance that might be imposed across the board on civilian and military agencies to determine mission accomplishment, the war "fell between the cracks." With everybody drawn into the act, it was a war belonging to no one in particular—perhaps not even President Lyndon Johnson, whose name was most often affixed to the conflict. Fragmentation of authority was paralleled by fragmentation of responsibility and, equally important, by fragmentation of the *sense* of responsibility. The attitude alleged to have governed much of US behavior in the later stages of the war—that the conflict not be lost "on our watch" but, by implication, on someone else's—was the final, bitter, and sterile incarnation of this erosion of responsibility, which in turn was born of the inability to impose a coherent vision of the war as a whole.

The US effort in Vietnam was not an intellectually, culturally, or technically neutral response to external problems created by an external enemy. Nor was it unaffected by its own internal dynamics—the American way of war which included a specific set of preferences for different groups about how best to use air power. Thus, what Americans thought about air power as they approached the problems of Southeast Asia became a distinct player in the conflict, affecting the war. Perhaps it would be better to say players in the plural, since there were disagreements.

Consciousness of these ideas and the self-limiting and self-restraining qualities they impose is the key for the future. Otherwise, we bind ourselves to unthinking misuse of our resources, and we risk misinterpreting the situation while we unconsciously protect our less-examined predilections.

The military services often seemed far more interested in jockeying with one another than the situation may have demanded, and this rivalry had several serious effects: (1) efforts to resolve conflicts over command and control and strategy went on far too long, perhaps too long to come to grips with the real problem; (2) a decision once agreed upon could not easily be overturned, since it represented either a delicate political compromise or too much invested effort and sunk cost; and (3) whatever the reality behind the service's motivations, the military seemed so self-serving as to undermine the authority they could have mustered with the executive branch, in the moments when it was open to advice, or with the Congress.

Interservice and intraservice rivalries, especially at lower levels, cannot be expected to vanish magically in wartime. Their resolution must receive high priority in peacetime if US forces are to be capable of handling the multifaceted aspects of a low-intensity conflict; and as such conflicts escalate to mid-level or above, the damage resulting from interservice rivalry becomes even more serious.

Successive administrations in the United States failed to make clear or unqualified commitments to what they wished to achieve in Southeast Asia. (The Nixon administration, once it set getting out of Vietnam as its maximum military *and* general policy priority, was a possible exception.) Even the Kennedy administration qualified—perhaps even contradicted—its own verbal commitment to counterinsurgency. It did so, for example, by leaping to emergency insertion of US combat-capable troops to buy time when the accepted view was that counterinsurgency must be handled slowly and gradually. That view of effective counterinsurgency also, in effect, contained the risk of loss and even general failure; but the Kennedy administration could not swallow it. The Johnson administration, despite the magnitude of its escalations, perceived that it was engaged in a continuing political process even more than in waging a war; but there is reason to suspect that the interpretation given to Johnson's ''language of military actions'' in Washington was different from that given in Hanoi.

Despite the desire to keep options open, an administration must take into account that the use of military force at various levels and in various combinations begins to impose certain limiting qualities on its freedom of action. Once a military option is to be considered, it must be assessed in terms of both its military and political effects. Further, for all the talk of responsiveness of military forces, civilians and military alike must remember that there are limits to both the responsiveness and the flexibility of any piece of bureaucratic machinery: a tactic can be changed faster in the mind than in the field, and a strategy can be jotted down faster on paper than it can be translated into force structure and deployment. Vietnam illustrated, among other things, that ideas and execution can be persistently out of phase. One would hesitate to say that virtually any one policy should have been maintained rather than risk a mess caused by changes in policy. Yet this view is useful enough to invite consideration.

The Vietnam War does not tell us whether we can effectively fight a counterinsurgency, since we were never fully dedicated to it. Counterinsurgency is therefore not a discredited or disproven concept. A similar logic applies to many technical and operational aspects of the war. In short, the subsets of the war—its practical matters—can be decoupled from some of its theoretical ones. Efficiency does not prove effectiveness. Efficiency means merely the skillful execution of a predetermined routine; effectiveness suggests that the routine had a useful purpose and that executing it achieved the predetermined goal. But ineffectiveness in Vietnam does not necessarily indicate probable ineffectiveness elsewhere.

CHAPTER 1

Air Power Theories, Air Force Thinking, and the Conflict in Vietnam
The Past Was Prologue

Ever since the First World War, Air Power has held political allure, seeming to offer the promise of almost painless victory. The promise has not always been fulfilled, but it is part of the nature of air power that its real effects are often difficult to separate from those claimed.

William Shawcross

How the Air Force and the other services interpreted the Vietnam War depended largely on what they thought about military power and its employment in general. Although events in Southeast Asia had discrete features, they looked different to observers according to their various perspectives. Different points of view generated different visions of war, sometimes calling for contrary solutions. And the war on the ground and in the air over Vietnam played against the war within the minds of military and civilian observers as to whose vision was right. Thus Air Force thinking and mentality became one among many autonomous variables in shaping and interpreting events in Vietnam.

As the United States became more involved in the war in Vietnam, it lacked a coherent understanding of air power—what it could do, what equipment it required, what organization it needed, and what conflicts it was best suited for. Nor was there even a common sense of what air power was. Did the term apply simply to anything that flew, or must it be reserved for special air vehicles organized in special ways? At the same time, despite the uncertainties concerning air power and how to use it, there were deep-seated hopes about its potential. The promise of air power persisted, no matter what difficulties had appeared in air operations in the decades before the Vietnam War. But the effort to fulfill the promise was fragmented, broken among the several military services and even among factions within them. The fragmentation so much a part of the history of air power came to bear on the war in Southeast Asia. Past debates over air power formed a complex prologue to Vietnam.

Ideas prominent in the Air Force in the early 1960s were rooted in decades of thinking by air power theorists about concepts and doctrines that were articulated with special force after 1947. These ideas carried forward in a direct line from the interwar years into the Vietnam era. Despite the diversity of views within the Air Force, there were broad areas of consensus: the importance of the strategic deterrent, the effectiveness of manned bombing, and the need for air superiority.

And, notwithstanding differences among the several services, there was interservice acceptance that the vertical dimension in modern warfare could not be evaded. Yet the closer one adhered to original ideas about air power or to their lineal descendants, the closer one came to developing an absolute model for the use of air power in warfare—one that might not only run afoul of competing interpretations, developed in the other services or even among civilians, but also force the realities of the war at hand to conform to the expectations of one's theory. The closer one's views about war in the 1960s conformed to air power theories shaped in the interwar years, the less might they respond to novel pressures and demands imposed by events or civilian authorities. The more one insisted upon the decisiveness of one form of air power, the greater the danger that other forms would languish. In this way, theories about air power and specific Air Force thinking about it became players in the conflicts of the 1950s and 1960s.

The distinctiveness of the way of war advocated by US exponents of air power is itself part of a broader scheme. The attractiveness of air power to Americans—even in its extreme or ideal forms—stems largely from its compatibility with deep-seated national tendencies and preferences as to the conduct of war. In *The American Way of War*, for example, historian Russell F. Weigley delineated the characteristic ways the United States has fought its wars. Americans have persistently seen themselves as outnumbered, whether against more numerous Indians in the seventeenth century, the so-called Yellow Peril of the nineteenth century, or the stereotypical Chinese hordes and Russian bear in the twentieth.

Occasionally, this feeling of insufficiency is fortified by isolated events such as the Custer massacre or perhaps the siege at Khe Sanh. In their desire to offset this perceived sense of numerical inferiority, US leaders have developed an intense reliance on firepower and technology. From firing cannon to overawe the Indians in colonial Virginia through the comparatively heavy use of firepower by Benjamin Church in King Philip's War to the increasing carnage of the US Civil War, these tendencies strengthened. As the sickening anxiety over attrition in World War I was added to the stored memories of earlier wars, bombardment aircraft seemed to offer a clean, scientific, and lifesaving means to attain security objectives in a manner that best suited the nation's peculiar strengths while minimizing its shortcomings.[1]

In part, the rise of air power to its integral place in US strategy and doctrine depended on an altered distinction between combatant and noncombatant. This process began in the Civil War with William Tecumseh Sherman and Ulysses S. Grant. Both of these Union generals accepted the idea of a people's war in which those civilian institutions that supported an enemy's military capability became legitimate military targets as a prototypical home front. This idea later became part of a larger reevaluation of Jominian and Clausewitzian strategic thinking that led to a broadened sense of permissible conduct in war. And on this, the structure of a strategic air offensive was ultimately built.

Gen Frederick C. Weyand, former chief of staff of the Army and the last head of the US Military Assistance Command, Vietnam, styled the US way of war as "particularly violent, deadly and dreadful. We believe in using 'things'—artillery, bombs, massive firepower—in order to conserve our soldiers' lives." General Weyand also noted that the enemies faced by the United States in Vietnam did nearly the opposite, compensating for a "lack of 'things' by expending men instead of machines."[2] The enemy were not only people and the materiel they could gather, but the very way in which war and its prosecution were conceived. Not only was the United States at war in Vietnam, but its whole way of thinking about conflict was at war, too. Serious reflection on the Korean War might have prepared the United States better for the kind of Vietcong and North Vietnamese commitment that was encountered in Vietnam; and failure to capitalize on that earlier experience suggested the persistence of this special US mentality about war. Actual conditions in the theater of conflict comprise only one part of a much broader phenomenon. The distinctive way US strategists view war is especially evident in the manner in which they have looked at air power and its role in combat.

The Thrust of US Air Power Theories

Several persistent themes have appeared amid the accumulation of ideas about air power in America, and these eventually influenced the use of air forces in Vietnam.[3] These themes derive their coherence less from how they interacted technically in the events of the 1960s and 1970s than from their common origin in the thinking done between World Wars I and II. First, air power's proponents, especially the most ardent, have typically stressed the essential novelty of the air age and the consequent irrelevance of historical experience. The new principles and practices of air power supposedly superseded old military lessons and dogmas, which had arisen in reflection on the character of surface warfare. New doctrines for air power risked ignoring the test of experience, which obviously could be formed only in the past. However much the advocates of air power would later seek evidence in its short history, validation for their contentions lay in theory itself. The emphasis on novelty was also made possible by a corollary feature so often discussed that it appears to be a separate theme. The advocates of air power developed an especially strong dependence upon technological innovation and a peculiar attachment to weapons and systems projected for the future rather than those of the more conventional present. Although land power and sea power theorists were also attracted to technology, air enthusiasts showed a special commitment because the movement and service they fostered owed their very identities to a comparatively recent technological breakthrough. While they accepted the importance of air forces as a constant and an absolute, they insisted on a diligent and permanent search for improved aircraft and weapons types to fulfill airpower's promise. The words of Gen Henry H. Arnold shortly after World War II exemplify this thrust:

> The first essential of air power necessary for peace and security is the preeminence in research. . . . We must count on scientific advances requiring us to replace about one-fifth of existing Air Forces equipment each year and we must be sure that these additions are the most advanced in the whole world.[4]

Although he wanted numbers, General Arnold regarded improved technology as essential. The result was a diminished opinion of the worth of those aircraft and weapons that were not of the most recent and most advanced design.

A third theme advanced by proponents of air power in this country has been the essentiality—perhaps the dominance—of the strategic air offensive. The best defense in a generic sense depended upon a force that could project an offense in the concrete sense. For example, defending the United States seemed to require an air force that could strike the enemy's heartland. In time, this attitude proved compatible with the formal strategy of deterrence. But because it had roots in a strategic vision that considered doing away with surface engagements, the Air Force and its forebearers gave considerably lower priority to some matters, such as the support of ground and sea forces, which were vital to the Army and Navy. At the very least, the Air Force showed this priority in ways which the other services found hard to accept.

Fourth, since the air around the world had no borders, theorists regarded it as an indivisible medium for military purposes. They thought that air power should likewise be unified in one military service. In fact, the argument for an autonomous air offensive was based in part on the idea that the atmosphere on the one hand and the land and sea on the other are completely separate theaters of warfare. This view clearly supported a separate air service, independent air campaigns, and the supremacy of air force personnel in control of air assets during joint operations. Later, aspirations of the various services matched the way each force looked at the medium in which it operated. For example, basic Air Force doctrine asserted that "the medium in which air forces operate—space—is an indivisible field of activity"; hence, it was necessary to preserve the independent command of air forces. This doctrine also implied that, in any supposed partnership among the services, the air component should be dominant even when the theater of operations was no more than regional. Thus, Air Force Manual (AFM) 1–2, *United States Air Force Basic Doctrine (1955)*, substantially contradicted Army doctrine expressed in Field Manual (FM) 100–5, *Operations,* which claimed preeminence for the ground forces precisely because they operated on land. The Navy took a rhetorical middle ground that satisfied neither the Army nor the Air Force. In US Naval Warfare Publication 10, the Navy emphasized that mobility, largely by sea, enhanced US ability to put pressure on enemy territory. Navy doctrine left the exact role of air power and air strategy undefined, describing it as being "in the process of historic development."[5]

A fifth theme is in some respects the most important. Air power enthusiasts and advocates tended to adopt a particular interpretation of what air power was; that is, what its dominant aspect was, and in what mode it could be used most effectively. They focused overwhelming attention on the strategic air offensive. Other considerations—even one so basic as air superiority—became largely the functional servants of the air offensive. Thinking about air power in a broader sense was noticeably lacking. Perhaps the case for air power's future significance and for the necessity of an independent air force hinged on its claim to the dominant strategic military role. Yet, however genuine their commitment to this vision, its authors narrowed the unspoken definition of air power while seeking to give it reality. Various thinkers, theorists, and practitioners of air power manifested these ideas in their various works. The themes meshed, blended, and interacted, forming a general context rather than an analytically precise list of particulars in the minds of air power advocates; but they altered the climate in which future conflicts were understood.

The Ascendancy of the Offensive

Gen William "Billy" Mitchell, a prophet and martyr in the cause of independent air power, sometimes defended a fundamental truth with a discomforting multitude of intelligent guesses. In a sense, the need to defend the infant air force encouraged the most optimistic interpretations of debatable and complex issues. In *Winged Defense* (1925), for example, Mitchell sought to emulate the sweeping power of Alfred T. Mahan by posting a whole defense system based on air power. He not only proclaimed air power's eminence as the new and dominant medium of transportation, but also saw useful peacetime roles for air power that supposedly made armies and navies wasteful and obsolete.[6] Yet there were differences in approach between Mahan and Mitchell that persisted in debates among their successors decades later. For one thing, Mahan's work was largely historical while Mitchell's was largely predictive.

Among the critical characteristics of Mahan's view of sea power, which was credible and valuable even for those outside the naval fraternity, were:

● It was neither bound to highly specific technologies nor threatened by changes in technology.

● Sea-lanes were limited and definable, despite the vastness of the oceans, and thus credibly open to dispute among competing powers.

● Sea power not only deterred enemies but promoted further economic growth.

● The size of a nation's navy should correlate realistically to the growth of the nation's shipping and the importance of the interests linked to it; and navy spending should relate to a measurable standard, matching seagoing force with seaborne interests.[7]

7

Unlike Mahan, who insisted that theories of sea power in the age of steam grew from experience in the age of sail, air power theorists had relatively little experience from which to project. They were therefore compelled to predict from theorizing and to extrapolate from the nature of available technologies.[8] Thus, air theorists were freed from the limitations often suggested by historical experience. But because their imaginations were unrestrained, air theorists ran the risk of subordinating strategic thought to advances in engineering and technology—a danger they seemed to recognize only reluctantly. The present was deemed to offer little that was applicable to the future, and the failures of current technology did relatively little to deter wide-ranging optimism about great and effective weapons that always seem just around the corner. This inclination tended to make strategy a hostage of machinery, and it invited reluctance to adapt doctrine to experience.

Dismissal of the past as irrelevant to the future pervaded Mitchell's *Winged Defense*. Contrasting the age of air power with its predecessors, Mitchell wrote:

> Hindenburg looked back to Hannibal's battle of Cannae, and made his dispositions to fight the Russians at Tannenberg. Napoleon studied the campaigns of Alexander the Great and Genghis Khan, the Mongol. The navies drew their inspiration from the battle of Actium in the time of the Romans and the sea fight of Trafalgar.
>
> In the development of air power, one has to look ahead and not backward and figure out what is going to happen, not too much what has happened. That is why the older services have been psychologically unfit to develop this new arm to the fullest extent practicable with the methods and means at hand.[9]

The Air Force's chronic impatience with history originated in such thinking. Moreover, Mitchell's ideas anticipated the penchant for reconciling apparent discrepancies in strategic thought and theory with optimistic predictions of new inventions. Thus, hardware served not only to carry out theory but to protect it. Whatever lessons experience seemed to offer, theories could always be defended by weapons yet to be built.

In prophesying aviation developments, Billy Mitchell adopted a tone of absolute certainty, irritating both ground and sea forces while rousing the spirits of his followers. In *Our Air Force* (1921), he contended "That airships will be a potent factor in all communications in a comparatively few years, there can be no doubt." The words "there can be no doubt" conveyed the certitude of a visionary, even though the prediction was never quite fulfilled.[10]

Mitchell's role may have been that of prophet more than strategist, but his pronouncements favored a doctrinal slant that was a significant and influential part of his legacy: the world of air power was too new to pay much attention to older experience and theory; ascendancy in the age of air power would depend upon technological superiority; and the medium of air would encourage a sweeping global perspective, dictating particular strategic concepts and force structures. Mitchell's successors debated the most effective way to employ air power and the most appropriate ways to assure and foster its future within the broad framework of Mitchell's assumptions.

Such ideas might have been dismissed as mere footnotes in the history of American military thought had they not become central forces in shaping the attitudes and institutions of our nascent air force. What Mitchell advocated eventually became part of the core of Air Service teaching. In 1921, Maj William C. Sherman, a faculty member at the Air Service Field Officers' School, underscored the need for independence from the doctrines of the other services: "In deriving the doctrine that must underlie all principles of employment of the air force, we must not be guided by conditions surrounding the use of ground troops, but must seek our own doctrine . . . in the element in which the air force operates."[11] Such thinking clearly pointed toward commitment to an independent air campaign, strengthening the interdependence of the air offensive and an autonomous force to carry it out. But it also suggested an especially firm view of doctrine as something deeper, broader, and more enduring than the conduct of war. Air power thinkers tended to base general doctrinal positions on specific hardware and systems while elevating the scientific principles behind the hardware to the status of law.[12]

The studies of officers in the Air Corps Tactical School during the 1920s and 1930s clearly reflected a tendency to emphasize the air offensive and aerial bombardment, and the War Department's insistence on a subordinate role for air power in combat strengthened the deep commitment of these officers to the idea of an air offensive.

But not all air officers were supportive of the independent air force concept. Suggestive of opposing views giving air forces a less central role was a 1928 paper on "The Doctrine of Air Force," forwarded by Air Service Lt Col C. C. Culver. He concluded that "the air component . . . always supports the ground forces, no matter how decisive its . . . operations may be, nor how indirect its support." Maj Gen James E. Fechet, who had become chief of the Air Corps in 1927, objected to the statement as defective, even if it did conform to War Department guidelines.

> The objective of war is to overcome the enemy's will to resist, and the defeat of his army, his fleet or the occupation of his territory is merely a means to this end and none of them is the true objective. If the true objective can be reached without the necessity of defeating or brushing aside the enemy force on the ground or water and the proper means furnished to subdue the enemy's will and bring the war to a close, and the object of war can be obtained with less destruction and lasting after effects than has heretofore been the case. At present the Air Force provides the only means for such an accomplishment.[13]

Such notions as brushing aside hostile armies conjured up visions of a relatively easy victory and pointed even more sharply to the widening gulf between air power thinkers and the leaders of ground and naval forces.

The Baker Board, in its mid-1934 report, widened the rift. The report expressed the established view of the War Department as to the Army's place in the scheme of defense.

> The idea that aviation can replace any of the other elements of our armed forces is found, on analysis, to be erroneous. . . . Since ground forces alone are capable of occupying territory, or, with certainty, preventing occupation of our own territory, the Army with its own air forces remains the ultimate decisive factor in war.[14]

Air power advocates have focused on this remark precisely because it opposed the formation of a separate and enlarged air force. It also provides an instructive clue about the conceptual underpinning of the Army.

Following the Baker Board's discouraging opinion, air power advocates redoubled their efforts. They recognized that escort aircraft might be needed and that control of the air was a critical variable, but they pinned their greatest hopes on independent air campaigns aimed at the deep sources of the enemy's strength and thus on the strategic bomber. Secretary of War Harry Woodring approved a report by the War Department Air Board, agreed to by Gen George Marshall: "The basis of Air Power is the bombardment plane."[15] Although this report did not settle the broader conceptual and strategic issue of the relative worth of air, land, and sea forces, it did provide authority to develop a force that air theorists saw as the very heart of air power.

This emphasis did not decline with the coming of World War II. The war did much to liberate the officers of the air service, but the realities did not conform to the fondest expectations of air power enthusiasts. And failure to establish old Air Corps views as current US defense policy was disturbing. Controversies over proper tactics and targeting for bombing, especially in the European theater, offset the satisfaction of achieving a de facto status of equality as an autonomous service. In fact, the war became a source of complaint for various air power purists. They attacked the decisions to rebuild the US Navy and conduct large-scale ground operations as fundamentally wrong and wasteful. They argued that the country would get better results by expending its resources on a more modern force—the air arm.

The most articulate proponent of this view was Alexander P. de Seversky. An aircraft designer and businessman as well as a theorist, and later a lecturer at the Air University, de Seversky saw no virtue in dispassion. He boldly claimed that air power could bring victory in the world war without much help from land and sea forces. He sought to supplant the navalism of Mahan, whose persuasiveness was a barrier to full-scale commitment to air power. Nevertheless, de Seversky borrowed heavily from Mahan's terminology. In his book *Victory Through Air Power* (1942), he referred explicitly to passages from Mahan's most famous text and elaborated on the notion of an enveloping "air ocean." He wrote of "dreadnoughts of the skies" that would wage "an interhemispheric war direct across oceans, with air power fighting not over this or that locality, but by longitude and latitude anywhere in the uninterpreted 'air ocean'." But while imitating Mahan's rhetoric, de Seversky departed from Mahan's theories. Rather than just learn from the experience of World War II, he debated the whole shape of the war even as it was being fought. De Seversky called for bold departures in force structure and strategy. He even claimed that military aviation in the war had shaped "new principles of warfare." This new way of making war had to be freed from ground and sea commanders who were fatally infected with older strategic ideas and, hence, unable to appreciate the true role of air power. Mincing no words, de Seversky described air power as

> a force that eludes static, orthodox minds no matter how brilliant they may be. Air power speaks a strategic language so new [despite his own borrowing from Mahan] that translation into the hackneyed idiom of the past is impossible. It calls not only for new machines and techniques of warmaking but for new men unencumbered by routine thinking.[16]

The visionary's impatience with evolutionary, gradual change had clearly not been the exclusive property of Billy Mitchell.

De Seversky could not conceal his disdain for minds that subjected the claims of air power enthusiasts to the test of its present technology. "The critics," he complained, "are unable to see the *potentialities* of air power *beyond the horizons of its present equipment* and its present tactics. They do not take in the full majestic sweep of the *inevitable progress* of aircraft; they base their thinking on aviation as we know it today" (emphasis added). Although de Seversky was referring here specifically to the need for an independent air service, his emphasis on the primacy of the future was nonetheless tinged with irony. He sought the adoption of a new policy based largely on a future technology to fight a current war. De Seversky saw "the chance *to skip intermediary stages of development* and reach out boldly beyond the present confines of aviation types," and he was convinced that the nation could do so during the current war (de Seversky's emphasis). He reached this conclusion partly because he saw that new technological developments were accumulating rapidly. But the idea of "skipping stages" also suggested a measure of faith that might run ahead of experience.[17]

With exuberant optimism, de Seversky pressed his view that aircraft with global capabilities were at hand. He claimed that rapid achievements in range were inevitable, and he demanded that the United States throw itself wholeheartedly into developing the best possible air force.

> We need only make the assumption of a vastly expanded aviation range—an assumption fully justified by the scientific aeronautical facts—and instantly the exposed position of America becomes evident. Imagine the reach of air power multiplied three to five times, and the tactical position of the United States becomes precisely the same as that of the British Isles today.
>
> The range of military aviation is being extended so rapidly that the Atlantic will be canceled out as a genuine obstacle within two years, the Pacific within three years. After that, in five years at the outside, the ultimate round-the-world range of 25,000 miles becomes inevitable. At that point any nation will be able to hurl its aerial might against any spot on the face of the globe without intermediary bases. By the same token every country will be subject to assault from any direction anywhere in the world. The blows will be delivered from the home bases, regardless of distance, with all oceans and bases in between turned into a no man's land [de Seversky's emphasis].[18]

Like earlier air theorists, de Seversky was far less generous in his estimate of what the ground and sea forces could gain from technology. He specifically rejected separate, sea-based aviation, partly to preserve the concept of undivided air power and partly to strengthen the case for an independent air force. He claimed that "the strategic offensive rests with aviation," thus denying the Navy a role in an area traditionally a part of its interest.

In assessing the British naval air operations of early World War II, de Seversky asserted that they were fundamentally deficient. He allowed no excuse for this weakness: "Students of aerial warfare saw in practice what they had foretold in the abstract, that the carrier-based planes would be like so many clay pigeons for land-based air power."[19] His dismissal of naval aviation was the reciprocal of his defense of land-based air power: "Of necessity encumbered with special take-off and landing paraphernalia for operation from their 'floating bases,' the carrier aircraft are no match in performance, type for type, against land-based aircraft."[20] In addition, the Germans had sullied pure air theory with the dust of ground combat. In assessing the German bombing effort against Britain, de Seversky arrived at a justification for dismissing critics who challenged the validity of air power per se. On the one hand, he deplored the insufficient defensive firepower of the German bombers; on the other, he decried the German emphasis on using air power to govern and support ground warfare as a distortion of the force structure, tactics, and strategy of the Luftwaffe.[21] If the air theorists' strategic conception was at issue, then theory drove experience; but if it was a competitor's strategy or tactics under fire, then current experience irrevocably impeached the theory.[22]

Actual US performance in World War II left much to be desired from de Seversky's perspective, but he lost no time in redoubling his calls for supreme reliance on strategic air power. In lectures at the Air University in 1946 and in a new work, *Air Power: Key to Survival* (published in 1950 on the eve of the Korean conflict), he expanded on themes first introduced in the widely read *Victory Through Air Power*. In 1942, de Seversky had emphasized the need to use the most advanced technology, criticizing what he called "the danger of obsession with numbers in planning for American security." In *Air Power: Key to Survival*, he added a specific injunction against the obsession with stockpiling atomic bombs—a concern for quantity of bombs could interfere with the quality of vehicles for their delivery. In a practical sense, the linchpin of de Seversky's whole conception of strategic dominance became essentially an operational one driven by specific aircraft technologies. He persisted in dismissing the growing and sometimes intriguing claims made for alternatives to the manned bomber wherever those claims originated.

A notable example was the development of missile-carrying submarines. De Seversky denied that technological progress could validate missile submarines or submarine-delivered mines or torpedoes. "In theory it is quite conceivable that submarines might lay atomic bombs in enemy harbors in the same way that they lay conventional mines. For the bomb to be effective, however, the submarine would have to penetrate to the very heart of the harbor."[23] Another alternative to manned air power thus faltered in de Seversky's view because of incorrect theory or inadmissible tactics. Moreover, although de Seversky would not foresee technological changes strengthening the offensive capability of sea forces, he confidently predicted that science would negate the submarine's one great advantage.

> Water will lose its ability to serve as a cloak and when we are able to detect underwater craft unerringly and keep them under constant surveillance, submergence will no longer offer protection. The submarine will then be a goldfish in a glass bowl.[24]

To de Seversky, technological limits not solved even in the 1980s were insignificant when compared to his vision of indomitable air power.

Such an understanding of the nature of air power favored a special understanding of the politico-military problems that developed in the world after 1945. During World War II, for example, de Seversky had observed that an aerial attack against an underdeveloped target area was "well-nigh futile," leaving in doubt the value of air strikes in lower level conflicts.[25] For practical purposes, de Seversky simply assumed the functional improbability—or perhaps unimportance—of war between nations unequal in power and industrial level. In the context of World War II, this may not have been hard to understand. But after the war was won, this view became increasingly inadequate. The most immediate postwar problems were well below the level of general or world war—in Poland and Czechoslovakia, in Greece and Iran, in Berlin, in China, and ultimately in Korea. De Seversky—an émigré from the Czarist air forces and a politically conservative industrialist—surely needed little prompting to view the wide range of problems in the world as directed centrally from Moscow. Within the context of East–West confrontation, there were thus no truly local problems; all became world problems.

Yet, in another sense, the emphasis on strategic, high-intensity air power inclined its advocates toward a global perspective lest the whole premise of air power and its practicality be impeached. Shortly after the outset of the Korean War, de Seversky pointed out that the Air Force was not designed to fight land wars in small and backward countries. The only solution de Seversky could reasonably deduce from his construction of air power was to go straight at the Soviet homeland. Thus he advocated penetration capability for strategic strike aircraft and a resolve to use it, and he wanted to make this clear to the Soviet Union. The notion of a local force acting independently in opposition to America or one of its allies made no sense to de Seversky.[26] To the extent that it embraced such views, the Air Force could not be expected to develop a wholehearted interest in low-intensity conflict.

Limited War as a Challenge to Doctrine

Although many Americans viewed all postwar problems as part of one grand strategic confrontation, many others looked towards limited war as an alternate to nuclear war. Such conflicts had been virtually forgotten in the sweep of two world wars, and they were decidedly overshadowed by a hypothetical nuclear war.

The genuinely new limits in war, unlike those of the eighteenth century, derived from an abundance of power rather than from a shortage; yet the political objective, the need to limit the scope and cost of wars actually fought, was substantially the same. And the desire to limit war strengthened despite a conscious effort to build a huge stockpile of yet more powerful weapons. World military conditions were splitting the war and its deterrence into two quite distinct parts: a succession of actual conventional wars and the prospect of a massive but still hypothetical nuclear war. In the short run, then, the ominous cloud at Hiroshima verified the central role the Air Force would play in the emerging policy of deterrence. But to the extent that it became tied to strategic nuclear deterrence, the Air Force risked focusing on hypothetical wars that might never happen. And if a war of lesser magnitude actually broke out, would the Air Force really be ready?[27]

The close association of the Air Force with strategic deterrence took on even more importance after the passage of the National Security Act of 1947. Debates over strategy now inevitably became battles over shares of the military budget and the relative importance of each service in overall defense. Army and Navy planners made concerted efforts to get a share of nuclear weapons, since they might dominate future wars. And the Truman administration made budgetary concessions to them to ensure enactment of the so-called unification legislation; but it nonetheless favored a strategic nuclear deterrent comprised primarily of a long-range bomber force. For this reason, and because of the president's close cooperation with Secretary of the Air Force Stuart Symington and other promoters of the Air Force, the Navy and (to a lesser extent) the Army regarded Truman with suspicion. And Truman viewed small or limited wars as incidents within a general confrontation between the great powers.[28]

With the outbreak of the Korean War, the United States had to make various changes in its strategic approach to world security—or at least in the nuances of its execution. The scope of deterrence was extended beyond the realm of general war. This change in the scope of deterrence was evident in the fact that, despite dissatisfaction with how Truman managed the Korean conflict, the Eisenhower administration did not reject involvement in small wars. The problems had supposedly come not from involvement in the war but from letting the enemy choose the weapons. The logic for avoiding or managing a future small war was revealed by Secretary of State John Foster Dulles. He believed that the truce agreement in Korea came because the North Koreans feared a bold US move; that is, that the fighting might soon spread beyond the limits and methods they had selected.

Eisenhower's decision to engage in "no more Koreas" did not mean abstention from low- and mid-level conflicts. Secretary of Defense Charles E. Wilson even suggested that US involvement in Indochina was possible. A US response might come as it had in Korea, but Wilson left deliberately opaque what form such action might take. Thus, the Eisenhower administration implied that smaller wars could be managed, that escalation might be contemplated, and that conflict might be swiftly terminated by the threat or use of force greater than that chosen by the enemy.[29] But it was a strategy that could work only if major powers actually did control these conflicts or could at least impose substantial pressure on the immediate aggressors. So, too, it required that the country adopting such an approach maintain clear strategic supremacy and effective defense of its own homeland.

Especially because the Air Force held views coincidentally similar to those of the administration, the service was well positioned for a windfall. After Korea, most airmen agreed that nuclear weapons should be the basis of our defense strategies; but the Army and Navy maintained that limited conflicts were most likely and would be fought with conventional weapons. The Air Force "espoused the strategy that forces equipped for general war would deter most forms of aggression; if deterrence failed, those forces could fight a limited war."[30] It remained to be seen, however, whether general forces could win specialized wars and how the limiting of a war might alter the effectiveness of those forces.

The high profile of massive retaliation during the Eisenhower years allowed the Air Force to formulate its own doctrine of strategic deterrence under the mantle of official policy. Official sanction of massive retaliation also lent practical support to the Air Force in its quest to fund its programs. But this tendency toward an organizational coherence and a unitary vision of war did not foster flexibility and versatility, whether in tactics, strategy, or force structure.

The Army and the Navy, by contrast, embarked on specific programs and wide-ranging reevaluations of their respective positions in defense. Capitalizing on its World War II experience, the Army gradually developed both practices and doctrine for psychological warfare and special operations, including the development of ranger units. During the 1950s, influential Army officers also gradually distilled an alternative strategic concept of "flexible response." It enjoyed some credibility because it accepted the possibility of nuclear warfare. Gen Maxwell D. Taylor, who pioneered this strategic approach, suggested that a nuclear war was actually winnable on a battlefield, thus justifying the maintenance of substantial ground forces. Meanwhile, the Navy pursued alternative weapon systems—notably the missile-armed submarine. In one sense, the Army and the Navy engaged in damage limitation to save their own interests. On another level, however, they were looking toward a brighter day whose dawning would come when a new strategic vision was accepted in the White House.

During the 1950s, more and more people came to share the belief that the United States needed a basic change in strategic outlook. Henry Kissinger, in his book *Nuclear Weapons and Foreign Policy* (1957), provided an example of this growing school of thought. Kissinger argued that weapons, planning, and operations differ radically between forces useful for all-out war and those for limited war. He dismissed the idea that building forces to deter all-out war would at the same time deter limited war. He believed that use of our strategic force as a dual-purpose force

15

would weaken the deterrent to an all-out war at the precise time when it should be strongest. Significantly, McGeorge Bundy, Lt Gen James M. Gavin, Roswell Gilpatric, and Paul Nitze, who were soon to influence national policy, shared Kissinger's views.[31]

Some within the Air Force feared that Air Force thinking about contemporary warfare and the appropriate role of air power had changed too little since World War II. In a report to Air Force Vice Chief of Staff Gen William McKee in 1963, Maj Gen Dale O. Smith accused the Air Force of backwardness and lack of imagination. He argued that the deplorable condition of aerospace power was largely the result of allowing Air Force doctrine to stagnate. Instead of a dynamic program to update doctrine, there was drift from the whim of one leader to another. He portrayed the Army as having risen brilliantly to a major position in national strategic thinking after a decade of suffering under the Air Force–led doctrine of massive retaliation. In contrast, he viewed the Air Force as a victim of "hardening of the categories" and as a candidate for further erosion. A continuing program of doctrinal research to counterbalance the one at the Army War College would help to redress the deficiency; but the key change needed was one of attitude and disposition, especially at the higher echelons. The Air Force needed to pay serious attention to new ideas and new national policy interests, and to relate them to the capabilities of air power in a forthright and realistic way.[32]

What General Smith saw as inflexibility in doctrine was strengthened by the absence of a firm and meaningful doctrinal statement. On one level, this absence reflected the persistent sense that the Air Force has never "found its Mahan." At another level, it allowed beliefs that had the force of doctrine to continue without having to be defended formally. Moreover, in 1948, an Air University staff study had pointed to the rapid development of air power as the chief obstacle to writing a doctrinal statement. Some senior officers even discouraged the effort to write such doctrine in the late 1940s and early 1950s, believing these statements too short-lived to warrant publication. Since formal doctrine suffered because of the brevity of air power's past, technology was thus substituted for history. The views of Gen Nathan F. Twining, acting chief of staff of the Air Force, exemplified this point. He believed that formal doctrine is tied to the past and to historical experience rather than to ongoing technological development: "The Air Force is not bound to any fixed doctrine or concept. It grew out of scientific achievement."[33] And Maj Gen Lloyd P. Hopwood, former commandant of the Air Command and Staff College, argued that we try to make our doctrine and strategy conform to glamorous hardware. He believed we should be studying modern conflict instead.

The beliefs of early air power advocates persisted into the 1950s, but those advocates tended to confuse the principles of air power with the instruments of air power. This tension between the demands of recent experience and current force structure on the one hand and an imbedded orientation toward the future on the other was typified in the Air Staff's rejection of Air University's revision of the service's doctrinal statement in 1958. There was disagreement as to whether the statement should reflect proven doctrine or project into the future. In a lecture at the Air War College in 1958, General Smith suggested that the search for doctrine was a frustrating process since technological change might make any doctrinal statement obsolescent. He argued that actions, not pronouncements, are the real indicators of doctrine. But the risk in this approach was that one might become unconscious of fundamental tenets, obscuring sources and discouraging revision. It is especially difficult to revise an unknown.

The closest thing to a compromise in doctrinal statements may have come in remarks made by Col Orin H. Moore at the Air Force's Squadron Officer School. He suggested that doctrine proven from past experience would govern local war while grander concepts of air power, untested in actual combat, would govern general nuclear war; but even this limited compromise did not win a servicewide following.[34]

Thus, at the start of the 1960s, the Air Force lacked a sense of doctrine that would combine the virtues of conviction with the advantages of flexibility. Indeed, some tended to regard flexibility largely as a matter of reallocating air assets from one place of combat to another. In an article published anonymously in 1961, two Air Force analysts indirectly impeached the pertinence of political, social, economic, and other considerations not specifically military. They argued that technology paces strategy and determines its nature, although strategy can place demands on technology in order to meet momentary requirements. The confidence of air power enthusiasts remained; concern over counterinsurgencies and lower level conflicts was limited. Gen William W. Momyer later recalled that the initial focus in lower level conflict pressed upon the armed forces was

> our "counterinsurgency." This focus was too far down the spectrum for many elements of our tactical air forces. Tactical airmen had serious reservations about putting so much attention on counterinsurgency when there was a need to restore the non-nuclear capability of our tactical forces.[35]

This attitude reflected a genuine desire to prepare the Air Force to meet its potential responsibilities. But it also reflected a divergence of views on what the responsibilities might be—a confusion that became persistent during the war in Indochina.

Vietnam and the Burden of the Past

In Vietnam, the Air Force provided essential supportive services for what was, on balance, a strategically defensive effort. The strategic objective was to defend and strengthen pro–US forces centered in Saigon against a combined Vietcong and North Vietnamese effort. The means for achieving this strategically defensive objective even included employing, for tactical defensive purposes, weapons with a primarily offensive image and generally strategic character. Yet the Air Force approached this task on the premise that a strong offense was the best defense and that the advantages of widening a theater of operations outweighed the political and military risks. This idea had permeated air theory in the 1930s and general defense theory in 1940s and 1950s, and it grew stronger in the debates over air defense during the 1950s and at the start of the 1960s. In discussing the budget for fiscal year 1961, for example, Gen Thomas D. White, Air Force chief of staff, justified diverting some funds from air defense to offensive programs by saying, "our philosophy is based on the fact that offense is the best defense."[36] Consistent with deterrence theory, this approach aimed at restraining one's most powerful potential adversaries. But how was this view pertinent to lower levels of conflict where wars seemed largely political in means as well as ends? This question especially challenged those military and political leaders who thought political issues were not relevant to the conduct of military forces. Yet General White's understanding of air and general defense theory could not easily be overthrown—partly because it grew from some fundamental truths, but also because it was enmeshed in decades-old Air Force ideas. These entrenched beliefs became a real problem for the Air Force when it tried to deal with the new Kennedy administration and the burgeoning war in Vietnam in the early 1960s.

The Air Force could not contribute effectively to the debate over strategy in Southeast Asia because it gave priority to questions other than Vietnam. Even though it was understandable that the Air Force would attend to its responsibilities at the strategic level, this made them seem reluctant to get on board with the administration's approach to the conflict in Southeast Asia.[37] Air Force leaders, given their lack of interest in counterinsurgency and limited war, focused on the global situation, which thrust Berlin and Cuba into the headlines, and on developing responses to such crises. At the same time, some have charged, the civilian and military planners closest to Presidents Kennedy and Johnson gave ever more complicated and (sometimes) false interpretations of the Vietnam problem so that any proposed remedies would become confusing in execution and inadequate in result.[38] Moreover, the most pressing Southeast Asian concerns of the Kennedy administration centered on Laos—not Vietnam. The political, economic, and social characteristics of the Laotian problem shaped a military response that differed significantly from what conditions in Vietnam invited. Thus, Vietnam ultimately seemed something of a sideshow, at least in the late 1950s and early 1960s—a distraction from major Air Force concerns and something of a threat to Air Force interests, since the emerging US approach in Vietnam placed renewed importance on a ground effort and hence on the Army.

Meanwhile, developments in the cold war in 1961 and 1962 worked to reinforce the Air Force's focus on strategic air power and deterrent strength. Construction of the Berlin Wall and concern over the city's future argued strongly that the strategic relationship between the United States and the Soviet Union was unstable. Even more, the Cuban missile crisis in 1962 was widely taken as evidence that the Air Force's emphasis on strategic superiority had been correct. Even Secretary of Defense Robert S. McNamara told Congress that the strategic forces had been decisive.

Khrushchev knew without any question whatsoever that he faced the full military power of the United States, including its nuclear weapons. That might be difficult to understand for some, but it is not difficult for me to understand, because we faced . . . the possibility of launching nuclear weapons and Khrushchev knew it, and that is the reason, and the only reason, why he withdrew those weapons.[39]

Yet to observers whose biases differed from those prevalent in the Air Force, the end of the Cuban missile crisis could also be viewed as a negotiated settlement—one where escalated military pressure yielded a favorable political outcome without actual conflict. They apparently felt that they had orchestrated the events with enough care so that Khrushchev could extricate himself safely from the showdown. Kennedy's advisers viewed the end of the confrontation as a triumph of gradualism; graduated responses and the possibility of negotiation were kept open at each successive level of the crisis. But many believe that Kennedy's determination to see the crisis as a direct confrontation between the United States and the Soviet Union permitted the clarity and bluntness with which the problem was managed.

The Cuban missile crisis did not indicate how the government should act when direct confrontation with the USSR was not the problem or was only part of it.[40] In Vietnam, for example, there was at least one extra remove—even if one assumed that the North Vietnamese dominated the Vietcong as early as the 1950s—in which a proxy of a proxy of the ultimate competitor was the problem. The further the remove, the less credible was the threat posed by strategic superiority. Further, the action the United States wanted the Soviet Union to undertake in the missile crisis was clearly theirs to do—not a third party's responsibility. Fidel Castro was left out of the flow of communications and out of the lines of accountability. Could the same have been done to Ho Chi Minh?

Although McNamara grasped the value of US strategic superiority, he mooted his praise by attributing Khrushchev's concession to US conventional as well as strategic nuclear capability. In this, Gen Earle Wheeler, the Army chief of staff, concurred. Moreover, Wheeler's perception of the Army's state of readiness—or lack of it—for the Cuban confrontation encouraged greater attention to conventional general purpose forces. Likewise, the serious drawdown in tactical aviation from other parts of the United States to concentrate it closer to Cuba underscored shortages in that category. The efficiency and evident adequacy of the Strategic Air Command during the crisis were not challenged, but the numbers and readiness of tactical aviation caused some concern. Gen Curtis E. LeMay nevertheless saw it as a vindication of Air Force emphasis on the strategic deterrent. At the same time, McNamara and his team thought it verified their own view that graduated response and measured force led to negotiation. Thus the crisis and its conclusion did little to close the gap between the Air Force and the White House.

Strategic forces remained the dominant concern of the Air Force and its top leaders. In remarks to Congress after the crisis had subsided, General LeMay reiterated: "If you have the power to stop a big war, certainly the same power ought to be capable of stopping a small war."[41] General LeMay, as Air Force chief of staff, spoke in favor of the Kennedy–McNamara effort to enhance conventional capabilities for lower level wars; but he did so only in the general context of higher defense budgets, which reduced the immediate risk of an abrupt drop in the funding of strategic forces.[42] LeMay's approval is best regarded as an endorsement of a general expansion of defense capabilities.

Other Air Force spokesmen likewise claimed a powerful role for strategic forces in deterring even low-level conflicts. Maj Gen David A. Burchinal, Air Force director of plans, defended the strengthening of strategic forces by arguing that superiority in this area would dissuade an enemy from engaging in a smaller war. "If you have a strategic capability which is clearly superior . . . ," he argued, "then you have established your ability to control . . . escalation in the lower levels." An enemy would presumably be unwilling to let a war expand when faced with the likelihood of defeat at the higher level of conflict. Thus, the United States would at least have controlled the intensity of conflict.[43] Indeed, according to this view, without superior forces one could not guarantee control of the level of conflict. Yet even with superiority, it was not obvious that one could. Were there no situations special enough to require equally special forces, tactics, and perhaps even strategies? Were some problems so fundamentally political in character as to invite the use of military measures in a primarily political role? Such questions survived the Cuban missile crisis but were perhaps too arcane to be addressed in Air Force doctrine.

The Air Force attempt to reconcile its force structure and doctrine to the growing concern over limited war did not much resemble that advocated for the Army by General Taylor; nor did it reflect a similar overall spirit. In a position paper presented on 24 April 1962, US Air Force Deputy Director of Aerospace Plans Brig Gen Jerry D. Page specified that overall superiority was essential to fighting effectively and to "fighting on our terms." In suggesting a linkage between strategic forces and the deterrence or regulation of lower level conflicts, General Page asserted that "limited war against Communist forces is not a separate entity from general war" and that consequently "our strategy and forces for limited war should not be separated from our overall strategy and force structure."[44] This clearly made sense to the extent that US freedom of action depended on the strength of its strategic forces. But it still left unclear precisely what measures were needed in limited war—let alone in genuine insurgencies. The risk was that emphasizing strategic capabilities might put discrete local conditions in second place when leaders developed strategies to meet local problems.

For General Page, the underlying prerequisite for effective conduct of limited war was superior capability for general war. To the extent that the United States could exploit air superiority and other superior capabilities, the concept was almost self-evident. But it remained to be seen whether a country with a weaker capability for general war would yield if the stronger one pushed a limited war to higher levels.

Although General Page thought the United States should not respond to a limited war with more force than necessary, he also specified that the nation with the superior technology must use it to offset deficiencies in manpower, conventional armaments, and so forth. He implied that conflict was shaped by one's adversary rather than by indigenous forces, and that control should be wrested from the adversary. He believed that a nation should conduct limited war to take advantage of its best capabilities rather than have choices forced upon it by the enemy. Hence, forces should be designed to possess range, speed, firepower delivery, flexibility, and mobility "that can perform in cold, limited and general war situations."[45] This concept for limited war suited Air Force doctrine better than it suited ground officers' thinking on counterinsurgency, but many outside the air power community doubted whether such views were suitable to the local conditions of insurgency and to low-level invasions executed in stages. The Army's advocates of airmobile operations clearly focused on meeting the enemy in local theaters rather than pressuring their patrons in the capital cities of major powers. Military and civilian advocates of Army Special Forces similarly focused on down-in-the-dirt fighting under local conditions. If General Page's statement really was an expression of "limited war," it only underscored how wide a range of meanings the word "limited" could take on.

The Air Force did, at length, respond in some measure to the challenges of counterinsurgency and low-intensity conflict—especially under prodding by the Kennedy administration. In April 1961, the Tactical Air Command established the 4400th Combat Application Crew Training Squadron at Eglin AFB, Florida. It was designed to counter the challenge of the Army's Special Forces, which were so highly prized by President Kennedy. Soon redesignated the 1st Air Commando Wing, the unit was to support the US Army Special Forces with air power and to train foreign air forces in special operations. Meanwhile, Air University introduced a two-week course dealing with counterinsurgency.[46] Advocates of an Air Force capability in low-intensity conflict could see them at least as first steps.

The effort to make Air Force doctrine compatible with Kennedy's perception of national strategy began, and McNamara's implementation began in earnest, only when Secretary of the Air Force Eugene Zuckert commissioned General LeMay to review Air Force prospects for the future. LeMay designated Gen Bernard Schriever to undertake a comprehensive study (Project Forecast) to assess the suitability of the Air Force to meet the needs of the 1965–75 period. The study's policy panel, headed by General Page, maintained the long-standing Air Force view that superior strategic forces deterred a nuclear holocaust; but it demurred on the matter of lower levels of conflict.

In insurgencies, insurrections, and civil wars, deterrence might not be the primary identifiable goal. During extended periods of danger and uncertainty, other considerations might be more important—such considerations as ensuring negotiating thresholds at various levels of escalation and maintaining survivable forces. Echoes of the Kennedy administration's views of the Cuban missile crisis

21

were discernible. Secretary Zuckert accepted these and other provisions of the policy review on 10 February 1964. And in the August 1964 version of AFM 1–1, *United States Air Force Basic Doctrine,* the Air Force dropped its earlier claim that air power was the best way to achieve decisive results in any conflict; it claimed only to be one part of a defense team. Such measures substantially recognized military as well as political realities of the day. Yet they came relatively late—perhaps too late to guide attitudes toward the problems of Vietnam. They also came abruptly—perhaps too abruptly to be absorbed effectively by the whole Air Force.[47]

Perhaps more significant than statements of theory or doctrine were ideas as they were perceived in action. For example, General Momyer said his understanding of the proper strategy for Vietnam grew from his World War II and Korean experience; but he actually reiterated traditional Air Force ideas, making them more concrete with historical illustrations. What he had seen in World War II governed his prescriptions for interdiction, air support, and counterair missions in Korea. Similarly, the experience of Korea as he understood it applied directly to Vietnam. Throughout, General Momyer embraced the independent air campaign as the economical, crucial, and determining ingredient. Moreover, in his book *Air Power in Three Wars,* he saw the air campaign as invariably relevant; history was a matter of relearning the obvious at precious cost. Indeed, the general message of Momyer's book was that the fundamental premises of air power and doctrines for its employment remained valid through World War II, Korea, and Vietnam. He acknowledged that some adjustments to interdiction were made possible by new weapons, but insisted that the central objective and proper means for its achievement were unaltered.[48] Commenting on Operation Linebacker II, he observed that the development of air strategy in World War II, Korea, and Vietnam had been a repetitious process—not an evolutionary, developmental, or incremental one.[49] In each case, he asserted, non–Air Force planners

> first perceived airpower as a subordinate part of a joint strategy that would employ an extensive ground campaign to end the war on favorable terms. On the other hand, airmen came increasingly to believe that airpower, in its own right, could produce decisive results. The validity of such a view was suggested by results of the Allies' combined bomber offensive in Europe and by the surrender of Japan in the 1940s. Additional evidence came from the skies over Hanoi in December 1972. In a concentrated 11–day test, our air strategy persuaded a determined adversary with a remarkably elaborate air defense system that overt aggression could not be sustained in the presence of unrestricted U.S. airpower.[50]

General Momyer's remarks testify to the persistence of traditional Air Force commitment to an independent air campaign and an inclination to shape the contours of conflict to suit perceived US advantages such as technology.[51]

Not surprisingly, General Momyer was less enthusiastic about measures taken by the Air Force to modify force structure to engage actively in counterinsurgency. He viewed the war in Southeast Asia as having passed beyond insurgency by 1961, well before most officers outside the Air Force date the change, for he wrote in *Air*

22

Power in Three Wars, "while we considered the merits of various approaches to counterinsurgency warfare, the fighting in parts of Southeast Asia had already passed through that stage of conflict."[52] Accordingly, he disapproved of establishing Jungle Jim teams as developed at Eglin—special units intended for "behind the lines" counterinsurgency work.

Secretary McNamara wanted the Vietnamese conflict to be a "laboratory for the conduct of sub-limited war." General Momyer and the Air Staff dissented: "CINCPACAF and the Air Staff had held the view that the main threat to US interests in the Far East was China and that PACAF's command structure should be designed to meet that threat."[53] They wanted air assets assigned to South Vietnam to be limited so as to maintain forces needed for possible duty in a larger war. General Momyer's vision of the war and his understanding of air power doctrine left him cool to such innovations as the use of B-52s in a tactical support role and the development of special counterinsurgency forces. Since he saw the Vietnam War as a largely conventional one, Momyer advocated a traditionally conceived air offensive aimed at destroying enemy war-making capability.

> Although most experienced airmen would have chosen to employ our strategic bombers against the enemy's major target systems and to have used them for close support only in emergencies, the use of B-52s for in-country missions was in consonance with the secretary's view that the place to destroy the enemy was in South Vietnam.[54]

Clearly, obedience to orders did not reflect agreement with the secretary's point of view.

Air Force leaders such as General Momyer tended to see the Vietnam War as an essentially simple conventional conflict masquerading as a subtle and complicated counterinsurgency. Non–Air Force military leaders saw it otherwise. Gen Donn A. Starry, USA, widely regarded as a capable soldier and military intellectual, perceived the war so differently from Momyer that a casual reader might wonder if they were describing the same conflict. General Starry accepted the view that the Vietcong were largely managed by North Vietnam, but he saw differences in the specific military threat from one province to another and from one year to the next.

> Perhaps the most unusual Viet Cong fighting technique was that of carrying on a different kind of war in each of South Vietnam's forty-four provinces. South Vietnamese defenders in the northeast highlands were confronted with enemy tactics that were in sharp contrast to those used in the broad southern deltas. Even more unusual was the fact that the level of conflict in each province varied surprisingly. Often one province would be simultaneously subjected to large-scale mobile attacks and guerrilla harassment, while a neighboring province was left entirely alone. This selective intensification of the war by the Viet Cong confused American observers, and hid the true nature of the conflict. The American image of the enemy as loosely organized groups of bandits or guerrillas was not real. The enemy had a plan and worked his plan well, so well in fact that by 1964 he was ready to make the transition to the last phase of the conflict, full-scale mobile war.[55]

Starry believed that the Vietcong had operated with some measure of autonomy during the earlier phases of US commitment and that they had kept it well into the war. Moreover, he suggested that they would sometimes change the level of conflict and alter their tactics. Further, Starry suggested that the war had not begun as a conventional ground-force engagement, but only culminated that way—precisely what Momyer ultimately regarded as wasteful and unnecessary. General Starry's assessment serves as a useful reminder that the debate over the proper use of air power was only one term in the complex equation; there was a parallel debate over what kind of ground forces to employ.[56]

A comprehensive and effective strategy in Southeast Asia required either a genuine consensus as to the character of the war or uncompromising decisiveness from the commander in chief. Neither was easy. Both were held hostage to the divergent ideas and doctrinal notions of differing constituencies within civilian and military sectors. In this way, historical experience and "institutional memory" of past disputes weighed down the armed forces in Southeast Asia.

The burden was especially great because there was no agreement on the lessons of conflicts before Vietnam. And specifically, there was no agreement on air power and its uses. Air power retained a powerful allure during the war in Southeast Asia, raising hope in some quarters that the scales might be tipped in favor of the United States and its allies. Yet it was not clear what practical steps were needed to achieve this result. Without agreement on how to fight, the war in Vietnam became a conflict among US military and political elements. The persistent themes in the history of each service thus became the prologue to their war in Vietnam.

NOTES

1. See Russell F. Weigley, *The American Way of War, A History of United States Military Strategy and Policy* (New York: Macmillan Publishing Co., Inc., 1973).

2. Quoted in Harry G. Summers, Jr., *On Strategy: The Vietnam War in Context* (Carlisle Barracks, Pa.: Strategic Studies Institute, US Army War College, 1981), 25.

3. These ideas will be developed more concretely in the balance of the chapter. Here the purpose is only to set out a framework in sharp relief.

4. Quoted in Robert Frank Futrell, *Ideas, Concepts, Doctrine: A History of Basic Thinking in the United States Air Force, 1907–1964* (Maxwell AFB, Ala.: Air University, 1971), 102.

5. Ibid., 206–7.

6. William Mitchell, *Winged Defense* (New York: G. P. Putnam's Sons, 1925). Also see Alfred F. Hurley, *Billy Mitchell, Crusader for Air Power* (Bloomington: Indiana University Press, 1975).

7. Alfred Thayer Mahan, *The Influence of Sea Power Upon History* (Boston: Little, Brown and Co., 1918).

8. Ibid., 2. Here Mahan deals with the pertinence of experience under sail to expectations under steam.

9. Mitchell, *Winged Defense*, 20.

10. William Mitchell, *Our Air Force* (New York: Dutton, 1921), 106. In this instance, Mitchell specifically meant lighter-than-air aircraft, whose decline he did not anticipate.

11. Quoted in Futrell, *Ideas, Concepts, Doctrine*, 2.

12. This may help to explain why a clear statement of doctrine seems almost impossible to obtain in any given period. The capability for a strategic offensive effectively became the dominant concern that made all other roles secondary. Consequently, all that remained was to debate the appropriate technologies for meeting this central concern.

13. Futrell, *Ideas, Concepts, Doctrine,* provides a succinct treatment of the Air Corps Tactical School, especially pages 31–48. The quotations appear on page 32.

14. Ibid., 34.

15. Ibid., 51.

16. Alexander P. de Seversky, *Victory Through Air Power* (New York: Simon and Schuster, 1942), 6, 16, 5. Also see de Seversky, "A Lecture on Air Power," Air University Quarterly Review 1, no. 2 (Fall 1947): 25–41; and 1, no. 3 (Winter 1947): 23–40.

17. De Seversky, *Victory Through Air Power,* 5, 291.

18. Ibid., 14.

19. Ibid., 125.

20. Ibid., 126.

21. Ibid., 53.

22. Ibid., 85.

23. Ibid., 63.

24. Alexander P. de Seversky, *Air Power: Key to Survival* (New York: Simon and Schuster, 1950), 84–85 passim.

25. De Seversky, *Victory Through Air Power,* 102.

26. De Seversky, *Air Power: Key to Survival,* xviii, ff.

27. Among early statements suggesting the quick acceptance of the concept of deterrence are: Memorandum by Artemus Gates to James Forrestal, 19 September 1945, Miscellaneous Files, "Atomic Energy Commission" folder, Forrestal Papers; Ralph A. Bard to James Forrestal, 11 December 1946, Miscellaneous Files, "Unification Letter" folder, Forrestal Papers; manuscript memorandum, George Elsey, April 1948, "Western Union" folder, Papers of George Elsey.

28. On the development of Truman's defense policy and its emphasis, see Donald J. Mrozek, "Peace Through Strength," unpublished doctoral dissertation, Rutgers University, 1972. An interesting and balanced appraisal of Truman's policies is found in Richard F. Haynes, *The Awesome Power, Harry S. Truman as Commander-in-Chief* (Baton Rouge: Louisiana State University Press, 1973).

29. Lt Gen E. R. Quesada, USAF Ret., "Tactical Air Power," *Air University Quarterly Review* 1, no. 4 (Spring 1948): 44–45.

30. Dulles is quoted in Futrell, *Ideas, Concepts, Doctrine,* 13; Wilson is quoted in Donald J. Mrozek, "A New Look at 'Balanced Forces': Defense Continues from Truman to Eisenhower," *Military Affairs* 38, no. 4 (December 1974): 145–51.

31. Gen William W. Momyer, USAF Ret., *Air Power in Three Wars* (n.p., 1978), 6, 248–49.

32. On the gradual development of Army special warfare, see Alfred H. Paddock, Jr., *US Army Special Warfare, Its Origins* (Fort Lesley J. McNair: National Defense University Press, 1982). For an example of Army thinking on war in the 1950s, see Theodore C. Mataxis and Seymour L. Goldberg, *Nuclear Tactics, Weapons, and Firepower in the Pentomic Division, Battle Group, and Company* (Harrisburg, Pa.: The Military Service Publishing Company, 1958); and Henry A. Kissinger, *Nuclear Weapons and Foreign Policy* (New York: Harper & Brothers, 1957), 156–57.

33. Quoted in Futrell, *Ideas, Concepts, Doctrine,* 406. Also see Dale O. Smith, *US Military Doctrine, A Study and Appraisal* (New York: Duell, Sloan and Pearce, 1955).

34. Quoted in Futrell, *Ideas, Concepts, Doctrine,* 2–6.

35. Ibid., 6.

36. "Are We Using Or Abusing Technology?" *Air Force/Space Digest,* October 1961, 45–48; Momyer, *Air Power in Three Wars,* 249.

37. Quoted in Futrell, *Ideas, Concepts, Doctrine,* 273.

38. Typical of those attributing the unsatisfactory outcome in Vietnam to civilians and overly sophisticated political analysis is Adm U. S. Grant Sharp, *Strategy for Defeat, Vietnam in Retrospect* (San Rafael, Calif.: Presidio Press, 1978). Also see Gen William C. Westmoreland, *A Soldier Reports* (Garden City, N.Y.: Doubleday & Co., 1976).

39. Futrell, *Ideas, Concepts, Doctrine*, 356–57.

40. It is hard not to see the Cuban crisis, understood this way, as a precedent for gradualism in Vietnam. On the assessment of the Cuban confrontation, see Futrell, 356. For a positive appraisal of political management in the crisis, see Robert F. Kennedy, *Thirteen Days, A Memoir of the Cuban Missile Crisis* (New York: W. W. Norton & Company, Inc., 1969); it also indicates that the incident confirmed President Kennedy's negative judgment of all his military advisers except General Taylor. Also see Elie Abel, *The Missile Crisis* (Philadelphia: J. B. Lippincott Co., 1966).

41. Futrell, *Ideas, Concepts, Doctrine*, 358–59.

42. Ibid., 360.

43. For information on the Air Force's effort to deal with the problem of limited war, see Futrell, *Ideas, Concepts, Doctrine*, 349–50. General LeMay is quoted on page 344.

44. Futrell, *Ideas, Concepts, Doctrine*, 344.

45. Ibid., 349.

46. Ibid.

47. Ibid., 408.

48. Ibid., 440–42.

49. Momyer, *Air Power*, iv.

50. Ibid., 34.

51. Ibid., 207.

52. Ibid., 21.

53. Ibid., 6–7.

54. Ibid., 10.

55. Ibid., 70.

56. Donn A. Starry, *Armored Combat in Vietnam* (Indianapolis: The Bobbs-Merrill Co., 1980), 14–15.

CHAPTER 2

Interservice Differences, Command and Control, and the Conduct of War in Southeast Asia

It may be improper to say we are at war with the Army. However, we believe that if the Army efforts are successful, they may have a long term adverse effect in the US military posture that could be more important than the battle presently being waged with the Viet Cong.

USAF Director of Plans, 1962

You can violate all the rules and regulations if you are successful in combat.

Maj Gen Delk Oden, USA, 1977

In December 1962, the Air Force director of plans observed that the Army had 199 aircraft in Vietnam while the Air Force had only 61. Eight Army generals were assigned to Vietnam, but there were only three from the Air Force. The very observation of this fact—and the criteria it used for comparison—reflected the interest of the Air Force in its position with respect to the Army as much as it showed interest in the Vietnam conflict per se. Vietnam was seen not simply on its own terms but also as a source of implications for future wars and for the relative roles of the services in national security. The persistent concern about roles and missions among the services affected not only proposals for how forces would be used in Vietnam but also the command and control system proposed for managing them. In this context, decisions about how air power was actually organized and employed were more than technical statements of operational capabilities—they were de facto statements of doctrine. The disposition of forces in Vietnam at the end of 1962 was, to a degree, a result of prior policy. But once these forces were deployed, they tended to shape subsequent policy. The present became enmeshed in the struggle for future security and service interests. Competing visions of the future, theories about the proper organization of forces, and differing understandings of the past intruded upon the conduct of the war itself.

Interservice rivalry was not invented during the Vietnam War nor, for that matter, in the twentieth century. But the absence of clear goals, clear strategy, and clear policy gave such rivalry unusual force in the era of Vietnam. Without a clearly stated common goal and a firm policy for its achievement, the military services are deprived of justification and motive to suspend their own doctrinal precepts and risk their institutional resources through self-sacrificial behavior. In its early stages, the Vietnam War seemed to justify such action very little. For one thing, the relatively low level of conflict early in the war (1959 through 1963) made it seem a sideshow, especially when compared with US involvement in the Bay of Pigs landing, the US–USSR confrontation over Berlin, and the Cuban missile crisis. These dramatic events strengthened the view that the relationship between the great powers remained the dominant military and political concern. In addition, Southeast Asia was only one of several third world trouble spots. Attention went to Africa, especially the Congo; and Kennedy's proposal of an Alliance for Progress showed concern over Latin America. Also, the urgency with which various US officials assessed the situation in Laos did not extend to Vietnam in the early years. As the military problem deepened in Vietnam, US intervention became largely a process of buying time rather than pursuing a neatly defined victory; the real goal was the emergence of a stable South Vietnamese government. But this required time and patience, and it depended on the South Vietnamese. Buying time for the South Vietnamese also bought time for the US armed forces, letting them persist in disagreement over how to manage the war. This problem was not new, but it was serious. It became one of the many separate wars fought either in Vietnam or over it.

Relationships among the services and such matters as civilian precedence deeply affected proposals for command and control structures. Many in the Army saw the ultimate goal of all command and control arrangements as maximizing the efficiency and effectiveness of ground war troops, including those providing air support. But others saw the Southeast Asian conflict as more complex, perhaps even more an air war than a ground war. Air war over North Vietnam obviously differed from air support for a ground war in the South. Put simply, how one interpreted the war tended to dictate which command and control arrangements seemed appropriate. Moreover, some officials gave more attention to political considerations than to the explicitly and concretely military ones. For them, political sensitivies in Thailand or South Vietnam might override sound military judgment. Behind the determination of command and control arrangements lay the question of which goal was the key. To say the objective was victory was surely too vague. The need was to decide where victory would occur and what would constitute it. Whatever else may be said, for good or ill, prosecution of the ground war did not enjoy consistent priority. Rivalries suggest that efforts to fight the war stumbled over confusion as to what the war really was; and without a common vision, the services were left to their own competing goals.

Interservice Differences in the
Post–World War II Context

In their rivalry over the organization and use of air power in Vietnam, the services continued their long dispute over roles and missions. This debate had special weight for the Air Force since it had been enmeshed in controversy with the other services through its whole history. Fighting for air power doctrines was a way of life for the Air Force, and this experience left it suspicious of the older services. The National Security Act of 1947 did not settle the problem of roles and missions. Even a major conference among the chiefs of staff and civilian defense officials at Key West the following year brought only limited and fragile agreement. As technological advancement yielded new weapons, the argument over how to control and use them was renewed; the greater the technological change, the greater was the pressure for each service to reassess its role. The push toward diversification of air power offers a pertinent example.

After World War II (and especially after 1947), the Air Force had sought to retain control over the general procurement of aircraft to guard against the possible development of a competing air element within the Army and to bar it from buying heavier planes. The contest with the Navy was ultimately less effective, although it attracted far more public attention. Army Gen Robert R. Williams, former head of the Airmobility Branch, Office of the Chief of Research and Development, and commander of the 1st Aviation Brigade in Vietnam, observed that such control would give the Air Force a powerful hand in constraining what they considered to be an unnecessary and undesirable expansion of Army aviation. The Air Force also sought control of all flight training.[1] In addition, some in the Air Force considered leaving air assets in the Army wasteful and duplicative.* This perception fostered opposition to a separate Army air transport service and an Army missile program that might displace attack aviation.[2] As General Williams noted, this also illustrated that "when you talk about roles and missions in the future, these are driven by hardware."[3] Army Brig Gen O. Glenn Goodhand made much the same point:

> When war comes you do whatever the equipment you've got will do. That's the reason people have to fight hard for equipment in the future because, you know, lead-times are such that you can't do anything with it during a war. I mean, roles and missions fly out the window when a war starts and equipment capability governs.[4]

The struggle for control of helicopter assets served as a case in point. The helicopter—which was to increase warfighting options in Vietnam—received enough exposure in the Korean War to become an object of competition among the services. The Army, the Air Force, and the Marine Corps all sought to gain the upper hand over the use of helicopters. For about a year and a half during the war,

---

*Perry McCoy Smith, in *The Air Force Plans for Peace, 1943–1945* (Baltimore: Johns Hopkins University Press, 1970), argues that proponents of the new Air Force felt it necessary to yield some air assets to the Army in order to win the service's assent to separate status for the Air Force. Smith sees this as leading to extreme emphasis on manned strategic bombing at the expense of some other potentially useful forms of air power.

29

both the Air Force and the Army claimed the medical evacuation role. The dispute came to a head when an Air Force major flying an Air Force H-12 helicopter ordered an Army crew to take a wounded soldier from an Army H-12, thus delaying the man's evacuation. The two service chiefs were summoned by Secretary of Defense Robert Lovett to discuss the issue in October 1952, and he decided to give the Army the medical evacuation mission and a key responsibility for troop transport. Meanwhile, some Army officers noted the Marines' use of helicopters for troop lift and supply and concluded that the airmobile concept would work as well for the Army as it had for the Marines.[5]

Through it all, Air Force Chief of Staff Gen Nathan F. Twining opposed the development of the Army's airmobile capability. He strongly objected to an Army proposal to establish a 12-battalion airmobile force. Army officers justified this step as providing logistical support behind the forward edge of the battle area (FEBA), and they claimed that it conformed to an earlier Joint Chiefs of Staff memorandum restricting them to the logistical role. But General Twining expected any substantial helicopter force to be transformed to undertake an assault role. When challenged by Joint Chiefs chairman Adm Arthur Radford on the survivability of helicopters, Army representatives defended themselves by noting that the Air Force and the Marines also wanted helicopters.[6] At its most important level, the issue was not technical but jurisdictional. As General Williams candidly remarked, "Many of us were thinking very strongly of the assault aspects, the airmobile aspects, but we were seriously inhibited in that there was no way we could use it as a justification."[7]

Although more visible between different services, jurisdictional tensions existed within each service as well.[8] Advocates of aviation and airmobility within the Army sought to use loyalty to the service to interest the various Army branches in air assets. During the mid–1960s, some branches did take up the cause for certain types of aircraft: the infantry advocated assault helicopters while armor pushed for attack helicopters; and each got what it wanted. The Army sought to generate enthusiasm and interest on the basis that they now owned them and they had the specific responsibility for developing the tactics, technique and doctrine for employing them.[9] This approach disarmed those who would have objected to a separate aviation branch out of concern that it would soon show separatist tendencies.[10] Proponents of Army aviation and airmobility favored close cooperation between ground forces and air components by stressing that aviators would identify themselves first with the traditional combat arms. They would be trained and identified as aviators only after primary training in other branches such as infantry or armor. Although this scheme never worked as smoothly as its advocates had hoped, it suggested how hard-nosed practical interests influenced the organization of air power. Army officers could not develop airmobility openly until they had won the basic weapons with which to carry it out; and they could not get those weapons without running into conflict with the Air Force. And in their fight for their own survival and recognition, Army aviators had little time to prepare for the war soon to confront them.

A significant body of literature on airmobility developed during the 1950s and early 1960s, authored by such prominent Army figures as Lt Gen James Gavin and Lt Gen Hamilton Howze. To Air Force leaders, however, these writings seemed to constitute an unwarranted challenge to Air Force missions and interests. In congressional testimony, Air Force Chief of Staff Gen Curtis E. LeMay said bluntly of the Army's arguments for airmobility: "What the Howze Board is advocating is in effect building another air force for the Army."[11] The discussion turned on technical issues. Specifically, could high-speed jet aircraft deliver close support for ground forces, and were slow rotary-winged aircraft too vulnerable for use in combat? But behind the technical arguments, it remained a dispute over "turf, that is, whether there would be needless duplication of force capabilities."[12]

These disagreements also reflected differences in view about the probable nature of future wars and how to fight them most effectively. Gen William W. Momyer, former commander of the Seventh Air Force in Southeast Asia and former commander of the Tactical Air Command, argued that Army and Navy commanders mistook the flexibility of air power as a justification to fragment it. Instead, Momyer insisted, its flexibility and effectiveness depended on the "centralized control of air power" in a theater of war.[13] He thought the use of air power in North Africa, Europe, and Korea proved "the need for a command structure that didn't arbitrarily divide forces between mission areas."[14] But unity of control had less appeal for those who saw air power only as ancillary in the Vietnam conflict. And even if one accepted air power as critical, there were many models of how best to use it. In particular, the use of helicopters in an airborne assault role raised questions about proper control. For example, the flexibility envisioned in airmobility centered on rapid movement and redeployment of troops; but among Air Force officers, it tended to mean versatility and using assets in successively varying roles.

While the Air Force favored a general and comprehensive view of what air power was and how it worked, the Army was developing a specific subset of air power with more restrictive uses in combat. Even so, the Army did not accurately foresee the actual combat role of airmobility in the 1960s. Airmobility was not conceived initially as a way of dealing with counterinsurgency or low-intensity conflict. According to General Williams, tests of the Army's air assault division were well under way before its designers gave any thought to using it in a Vietnam type of operation. During the development stages, Army Chief of Staff Gen Harold K. Johnson asked how the airmobile division would do in Vietnam. The question "really came as quite a surprise to me," General Williams remembered.[15] Similarly, in reflecting on discussions of this issue with Gen Harry Kinnard, Maj Gen Delk Oden recalled that the 1st Cavalry, going to Vietnam, expected to fight a mid-intensity war but actually fought a brushfire war. Maj Gen George P. Seneff, the first commander of the 1st Aviation Brigade in Vietnam, showed even greater surprise. He was told by Gen Creighton W. Abrams in the autumn of 1962 that the forerunner of the 1st Aviation Brigade, the Utility Tactical Transport Company, was to deploy to Vietnam as a de facto gunship unit. General Seneff later said, ''I damn near rolled on the floor.'' He elaborated on the move.

> It was a decision of expediency. They needed something they could get over there in a hurry, and the central highlands was selected as the area where they could best operate. They had the capability of getting back into Pleiku when nothing else could because the roads had been closed for years.[16]

In part, advocates of airmobility in the Army were so eager to justify an airmobile capability that original plans for the airmobile division became secondary. To some degree, this resulted from a need to defend the project from what Army officers saw as opposition from the Air Force. An example of this interservice infighting suggests the mood of the time. The Army chartered a distinguished board headed by General Howze to assess the worth and role of the airmobile division and air assault concepts. The Air Force quickly responded and set up a parallel board under Lt Gen Gabriel P. Disosway. The Disosway Board, under Strike Command (STRICOM), was to assess the ability of the Air Force to provide support comparable to that offered by Army organic aviation. The suspicions the two services harbored put claims on time and talent. War with the foreign enemy was the ultimate challenge, but jousting with one's brother officers was the more immediate and pressing task.[17] The tangles over equipment and roles from World War II through the 1950s substantially influenced the armed forces as to what command and control systems were needed in Vietnam.

The Search for Simplicity in the Complexity of Southeast Asia

The command and control arrangements for Vietnam and Southeast Asia may make more sense when viewed as a political phenomenon than as a strictly military one. They evolved over time as competing interests and perceived needs varied and changed. Command and control is basically a question of who has the authority to order whom to do what and what means are available to ensure that it gets done. These two issues have great doctrinal weight, and interservice differences show themselves here readily. For each service, the vision of objective reality passes through a subjective lens of service history and doctrine. The result is often competition among varying alternatives, each meant to serve the nation's security. Commonly, each proposal favors the interest of the service advancing it. Irrespective of motive, the services offered the simplest possible answers to the complex problems of Southeast Asia. In itself, the search for simplicity was only an effort to follow a principle of war. Yet finding a solution that worked proved as elusive as a common vision of the war itself. Even the belief that a single or simple solution was thinkable may have been a problem in itself, given the complexity of the war. What developed, in fact, was not a single system but a network of interlocking arrangements of command authorities and controlling agents. Meanwhile, since it was essential to firm up the political image and the actual strength of the Saigon government, the US government had to restrain itself lest it confirm charges of US imperialism. The challenge was to create satisfactory command and control systems despite the complexity of the problems being faced and differences over how to meet them.

In a simple sense, the issue boiled down to: satisfactory to whom? A unified command and control system over all of Southeast Asia made a good deal of sense from a military perspective. But because the war crossed political boundaries, State Department officials also took interest in the matter; and they often sided with the Southeast Asian leaders who wanted command and control systems that respected their borders. And no matter how one defined the boundaries of a given theater, the services could still disagree over what form of control was needed within it. In addition, the simultaneous operation of US, South Vietnamese, and other free world forces turned command and control into an international issue. What might be best from one nation's vantage point might be genuinely frustrating from another; the optimum solution to one problem might produce confusion and disarray in another area. Although all parties seemed to seek the virtues of simplicity, each simple solution seemed to its detractors to handle only one part of the multifaceted Southeast Asian problem.

Command and control requirements in Southeast Asia were driven in part by the growing commitment in numbers and kinds of units. But perceptions about the war had great force, and this allowed an essentially internal US issue to affect the military scene in Vietnam and Southeast Asia just as surely as the war itself affected the status of US forces. Late in 1961, for example, the Joint Chiefs of Staff (JCS) proposed that a unified command reporting directly to the JCS be established in Vietnam to control all US forces in the country. There would thus be one voice for all US military efforts in Vietnam. Yet this plan presupposed that the war was confined to Vietnam and could be separated from action elsewhere. But, Adm Harry D. Felt, commander in chief, Pacific Command (CINCPAC), argued that the proposed Military Assistance Command Vietnam (MACV) should not report directly to the Joint Chiefs. Admiral Felt envisioned a general Communist threat throughout all of Southeast Asia and argued that the command in Vietnam should be unified and subordinated under the Pacific Command. This disagreement showed more than bureaucratic infighting; it illustrated how one's perceptions of the conflict shaped judgments on how to fight it.[18]

CINCPAC also fostered an unusual command arrangement: The 2d Air Division (located at Tan Son Nhut Air Base), which succeeded the 2d Air Division Advanced Echelon (ADVON), not only exercised operational control of Air Force units in COMUSMACTHAI's (commander, US Military Assistance Command Thailand) area of activity on behalf of the commander in chief, Pacific Air Forces (PACAF), Maj Gen Emmett O'Donnell, Jr., but also exercised administrative control of Thirteenth Air Force units located in South Vietnam. Admiral Felt's goal, in which

General O'Donnell concurred, was to ensure control of the broader air war outside South Vietnam. They based this on the supposition that Air Force units in Thailand would play a key role in the air war against Laos and North Vietnam. On the other hand, Thai and South Vietnamese sensitivities also encouraged improvisation. As the US commitment increased in 1965, sharpening a separation between Thailand and South Vietnam became diplomatically important. In particular, the Thais were unwilling to have a commander located in South Vietnam exercise control over air power based in their country; but the means of assuring this emerged only as the war expanded.[19]

The war included business-as-usual interservice relationships as well as adaptation to circumstances. Conditions in Vietnam changed, but established ideas about organizing for war in general held sway. Contingency planning for unilateral US action in Southeast Asia or for joint action through Southeast Asia Treaty Organization (SEATO) had specified that the deputy commander in chief, US Army Pacific, was to serve not only as overall field commander but also as commander of his own Army component. This met Admiral Felt's recommendations. On 8 February 1962, with the approval of President Kennedy and Secretary McNamara and by order of the JCS, Admiral Felt established the US Military Assistance Command Vietnam as a subordinate unified command under his control. Lt Gen Paul D. Harkins became the commander of MACV (COMUSMACV) and was promoted to general. As something of a compromise, MACV could theoretically be either subsumed into a joint/combined headquarters in Thailand if the war expanded or deactivated if the enemy were swiftly defeated. Since the command was to be withdrawn with reasonable speed after the Vietcong insurgency had been squelched, the Military Assistance Advisory Group (MAAG), now under Maj Gen Charles J. Timmes, was continued and placed temporarily under the authority of MACV. Thus, General Harkins could not concentrate solely on his duties in Vietnam. Admiral Felt also ordered him to plan on assisting the Pacific Command if insurgency or conventional war should spread throughout Southeast Asia. Although logically a part of his responsibilities within the Pacific Command, this may have distracted him somewhat from the events in Vietnam.[20]

General Harkins' task as the COMUSMACV was further complicated when Admiral Felt established the US Military Assistance Command Thailand and made Harkins commander of that group, too. This action, taken on 15 May 1962, reflected Admiral Felt's holistic view of the war; it represented an effort to achieve some simplicity, clarity, and effectiveness in the command structure. Admiral Felt appears to have envisioned General Harkins as operating with sustained authority over a widening theater, but Harkins was forced to deal with steadily more numerous and diverse problems. The technical overlap between MACV and MAAG was mitigated somewhat by Harkins' delegation of control over ground forces in Vietnam to General Timmes, but this measure could not in itself secure the unity that Admiral Felt was so intent on achieving.

Eventually, General Harkins seems to have come to similar conclusions. In March 1964, he proposed changes in command and control arrangements that would end MAAG because it created a needless extra step in MACV's response to South Vietnamese requests for assistance. He also urged that MACV be a specified command of the Army, reporting directly to the JCS rather than to a subordinate unified command. The air and naval sections of the MAAG would become advisory groups to the Army command with the commanders of each section exercising actual control over these advisory units. Adm U. S. Grant Sharp, who had succeeded Admiral Felt, objected to this arrangement. He claimed that it would, in effect, establish two additional MAAGs—one for each service—under Harkins' Army MACV. He thought the idea of Harkins reporting directly to the JCS undermined the ability of the Pacific Command to support a comprehensive effort, and he believed that the COMUSMACV would be overburdened and spread too thin with this widened span of control. Instead, Sharp proposed a limited measure that would have made reporting procedures more manageable without significantly altering operations. The JCS approved the essence of General Harkins' plan early in April 1964, but they refused to let MACV operate as an Army specified command. The goal of efficiency and simplicity survived efforts to reform command and control arrangements but continued to spark controversy.

General Harkins' appointment as the COMUSMACV also led to lasting differences with the Air Force, Navy, and Marines over the distribution of authority. Joint service doctrine indicated that a joint headquarters should reflect the composition of forces assigned; and to the extent that the war in Vietnam was a ground war, the dominance of ground officers in MACV might seem justified. But the Air Force leadership soon became convinced that the MACV staff was dangerously overloaded with Army personnel. General LeMay considered Army dominance at MACV a detriment to the effective employment of air power. By early 1962, he had concluded that air power was being used too slowly and that the command system was too sluggish. The Air Force had committed itself to support outlying posts in Operation Farm Gate, using relatively small and slow aircraft. Now General LeMay used the Farm Gate program to claim a greater Air Force presence in MACV, arguing that Farm Gate could be more effective if more Air Force personnel had authority at higher command levels.[21]

Reaction to General LeMay's proposal, from the Air Force point of view, left much to be desired. And reports were even more alarming later. A message from Thirteenth Air Force to PACAF in October 1962 equated prospects for success in Vietnam with the interests of the Air Force.

> USAF interests are suffering in SEA. The trend toward an Army dominated or controlled COIN (Counter-insurgency) effort is clear. Because the USAF position in COMUSMACV's structure is weak in both numbers and rank, the Army is able to impose their will. . . . Their case will cost the USAF in roles and missions and will cost US lives in future actions. Army people are, in effect, being trained to consider our tactics ineffective and our capability limited, while being oversold on Army organic air.[22]

The Air Force was not alone in thinking itself aggrieved. In October 1962, based on the unified action armed forces doctrine, Admiral Felt placed an Army combat cargo group under control of the 2d Air Division, much to the distaste of the Army. The Army resented losing control over assets such as the CV-2 Caribou, especially since the Air Force insisted that it had responsibility for coordinating all air activities through the tactical air control system.

Control of air power over the battlefield kept the Army and Air Force at odds. Rooted in genuine concerns, this issue had many practical consequences. Air space had to be allocated usefully, scarce air assets had to be used to greatest effect, and maintenance/reliability had to be considered. There were many other practical problems to be resolved, and various officers were no doubt sincere in their proposals. But sincerity was not the point. The heart of the matter was that failure to set out a clear vision of the war frustrated the effort to determine clear and agreed means of fighting it. And without unity, the separate and specialized perspectives of the service branches all but inevitably retained great force. The Air Force held that air power used over the battlefield was its responsibility; the Army argued that its own aircraft (primarily helicopters) supported the ground commander in much the same way that jeeps or trucks did and should be controlled directly by him. The decision to give the Air Force control of Caribou fixed-wing tactical airlift assets while the Army retained its helicopters was a compromise that leaders of the two services could live with. But it satisfied no one completely. Army and Air Force air operations were ultimately coordinated through the combined USAF–VNAF Air Operations Center (AOC) (the US Army AOC was now collocated at the same site).[23] Although this particular matter was resolved on grounds generally favorable to the Air Force, the basic problem of air operations control continued to rankle Air Force leaders. To those Air Force officers who had predicted that the Army would seek to increase the size of its aircraft, the Caribou seemed to be concrete proof; and to those who feared that the Army wanted to develop a separate air component, the increasing interest in helicopters offered confirmation.

Such interservice differences continued to sour relations among some high military officials throughout the war. Gen William C. Westmoreland acknowledged in his memoirs that the "tendency for US Army advisors to rely on helicopters rather than fighter planes contributed to a long-held US Air Force concern that the US Army was trying to usurp the Air Force role." Westmoreland said that General LeMay criticized him on this very score when they met in Washington late in 1964. He later said that General LeMay administered a tongue-lashing to Maj Gen Joseph H. Moore, then the highest Air Force officer in MACV, for failure to uphold Air Force doctrine.

Westmoreland suggested that LeMay might have adopted a more lenient attitude if he had visited Vietnam during Westmoreland's command and examined the war firsthand. "Had he done so, he might have learned that counterinsurgency warfare required many variations from conventional practices and that there was room enough amid the myriad requirements for close air support in Vietnam for both fighter plane and helicopter gunship.''[24] But this remark ignores the widely held Air Force feeling that the war in 1964 could no longer be correctly described as a counterinsurgency. It also reflects how perceptions of the war's character affected the war's conduct.

Problems indigenous to the theater of operations often interlocked with interservice tensions. As action in Vietnam intensified, some revision in command and control became increasingly necessary. On 10 July 1965, the duties of the MACV commander and the MACTHAI commander were separated, permitting General Westmoreland (who had succeeded General Harkins in Saigon) to focus on Vietnam. This decision required more than a year of discussions at Pacific Command headquarters and in the Department of Defense. A unified command for the region remained preferable for some, primarily on grounds that the military situation would be ill-served by fragmenting the command. But political considerations of high importance, notably the resentment among the Thais that their affairs were managed from Saigon, suggested separation and division into two different command lines. When this latter view prevailed, Gen Ernest F. Easterbrook, MAAG commander in Thailand, assumed command of the new Military Assistance Command Thailand (MACTHAI). He also retained control of the advisory group there until the two were consolidated late in 1965.[25]

Ironically, providing the most appropriate match between US forces and their South Vietnamese counterparts did not yield a simple system. The commander of the naval advisory group reported to the naval component commander in MACV, who was also the commander of US Naval Forces, Vietnam. Likewise, the chief of the Air Force advisory group was also both the commander of the 2d Air Division and the Air Force component commander in Vietnam. Both naval and air component commanders received guidance and direction from the COMUSMACV. In contrast, Army advisers were directly under the operational control of the COMUSMACV: nine Army advisory groups reported directly to General Westmoreland rather than to a separate Army component commander. When the III Marine Amphibious Force arrived in 1965, adviser control was given to the commanding general of the Marine Amphibious Force (MAF); yet the previously responsible Army colonel continued to serve as deputy senior adviser. This meant that MACV had, for working purposes, both a Marine Corps and Navy component commander.

From one perspective, General Westmoreland's serving as his own Army component commander promised simplicity in command and control. Seen from another point of view, however, this arrangement cast a constant shadow of doubt upon Westmoreland's objectivity. How could he see the relative roles of air, sea, and ground forces in a balanced fashion when he was specifically responsible for carrying out as his own ground force commander orders which he issued as the COMUSMACV? Gen Douglas MacArthur's role as both unified and ground force commander in World War II and the Korean War provided a historical precedent for Westmoreland's course of action, and this arrangement was compatible with Army doctrine; but when tested against joint doctrine, the command arrangement in Southeast Asia seemed to be more improvisation than simplification.[26]

Integration of command over US and South Vietnamese forces proved similarly elusive. The US military substantially favored a combined US–South Vietnamese headquarters with a US commander and a South Vietnamese deputy, and the arrival of US combat forces and other free world forces encouraged General Westmoreland to favor this approach. But after short-lived hope that the South Vietnamese might receive it well, the concept of a combined command met with resistance. The political problem ultimately proved insurmountable, as the Saigon government sought to keep the public face of independence. In the end, coordination was the only available option; having lost the battle for what many US officers regarded as the ideal command arrangement, the US military acquiesced and adapted to its South Vietnamese counterpart.[27]

One of the main advantages seen in having General Westmoreland serve as COMUSMACV and as his own Army component commander was that it paralleled the Army of the Republic of Vietnam (ARVN) structure. Moreover, South Vietnamese officers sometimes voiced their dissatisfaction with various alternatives either contemplated or executed by the United States. In II Corps, for example, after Task Force Alpha was replaced by Field Forces, Vietnam, the commanding general of the Vietnamese II Corps objected to the fact that he was advised by the commanding general of US field forces rather than by the senior US officer in his area. In response to his complaint, the field forces commander was named senior adviser to the Vietnamese II Corps commanding general. Comparable changes were made in III Corps; but since General Westmoreland commanded the advisory group in IV Corps, there could be little resentment there as to the authority and rank of the senior American adviser.[28] The degree to which other Vietnamese concerns complicated command and control arrangements is suggested by Maj Gen George S. Eckhardt's remark that the American system in 1965 was compatible with the command and control system of the Vietnamese army, in which operational control of army forces rested with the South Vietnamese joint general staff, while the Vietnamese naval and air forces were under operational control of their respective commanders.[29] Such measures met Vietnamese sensitivities and built a system parallel to theirs more than they simplified management of the US contribution to the war effort.

Pressures for Change

Just as political and doctrinal interests created various pressures and enlivened the differences among the services, so did the practical problems of managing forces as they were committed. Again, the absence of a clear view of the war meant an absence of shared criteria. Whatever the apparent problem—technical, administrative, doctrinal—the underlying question was who would run the war. Implicitly, this also shaped how the war was to be fought.

The major buildup of US forces in South Vietnam during 1965 and 1966, and the arrival of allied forces in combat and support roles, exemplified changes in the command and control system. Both factors added to the burgeoning complexity of the machinery of war management, but they did not create pressure for a simplified or centralized system of command and control. The sheer increase in numbers created strains of its own. Contingency planning for such a buildup began late in 1964 and continued into the following year. The Army Support Command, Vietnam—created in 1964 in response to pressures generated by previous increases in US force levels—had its own specialized duties, which hindered its reorganization into a comprehensive logistical command even though earlier contingency planning had envisioned such a reorganization. Thus, Army Chief of Staff General Johnson proposed a new US command to manage logistical and administrative matters for Army forces in Vietnam. He specified that operational control of this command be given to the MACV commander. Admiral Sharp, as commander in chief, Pacific Command, opposed this measure; so did General Westmoreland. Discussions continued from March 1965, when General Johnson proposed his measure to the JCS, into July 1965. Gen John K. Waters, commander in chief, US Army, Pacific, continued to represent the views advanced by General Johnson. General Westmoreland, seeking to maximize his flexibility and authority in Vietnam, proposed a series of measures: to redesignate the US Army Support Command as US Army, Vietnam (USARV); to retain for the MACV commander the responsibilities of the US Army component commander in the capacity of commanding general, US Army, Vietnam; to assign all US Army units in Vietnam to USARV; and to establish a series of corps headquarters in Vietnam to conduct combat operations in their respective zones under Westmoreland's operational control. General Waters and the Department of the Army approved this plan and instructions came from US Army, Pacific, on 20 July 1965. General Eckhardt criticized this arrangement.

> The appointment of General Westmoreland as USARV's commanding general was a step away from the creation of a true Army component commander. Although the MACV commander had been the Army component commander since August 1963, the senior Army headquarters in Vietnam had had its own commanding general. With the change of July 1965, both positions were occupied by the same individual, General Westmoreland. Thus he was put in the position of having to serve two masters: the commander in chief, Pacific, and the commander in chief, US Army, Pacific. Similarly, US Army organizations in Vietnam were responsible to the head of the Military Assistance Command for combat operations and to the commander in chief of US Army, Pacific, for Army matters. The overlapping chains of command resulted in duplication and confusion within the MACV-USARV structure.[30]

The command of air power in Southeast Asia also came in a complex package. The 2d Air Division Advanced Echelon yielded to a reinforced air division as the use of air power increased in the early 1960s, and the growth of the war in 1965 and 1966 forced new thinking on how to structure operational and administrative support. In March 1966, the 2d Air Division was deactivated. In its place, the

Seventh Air Force was established at Tan Son Nhut Air Base. But even though it served as the Air Force element in MACV, Seventh Air Force was not truly an air component command because it did not exert control over marine and navy aviation.[31] In this sense, it remained a single service command. Coordinating the various elements of air power thus remained knotty. General Westmoreland disapproved of a proposal, favored by the Air Staff, to name an Air Force officer as his deputy commander in MACV. Westmoreland's opposition probably stemmed from his view of the Vietnam conflict as essentially a ground war; and there is no evidence to suggest that Westmoreland anticipated needing someone capable of unifying air power in Vietnam. The Air Staff disliked the idea of settling for a deputy for air operations whose role might be largely advisory; the Air Force wanted to maximize its doctrinal impact within MACV. But the decision to have a deputy for air operations was sustained. The air deputy was to provide a central focus for operational control of air power but was not given control of Marine aviation or Army helicopters.[32] And the Navy insisted on its need for autonomy.

Nor was the issue of control of air power only an interservice issue; differences within the Air Force also contributed. And the desire of officials in Washington to maximize their direction of the war further complicated the issue of who would control air power. The net effect was to increase both improvisation and compromise. The control of Strategic Air Command (SAC) bomber and tanker forces was a likely object of such compromise and improvisation. In previous wars, strategic aircraft used in support of theater operations had been placed under operational control of the theater commander. For example, World War II bomber forces in Northwest Africa and in the invasion of Europe were placed under the operational control of Supreme Headquarters, Allied Expeditionary Forces (SHAEF). And in the Korean War, the JCS directed SAC to put strategic bombing forces under the operational control of General MacArthur through his Air Force component command, the Far East Air Forces (FEAF).[33]

Notwithstanding such historical precedents, the conditions of war in Southeast Asia militated in favor of a different course of action. For one thing, the COMUSMACV was responsible for operations only in South Vietnam rather than in Southeast Asia as a whole. Moreover, the COMUSMACV did not even control all air power operating in South Vietnam, let alone Southeast Asia. Theoretically, then, the lowest level to which authority over SAC forces could have been delegated was CINCPAC, although CINCPAC could have delegated authority to commander in chief, Pacific Air Forces—perhaps even to Seventh Air Force. In any case, the complexities of the Vietnam conflict and the Southeast Asian settings weighed against unified direction of air operations.[34]

Additional arguments against putting a theater commander in charge of strategic bombers came from SAC and from considerations of national strategy. The role of B-52s in a possible nuclear strike against the Soviet Union made it important to preserve the credibility of the bomber forces. Losing B-52 aircraft in the Vietnam conflict might degrade SAC's credibility; and placing them under a theater commander might delay their transfer back to SAC in the event of a strategic crisis. Such arguments might not have been sufficient in themselves to determine the outcome of the issue of operational control, but they meshed well with the decision in Washington to retain control over targeting and to follow there the progress of the B-52 actions. These improvisations and compromises stemmed from the desire to retain rapid response capability and from the impulse to hold control as closely as possible in the hands of civilian authorities. And these competing interests contributed to the need for further improvisation in the control of air power.[35]

The series of ad hoc measures to coordinate the actions of SAC, MACV, and other interested parties created a long process for approving targets and authorizing operations: Ground commanders and the Seventh Air Force nominated targets to MACV; MACV approved them and sent a list to CINCPAC; CINCPAC sent the list to JCS; JCS sent it to the secretary of defense; and the secretary of defense coordinated with the secretary of state before sending it to the president. Delay was inevitable. Meanwhile, to facilitate proper use of the B-52s, a SAC liaison team was assigned to MACV. This team represented a force operating throughout the theater even though they were located at a headquarters that dealt with only a part of it; and SAC itself was never placed under the authority of those who were responsible for the prosecution of the war within South Vietnam.

That an alternative arrangement could have made the B-52s more responsive to the demands of the ground war than they were is by no means clear. But the arrangement actually used tended to suggest that strategic bombers were likely to be committed only where bombing missions would give maximum benefit.[36] Moreover, since the discussions among JCS, CINCPAC, COMUSMACV, and others had generated a compromise that often distinguished between operations within South Vietnam and those outside the country, multiple (and, arguably, redundant) tactical air control centers (TACCs) were established; but tactical aircraft and strategic aircraft still had to be coordinated. Direct air support centers (DASCs) were also set up in each of the four military regions (I through IV), with Vietnamese air force (VNAF) personnel controlling VNAF operations while US Air Force personnel ran US Air Force operations. And redundant DASCs were established in military regions I and III. (In the former, DASC Victor served US Air Force and DASC Horn served the Marines while I DASC handled VNAF; in the latter, DASC Alpha supported US forces while III DASC supported ARVN.) None of this did much to simplify things.[37]

The introduction of US combat forces in large numbers bought time, but the disagreements and confusions of earlier months continued. To the extent that these larger numbers seemed to contain the pressing nature of problems with the insurgency, the pressure for decisive clarification of administrative arrangements slackened. Indeed, one of the most curious and troubling aspects of the Vietnam conflict was the persistence of differences over command and control during phases of the war seen then and later as pivotal.

The Marine defense of Khe Sanh showed the persistence of competing views about the use of air power and raised questions about their resolution. As the effort to defend Khe Sanh against massing enemy forces intensified early in 1968, General Westmoreland established a MACV Forward headquarters at Hue-Phu Bai with General Abrams in command. General Abrams exercised control over all joint combat and logistical forces in the area. Air Force air efforts were controlled through Seventh Air Force and SAC, while III MAF had primary responsibility for Marine air support. In contrast, control on the ground was clarified. After negotiations between Lt Gen Robert E. Cushman, commanding general of the III MAF, and General Momyer, commander of the Seventh Air Force, the Marines had control of the Khe Sanh tactical air region. General Cushman then delegated to Col David Lownds, commander on the ground at Khe Sanh, the authority to control all supporting fire (including air strikes) within range of the regiment's 155-mm howitzers. But operational difficulties caused Westmoreland to reconsider the control of air assets; and by mid-February, overall control was given to the commander of the Seventh Air Force through the airborne command and control center (ABCCC), which normally operated outside South Vietnam. Only after the crisis at Khe Sanh had passed did Westmoreland appoint General Momyer as his deputy for air operations.[38]

General Momyer had repeatedly pressed for an air operations deputy, especially throughout the siege of Khe Sanh.[39] So what one service element regarded as the proper tactical air control system for Khe Sanh was established only after the battle had crested. More significant, it took place only as part of a pattern of changes. Other changes included MACV Forward becoming the provisional corps headquarters (provisional corps encompassed those troops in the northern part of I Corps). I Corps itself retained control of troops in the southern half. The provisional corps headquarters, under Army Lt Gen William B. Rosson, had operational control over the 3d Marine Division, the 1st Cavalry Division, the 101st Airborne Division, and other units. Meanwhile, Marine General Cushman was to concentrate on such efforts as civil operations and rural development support programs throughout I Corps.

These measures did not please everyone, nor did they respond only to US pressures. Creation of the provisional corps led to establishment of DASC Victor, which was subordinate to the joint USAF–VNAF DASC in I Corps. But the South Vietnamese opposed the US proposal to merge DASC Victor and the I Corps DASC with the Marine tactical air direction center (TADC) at Camp Horn. While US officers pressed centralization to maximize the effectiveness of air power, VNAF officials resisted losing control of their aircraft. Political considerations prevailed. The I Corps DASC continued to operate for the VNAF while Horn and Victor DASCs operated for US forces.[40]

Given the outcome at Khe Sanh, it would be glib, and somewhat doubtful, to claim that control arrangements were a failure. Yet there was a failure to anticipate and establish the kind of control arrangements that were ultimately accepted as necessary. It was not that the United States could not plan ahead. Careful preparation had been given to the placement of sensors and to gathering intelligence by other means, and MACV specifically expected a major enemy effort at Khe Sanh. So the delays in command and control cannot be attributed to enemy surprises.[41] At length, in early March, a single commander and a single tactical air control system for the Khe Sanh area and northern I Corps were agreed upon. It would be hard to say that urgency had shown itself in haste.[42]

The changes that were not made serve as a commentary on priorities. An example is the issue of communication with strike aircraft when they are flying in direct support of ground operations. Throughout the war, air-to-ground communications were restricted so that strike aircraft could not directly monitor ground forces radio. Some urged that strike aircraft be equipped with VHF and FM equipment so that pilots could better comprehend their intended roles, but three arguments were advanced against this measure. One was that the aircraft lacked the necessary space. A second was that pilots would be distracted by irrelevant information. The third was that ground commanders might call directly upon pilots of strike aircraft to assist them, further diminishing centralization. In July 1968, after a study by Seventh Air Force, an operational requirement was submitted for VHF and FM radios in F-4 and F-100 aircraft. Upgraded to required-operational-capability status in January 1969, it was canceled in September 1969 without having received an operational evaluation.[43] Such a radio capability could have reduced the chances of some US pilots being shot down, had the ground forces been able to warn them of enemy antiaircraft capabilities.[44] Support of ground operations might also have been enhanced.

To what purposes were command and control really dedicated? And which purpose was primary, which others secondary? The long-run issue was how to adopt an essentially functionalist approach, but the short run persistently intruded. A hint of how issues other than operational efficiency affected control issues came in the reluctance of the Air Force to support fully the development of the Southeast Asia integrated tactical air control system (SEAITACS). On purely operational grounds, SEAITACS was an improvement. The air control system prior to 1965 had consisted of relatively old mobile assets and had not met the demands of the air war. A survey team from Headquarters USAF, TAC, and Thirteenth Air Force developed SEAITACS specifically to meet the projected operational needs. But the Air Staff was reluctant to spend Air Force funds for a system designed to accommodate the air power of the other services. The Air Force did agree to support SEAITACS, but the Air Staff's reluctance suggests how easily a doctrinally acceptable goal could be endangered.[45]

New technologies held out the possibility of providing solutions to the command and control problems in Southeast Asia, but new technologies were not politically neutral. And hardware created to bring solutions to existing problems sometimes generate new problems. Individuals expert in the concepts and techniques of command and control might not be expert in the technologies of automation. Thus, discrepancies could develop unintentionally; and there was no reason to assume that some deliberate skewing would not occur. Many problems could be overcome, but as Lt Col John J. Lane, Jr., concluded, efforts often failed because they sought inappropriately to standardize hardware for diverse operational requirements. For example, the Seek Data II system was designed to automate various manpower-intensive functions of the TACC while the Pacific integrated automated command and control system (PIACCS) program sought to do the same for the communications center. Yet although the two systems were to be linked, the final result was not well integrated. One problem was a tendency to give priority to the efficiency of the hardware itself rather than to the operations it was intended to support. The automatic digital network (AUTODIN), automatic voice switching network (AUTOVON), and automatic secure voice communications (AUTOSEVOCOM) systems were generally successful; and the backbone transmission system in South Vietnam was "technically successful, but at an operational cost." In contrast, the digital subscriber terminal equipment (DSTE) system "was fraught throughout with problems."[46]

Apart from matters of technological efficiency, a persistent problem of organizational interest lurked beneath the surface.

> If an automated command-and-control system is to interface directly with an automated communications network, which organization should provide the interface mechanisms? Questions of this nature are of more than merely academic interest, since their answer, in practice, can be based on organizational interests rather than technical imperatives.[47]

In other words, technical systems were far from neutral. Their design could reflect specific command concerns and aim at particular patterns of control.

Doctrine and Complexity

The command and control arrangements for the Vietnam conflict were a peculiar mixture of doctrine based on experience, reaction to changing circumstances in Southeast Asia, and competing demands within the US national security system. General Eckhardt described it in the Army's official history on command and control: "In Vietnam the doctrine of command and control drew heavily on historical precedent, but its application tended to be more complex than it had been in the past and became more involved as the mission of the US command expanded."[48] Since future Vietnams cannot be ruled out, General Eckhardt urged that the problems of complexity be dealt with forthrightly. He outlined the specific principles: unified command directly under the JCS; unified command control over the forces of the host country, at least initially; combined operational and planning staffs at the theater level and at major subordinate operating commands; component headquarters control over their respective US branches, translating guidance from the theater commander into specific performance; component command control over MAAGs; field force or corps-level commands; an organization such as CORDS (Coherent On Receive Doppler System) with control apparently centering on civilian activities; field- or corps-level control of combat support units and service units; and single-manager logistic support.[49]

The scrambling required to piece together a workable system may have added to delay in prosecuting the war. If there is any truth to the often repeated statement that the people of the United States will not fight a long war, then it is imperative to make the war as short as possible. Whether the Vietnam War could have been shorter may never be clearly known, but the ability of the United States to fight effectively seems to have come only after distinct delays following insertion of US forces. Whether it was a case of building sufficient forces, equipping them amply, organizing them effectively, or developing new weapons and tactics, the net effect was a lag between the apparent and real starts of the US commitment. Thus, a kind of unpreparedness rooted in attitudes ensured that the war would be perceived as a long one by the US population and even by their government.

For several reasons, one cannot pass off delays and disagreements on command and control by saying that the United States ultimately muddled through.[50] First, it may have done so with a diminished capacity to meet the demands of the war. Second, it may encourage a dangerous and destructive precedent. (The long lulls required for resolving some issues in Vietnam may not be available in a future war.) Finally, whatever added to the length of the war strained the patience required to conduct it. Technological and tactical innovations do not diminish the need for relevant and agreed-upon doctrine. In fact, doctrinal unpreparedness may have been more troublesome than technological unpreparedness; the latter often depended on the former.

The command and control system for the war in Southeast Asia was pieced together incrementally, much as the war itself was pieced together. The original tactical air control system instituted to support the Vietnamese air force aimed at handling an estimated volume of traffic under projected conditions. It also conformed to the political needs of Saigon. As additional forces came to South Vietnam and elsewhere in Southeast Asia, demands changed. The command and control system that emerged was governed neither by pure doctrine nor by pure experience; it rested in a middle ground, which satisfied the demands of neither.[51]

It has been suggested that doctrine concerning command and control was largely disregarded during the Vietnam conflict.[52] To be more precise, one should say that various doctrinal alternatives gained favor at successive stages of the war. The problem was not that certain factions might frivolously ignore doctrinal views developed through experience, but that different parties held differing positions. Thus, a doctrinal view held by one service could be viewed by the other services as a disregard of proper doctrine. Seen this way, the Vietnam conflict suggests that disagreement among the services cannot be expected to vanish in wartime.

If clear doctrine and real adherence to it are to prevail in war, they must be obtained in peace. Wartime conditions do not necessarily create a sense of urgency sufficient to overcome military and civilian disputes about proper doctrine. Nor does citing the political challenge involved in resolving these disagreements during peacetime excuse failure to do so. Commenting on the limitations of the command and control system for the air war over North Vietnam, General Momyer pointed to how peacetime differences persisted in wartime. He perceived much of the difficulty in waging the air war as arising from competing doctrinal views that should have been reconciled in peacetime. The issue of controlling "two air forces from two different services" had appeared in the Korean War, he noted, and it would probably be "exceedingly costly in some future conflict such as, for instance, a NATO war." General Momyer focused on maintaining the unity of air power rather than on the particular time by which that unity must be assured, but experience suggests that centralized control cannot be safely deferred until air forces from two services are already in place.[53]

In Vietnam, issues of command having to do with precedence and authority proved to be more compelling than concern about maximizing effectiveness in actual operations. For example, the use of coordinating authority by CINCPAC to mesh the efforts of the Navy and the Air Force was more suitable for planning than for operations.[54] A given service could genuinely equate its own doctrine and operational effectiveness with likelihood for overall success in the war effort. The gravest indictment of the command structure in Vietnam may rest, as some have said, in the failure to apply maximum aerial firepower. Yet this may have followed from failure to effectively match air power to the character of the war itself. Certainty on this matter is elusive precisely because the various visions of the war were projected through the lenses of doctrines that have yet to be reconciled.

NOTES

1. Gen Robert R. Williams, USA, interview with Col Ralph J. Powell and Lt Col Philip E. Courts, 1977, US Army Military History Research Institute, Oral History Series, The History of Army Aviation, 2.

2. Ibid., 17–18.

3. Ibid.

4. Brig Gen O. Glenn Goodhand, USA, interview with Col Bryce R. Kramer and Lt Col Ronald K. Andersen, 9 May 1978, US Army Military History Research Institute, Oral History Series, The History of Army Aviation, 40.

5. General Williams interview, 37.

6. Ibid., 42–44.

7. Ibid., 44.

8. Ibid., 45.

9. General Williams interview, 25.

10. The concern over possible separatist tendencies among Army aviators became part of the argument against forming a separate Aviation Branch within the Army, but deficiencies in the system as it had operated were seen to have created sufficient personnel pressures so as to outweigh the preponderance of concerns; the Aviation Branch was approved in 1983.

11. House, *Sundry Legislation Affecting the Naval and Military Establishment*, 88th Cong., 1st sess., 1963, vol. 3, 6072.

12. Robert Frank Futrell, *Ideas, Concepts, Doctrine: A History of Basic Thinking in the United States Air Force, 1907–1964* (Maxwell AFB, Ala.: Air University, 1971), 410–11.

13. Gen William W. Momyer, USAF (Ret.), *Air Power in Three Wars* (n.p., 1978), 107–8.

14. Ibid., 62.

15. General Williams interview, 60–62.

16. Gen George P. Seneff, USA, interview with Lt Col Ronald K. Andersen, US Army Military History Institute, Oral History Series, The History of Army Aviation, 37.

17. General Williams interview, 64–65.

18. For information concerning Adm Harry D. Felt and references to various documents, see Maj Gen George S. Eckhardt, *Command and Control, 1950–1969,* Vietnam Studies (Washington, D.C.: Department of the Army, 1974), 26–27.

19. Lt Col John J. Lane, Jr., USAF, *Command and Control and Communications Structures in Southeast Asia* (Maxwell AFB, Ala.: Airpower Research Institute, 1981), 58–59.

20. Eckhardt, *Command and Control,* 26–27; Lane, *Command and Control and Communications,* 40.

21. Momyer, *Air Power,* 73; Lane, *Command and Control and Communications,* 41.

22. Quoted in Earl Tilford, *The USAF Search and Rescue in Southeast Asia* (Washington, D.C.: Office of Air Force History, 1980).

23. Eckhardt, *Command and Control,* 37–38; Lane, *Command and Control and Communications,* 51.

24. Gen William C. Westmoreland, *A Soldier Reports* (Garden City, N.Y.: Doubleday & Co., 1976), 86–87.

25. Eckhardt, *Command and Control,* 46.

26. Lane, *Command and Control and Communications,* 41–42.

27. Eckhardt, *Command and Control,* 59; Lane, *Command and Control and Communications,* 42.

28. Eckhardt, *Command and Control,* 56–57.

29. Ibid., 58–59.

30. Ibid., 51.

31. Momyer, *Air Power,* 72; Lane, *Command and Control and Communications,* 46.

32. Lane, *Command and Control and Communications,* 48, 50–51.

33. Ibid., 53–54.

34. Ibid., 54.

35. Ibid., 54–55.

36. Ibid., 55–56.

37. Ibid., 100–101.

38. Eckhardt, *Command and Control,* 73–75.

39. Moyers S. Shore II, *The Battle for Khe Sanh* (Washington, D.C.: Historical Branch, G-3 Division, Headquarters US Marine Corps, 1969), 94; on ABCCC, Lane, *Command and Control and Communications,* 80.

40. Lane, *Command and Control and Communications,* 83–84.

41. Eckhardt, *Command and Control,* 73–75.

42. Bernard C. Nalty, *Air Power and the Fight for Khe Sanh* (Washington, D.C.: Office of Air Force History, 1973), 68–81.

43. Lane, *Command and Control and Communications,* 115.

44. A case suggestive of the problem was that of Col Bobby Bagley, whose RF-101 was shot down when he could not be warned that he had been detected. Bagley spent six years as a POW.

45. On the SEAITACS issue, see Lane, *Command and Control and Communications,* 75.

46. Ibid., 156.

47. Ibid., 152–53.

48. Eckhardt, *Command and Control,* 88.

49. Ibid., 85–87.

50. Lane, *Command and Control and Communications*, 70, focuses on the problem of dangerous precedent in muddling through. My emphasis is on the destructive effect of the time element.

51. Ibid., 103.

52. An example of this view is Lane, *Command and Control and Communications*, 150.

53. Momyer, *Air Power*, 96.

54. Lane, *Command and Control and Communications*, 65.

CHAPTER 3

War Making and War Politics
Civilian Officials and the Uses of Military Power

Efforts to impose the requirements of careful crisis management on the use of military force often exacerbate the latent tensions between competing political and military considerations in limited warfare. Crisis management requires novel concepts of military planning, operations, and control that strain the experience, imagination, and patience of military professionals. The civilians' effort to transform military force into a highly discriminating instrument suitable for effective management of crises eventually breaks if pushed too far.

Alexander L. George

The house will be built with the bricks that are there.

Bertolt Brecht

Notwithstanding the claims of their critics, civilian officials and advisers in Washington always saw the problems of Vietnam as fundamentally political. The priority they gave to the political underpinnings of the situation in Southeast Asia had as its corollary a lessened attention to the concrete demands of making war. It was as if the old dictum that war is a continuation of politics by other means had been perverted to mean that war was no different from nonviolent politics and could be conducted in the same way. The risk created by this peculiar notion was that instruments of policy would be used for inappropriate tasks or applied inappropriately to worthwhile objectives—rather like using a chain saw for brain surgery or playing golf with a sledge hammer. Personnel and weapons constituted such instruments; and, although they could be changed, they could not be changed overnight by presidential directive.

The process of escalation, for example, which was largely a debate through action, aimed principally at creating political pressures, albeit through physical threat and material damage. But mounting that threat and imposing that damage were rarely considered on their own terms by those civilians responsible for policy. More curiously, they were rarely considered by those responsible for analysis. The former focused on political advantages to be won while the latter concentrated on depicting the state of political will and/or material capability at various points on the continuum of escalation. Neither paid much attention to how the material requirements of war and the way the armed forces were structured might rightly influence the policies to be established. Analysts attempted to assess what had happened, but they rarely emphasized *how* something must be done. Rather than build US involvement in Vietnam with the material available, civilian officials added some imaginary bricks and precarious experiments.[1]

Civilian authorities commonly viewed military undertakings as emergency reactions to political crises in the Saigon regime or as compensations for Saigon's diplomatic weakness. Even when Vietcong or North Vietnamese military action sharpened the apparent urgency of intervention, the political theme remained the constant undercurrent, inviting new schemes for buying time. The US perception of South Vietnam's weaknesses sometimes encouraged self-contradictory behavior; for example, advocates of long-run political solutions resorting to quickly mounted military actions. Political analysis of the war was highly complex, filled with subtleties, and often confusing.

Unfortunately, civilian authorities in Washington seem to have had a fragmented sense of what military power was and how it could be applied to political problems. In particular, they lacked a sense of what air power was and what it could do; and whatever understandings did exist were largely nontechnical and often abstract. For the military, who were also divided on what air power could do and how it ought to be organized, the civilians' difficulties constituted an added problem. This might have been only a footnote to the Vietnam War if these civilian authorities had not exercised general control; but they did, and despite the growing size of US forces in Southeast Asia, they never yielded basic control. Thus, civilian officials and advisers shaped what could be attempted with air power and, just as important, how and when to attempt it.

Some have argued that civilian officials progressively conceded the governance of the war and its dimensions to the military, but increases in military personnel deployed, operations undertaken, sorties flown, ordnance dropped, targets permitted, and rounds expended are not themselves meaningful determinants of whether the conflict had been militarized. They do suggest an increase in violence, who determined how it would be orchestrated, and whose purposes it was expected to serve. The focus on *whether* the approach to the Vietnam problem was more political or military obscures the deeper issue of *how* concern over a political problem manifested itself in military form.[2]

Political Action as a Counterguerrilla War

At the heart of the effort by the Kennedy and Johnson administrations to deal with guerrilla warfare was the belief that it was essentially political in form and local in origin. Political action was seen as the key means of waging counterguerrilla warfare, even though it was to be coupled with military and police force. As it prepared to take office, the Kennedy administration showed deep concern about losses at the hands of guerrilla forces. In a memorandum prepared for Secretary of State Dean Rusk, dated 6 January 1961, Walt Rostow wrote of the need to avert a "substantial setback on the world scene" while avoiding the resort to nuclear weapons. Rostow observed that the importance of limited-war doctrine had sharply increased for this very reason, especially within the Army and Navy. He strongly recommended a "country approach" that emphasized nonmilitary solutions to insurgency. Political, military, and economic officers should look at situations concretely, escaping "the somewhat abstract and theological cast of the debate on military policy." However conditions in each country might shape the US assistance program there, the success of counterguerrilla efforts would depend on "a mixture of attractive political and economic programs in the underdeveloped areas and a ruthless projection to the peasantry that the central government intends to be the local wave of the future." Despite the ominous talk of a ruthless enlistment of the agrarian sector, the primacy of nonmilitary measures to end the insurgency was clear. Indeed, the military was expected not just to conduct military operations but also to gain respect and influence by contributing to the economic development process, thus helping to make rural areas unfriendly to insurgents.[3]

Although Kennedy's advisers and supporters agreed that insurgency was a complex and integrated problem, they had trouble in providing a concrete, integrated remedy. Their advice was often general, devoid of persuasive solutions. Even before fighting in Vietnam reached clearly critical proportions, Ambassador Chester Bowles cautioned President Kennedy that reaction to Southeast Asian problems must not be largely military and paramilitary. Bowles worried that "the military nature of the Laotian and Cuban emergencies" detracted from more "positive objectives in world developments" (economic and social improvement). Crisis-consciousness distorted these positive goals, encouraging intervention weighted heavily toward military measures. The long-term solution required that military intervention be only a lesser part of a much larger package, but the short-term urgency raised military measures to an importance that had no discernible end; and focusing on the political demands apparently meant risking failure to cope with immediate pressures.[4]

Bowles charged in a letter to the president in December 1962 that the developing world received "only the most cursory attention" from Kennedy's top advisers. They showed this low priority by referring to these regions as the outlying areas; Bowles pointedly described them as "the rest of the world where most of the human race lives." As he saw it, Kennedy's advisers handled third world issues with peevish reluctance. As a result, he felt, the United States failed to adequately "relate military action to clearly established *political* objectives" (Bowles' emphasis). Bowles exemplified the belief that the problems of emerging nations required fundamentally political solutions. If he was regarded as peevish by some whom he criticized, it was not for advocating political remedies but for missing the extent to which Kennedy's close advisers did the same.[5]

Officials in Washington knew that close coordination of all agencies was crucial to the US assistance program in Vietnam, but they had great difficulty in hammering out a system to achieve it. On 4 April 1961, for example, National Security Adviser McGeorge Bundy sent a memorandum to President Kennedy urging that specific talented individuals be given clear responsibility over problem areas. The alternative was to trust men of goodwill whose interests were divided and whose habit was to coordinate rather than control. Vietnam was targeted for special attention. Bundy emphasized that an assignment to this area should be seen as a long job that called for persons of established reputation and self-confidence. He urged that disorganized task forces be transformed under firm leadership into country team, unifying military, political, social, and economic efforts.[6]

Yet such calls were, after all, only words. Implementing them posed large problems. Even though a special group (CI) comprising Attorney General Robert Kennedy, Deputy Secretary of Defense Roswell Gilpatric, and Robert Komer from the State Department, among others, was established to coordinate counterinsurgency planning and policy, it was difficult to develop coherent programs for troubled countries. For example, CIA Director Allen Dulles specifically cautioned President Kennedy that the US government's program for training foreign guerrillas had no clear-cut line of authority. And in a White House meeting with the president on 26 January 1961, Dulles warned that the Military Assistance Advisory Group (MAAG) organization made no adequate provision for paramilitary forces, which were crucial to Kennedy's concept of effective counterinsurgency. Even more, there was no clear authority in Washington, symbolized in part by Dulles' own unwillingness to have the CIA do more than train men to seek out and identify dangerous Communists. Despite such reticence among agency officials and confusion over counterinsurgency control, the president wanted guerrillas to operate in the north. But discrepancies between goals and means, between aspiration and management, persisted throughout the war.[7]

Competing Visions of the Vietnam War

High officials in Washington also disagreed over the source of threats to pro-Western factions in the emerging nations. Some emphasized the local origins of insurgencies while others pointed to outside aid. Some claimed that the rebels were governed from a central Communist source. Differences over how to defeat insurgencies were inevitable. And beneath it all lay a general lack of enthusiasm for counterinsurgency that warped the debate over how it should be conducted. President Kennedy and his advisers strongly advocated counterinsurgency through special warfare, adopting somewhat the techniques of the enemy while exploiting the advantages of his culture—all beneath the umbrella of political warfare. Those not keen on counterinsurgency thought it used men and materiel wastefully, preferring to fight on a higher and broader scale in hopes of a swift and victorious end.

For all observers, the mere persistence of the problem lent a sense of urgency that inclined them to accept half-measures, compromises, and other stop-gap measures. The war became a creature with no creator. As it grew beyond the will of any master, it stole clarity—leaving either the pathetic comfort of self-deception or the ache of irresolution. And the Kennedy administration, while insisting that insurgencies were a long-range problem demanding patience, fell through the trapdoor of its own crisis-consciousness into military measures that compromised its long-range goals.

Competing notions about military power itself also guided how various groups approached the war. Discussions held in Washington in 1961 about Pathet Lao advances in Laos cast some light on this process. There was a semblance of agreement that special warfare and counterinsurgency were on the rise, but differences over ways to handle the emergency in Laos soon appeared. One such instance came on 19 April 1961 at a meeting that included Secretary of State Rusk, Secretary of Defense Robert S. McNamara, Attorney General Kennedy, National Security Adviser Bundy, Gens Curtis LeMay, David Shoup, and George Decker, Adm Arleigh Burke, and others. General LeMay argued boldly that air power could protect even a few relatively isolated centers, "letting the enemy have all of the countryside," and insisted that "the PL [Pathet Lao] could be stopped by air power." Army Chief of Staff Decker cautioned that the United States could not win a conventional war in Southeast Asia: "All the advantages we have in heavy equipment would be lost in the difficult terrain of Laos where we would be at the mercy of the guerrillas." But Decker declined to call for a full-blown counterinsurgency, and so he risked having to choose between withdrawal and a major air campaign. Secretary Rusk suggested that US troops placed in Vientiane could always be removed by helicopter to avoid a disaster, but he skirted the logistical questions that such an operation could raise. Attorney General Kennedy asked whether air power would make "an appreciable dent" on operations by the guerrillas. General LeMay responded affirmatively, but the only clear agreement was the general desire to prevent further deterioration in Laos. An issue not openly discussed was whether pressure applied in one area would reliably produce results in another area. The questions raised about what air power could do in Southeast Asia suggested alternative rather than comprehensive thoughts on how to use it.[8]

The president's aides and other civilian officials showed a sincere eagerness to turn Kennedy's preferences into practice. They fostered the development of forces adequately trained and numerically sufficient for the counterinsurgency tasks anticipated. Studies, reports, and memoranda outlined past failures to use counterinsurgency and special warfare forces effectively. On 23 February 1961, for example, Rostow reported that some 1,100 Army personnel had passed through the Special Warfare Training Center at Fort Bragg and were available for work in the field but that nearly all of them (946) were assigned to duties that did not utilize their special skills. In Laos, where matters were most severe, only 146 graduates of the program were in the field. No guerrilla operations were being undertaken in Vietminh territory (much to Kennedy's dismay), nor had any decision been made for possible future operations. MAAG missions were reportedly still dominated by old infantry concepts rather than counterinsurgency doctrine. Impatient over this inertia and eager to restructure these forces, Kennedy and Rostow kept pressing for counterinsurgency training within the US armed forces. They were also drawn to oversee actively the implementation of whatever counterinsurgency was attempted.[9]

Even strong supporters of counterinsurgency had to feel their way on how to implement it. Rostow's "Counter-Guerrilla Programs," dated 3 April 1961, enumerated some options; a State Department policy study entitled "Internal Warfare and the Security of the Underdeveloped States" pointed to the political basis of military threat; and Edward Lansdale's 1 February 1961 report, "Binh Hung: A Counter-Guerrilla Case Study," offered an example of political pacification under the aegis of armed force. Still, their sense of the problem in Vietnam as fundamentally political kept the counterinsurgency faction in Washington from translating their general views into hard-hitting actions. Political pressure from third-party countries and inducements from the United States became critical. In a memorandum to Kennedy on 29 July 1961, Rostow listed what he and Gen Maxwell D. Taylor believed a military mission to South Vietnam must explore. The focus was on the attitudes and capabilities of the South Vietnamese government and its armed forces, especially in unconventional warfare. Rostow wanted Saigon to produce a coherent plan for systematic elimination of the Vietcong. He also wanted to know what the possibilities for offensive action by Diem's forces against North Vietnam were, whether current counterguerrilla training efforts in South Vietnam were adequate, and whether sufficient US Special Forces personnel had been assigned to this task.[10]

While the Kennedy administration had some difficulty selling its views to Diem, it continued to needle, coax, and pressure demurring elements in Washington. The president sought aggressive action by the CIA, asking on 28 January 1961 whether guerrilla forces could be mounted in the Vietminh area. He was determined that the United States be "better off in three months than we are now." But Deputy Secretary of Defense Gilpatric cautioned Kennedy on 9 March 1961 that progress had been limited, and suggested that the Defense Department might dance more spryly to Kennedy's tune than had the CIA. Still later, after a state visit to West Germany, Kennedy questioned why a Special Forces unit was located there. Such personnel were better assigned to the underdeveloped world, he thought, where they could run covert operations and use their special skills. The president's interests even touched on the character of the armed services themselves. He saw limited war as decoupled from strategic security; that is, a separate problem needing Special Forces. As late as 7 November 1963, Kennedy was still prodding military officials. In a memorandum to Secretary of the Navy Paul Nitze and Chief of Naval Operations Thomas McDonald, he insisted that they pay more attention to Special Forces. These would become increasingly critical, the president explained, "as missiles assume more and more of the nuclear deterrent role and as your limited war mission grows."[11]

To be sure, effort spent in advocating counterinsurgency was effort lost carrying it out—a particularly grave problem, given the commitment and staying power demanded by such an enterprise. Moreover, since the effectiveness of counterinsurgency depended on the real enthusiasm of those conducting it, formal compliance with presidential will was not enough. Anything less than real fervor could whittle away the strength of the counterinsurgency effort. Yet, commitment lagged, divisions over the nature of the war persisted, and institutional tensions within the armed forces lingered.[12]

The gap between the administration and its official military advisers, who were fast receding to the status of technicians, showed itself in a single package of documents prepared by the Joint Chiefs for the President's Special Group (CI). Charged with overseeing and promoting a vigorous counterinsurgency effort, the special group asked the Joint Chiefs to outline the armed forces' organization in the area of counterinsurgency and special warfare. Gen Lyman Lemnitzer, chairman of the JCS, sent a series of memoranda and enclosures on 17 July 1962. In this report, "Summary of U.S. Military Counterinsurgency Accomplishments Since 1 January 1961," military personnel called President Kennedy's emphasis on counterguerrilla action sustained strategy requiring "a major reorientation in military thinking in organization and in materiel." Yet the Air Force enclosure specified that existing Air Staff organization and staff agencies would assume responsibility for counterinsurgency. The Air Force specified no high-level advocate for counterinsurgency, but it did establish a Counterinsurgency Division within the Directorate of Operations under the Deputy Chief of Staff, Operations; and a Limited War Division under the Deputy Chief of Staff, Research and Technology. The claim that these agencies could "spread counterinsurgency knowledge and know-how throughout the Air Staff," however, was overly optimistic at best.[13]

The Air Force's experience suggested that special operations and counterinsurgency could not be evaluated apart from interservice differences and competition. Some motion toward special warfare became imperative to ensure that the Air Force's relations with the White House did not become completely unsatisfactory. Yet General LeMay's support for special warfare forces within the Air Force seemed lukewarm. Indications are that his formal advocacy of special warfare programs may have been largely a concession to presidential will. Debate developed over exactly what the Air Force had agreed to do. Air Force and Army personnel argued over the use of air assets in Swift Strike exercises, notably in Swift Strike III. The underlying issue was whether the Army would determine doctrine and, by extension, the use of Air Force units. Thus, the question of what each service would do and what it would control became enmeshed with assessing the operational merits of special warfare. And beneath the fear of Army domination lay general concern over service roles and missions, especially the enduring Air Force suspicion that the Army wanted its own integral air force. Air Force interest in special warfare intensified as the Army effort grew. Yet the Air Force continued to lag in providing an organization to advocate its own doctrinal preferences. Brig Gen Gilbert L. Pritchard, commander of the USAF Special Warfare Center, put it this way: "Our fragmented special warfare efforts throughout the various elements of the air staff are simply not capable of coping with [Army General] Bill Rosson's professional, centralized staff working towards their established and equally well understood specific goals.''[14]

General Pritchard's warning that the Air Force lacked an institution to advocate its version of counterinsurgency seemed especially timely, given a special Army study demanding that a specific agent be named to fight insurgents. Directed by retired Army Gen James A. Van Fleet, this study also showed the divergence of views on the subject within the military. General Van Fleet had reviewed the training activities at the Army's Special Warfare Center at Fort Bragg, North Carolina, not long before General Lemnitzer submitted his report to the special group, and he had determined that the Special Forces needed autonomy if they were to achieve maximum effectiveness. Although complimentary of Gen William P. Yarborough and his staff, General Van Fleet urged that the program be enlarged apart from the administration's ambiguity as to which countries most needed assistance. The problems most bothersome to Van Fleet pertained to personnel management and administrative accountability.

The personnel problem—especially the need to ensure that the best-trained counterinsurgents go to the most appropriate trouble spots—seemed to flow from the existing administrative arrangements. Van Fleet wanted the Army Special Warfare Center to answer to the US Continental Army Command (USCONARC) rather than to the Third Army. In his view, this step would have enhanced the center's autonomy and operational independence. Even though the Army evidently had the best counterinsurgency program (which was rather the darling of the president), General Van Fleet told Secretary of the Army Elvis J. Stahr, Jr., that the Army had failed to embrace heartily the implications of counterinsurgency. He could find no tangible evidence of an organization equipped with integral aviation and charged with fighting in rugged and isolated areas of the world. Advocating deterrence and control, Van Fleet observed that strategically located light combat task forces could give real meaning to the word ''restraint.''

When influential members of the administration compared Van Fleet's report with Lemnitzer's composite report, they were left with confusing signals. Van Fleet envisioned administrative realignment of the armed forces, but the message from Lemnitzer strongly suggested that political realities and institutional inertia would frustrate reorganization.[15]

Occasional remarks by General Lemnitzer and others added to the misgivings of administration officials in and out of the special group. Partly to temper the enthusiasm of the special group, and to steal their thunder, General Lemnitzer sent them a memorandum on 30 January 1962 putting past efforts in the most favorable light. He claimed that the military services greatly emphasized counterinsurgency and expressed hope of dispelling any lingering misconceptions. Personnel in MAAG and attaché assignments were presented as having knowledge ''related'' to guerrilla warfare and counterinsurgency. He conceded only that the scope varied in proportion to ''the years the individual has spent in the Military Service.'' In an addendum which cannot have heartened the special group, Lemnitzer claimed that the services had "from their inception" dealt with politico-military problems of many kinds. If the chairman of the Joint Chiefs of Staff saw no distinction between present difficulties and past situations, could the armed forces be expected to prepare in a special way and with new vigor?[16]

The military's efforts did not look all that convincing, even on paper. General Lemnitzer took pride that 41 special organizations of 12 different types including some 7,500 men had been "created expressly for the counterinsurgency task." Yet they were scattered among the different services and fell short of the president's vision. And they were even less awesome when compared to US conventional forces. Lemnitzer forwarded papers recognizing that the greatest change needed was to reorient the armed forces to favor counterinsurgency especially to include "peaceful" means. Military and development aid projects, however, did not show that such a reorientation was under way.

By contrast, the curricula of the war colleges were adjusted to include an average increase of 53 hours of instruction in counterinsurgency; but this step did not guarantee acceptance of the concept by the students. So too, the Joint Chiefs issued "Joint Counterinsurgency Concept and Doctrinal Guidance" in April 1962 to fill a doctrinal void. Films were produced, book lists compiled, and a host of other measures undertaken. But sanguine estimates of accommodation to counterinsurgency by the armed forces skirted the problems of long-held beliefs, imbedded traditions, and quiet disdain for counterinsurgency as a dangerous fad.[17]

Self-Defeating Aspects of the US Commitment to Counterinsurgency

The divergence of views about the conflict in Southeast Asia and the divisions among the services over the administration's policy were serious problems. But they might have had less impact if the most powerful officials had been rock-steady. Despite Kennedy's interest in counterinsurgency, there were limits beyond which his administration would not tread—lines drawn less in the soil of Southeast Asia than in the minds of the president and his advisers. Compromise and vacillation within his administration assured that the agency of government most capable of creating a unified front failed to set firm criteria. International political concerns did much to determine the limits of US involvement. The administration that had declared itself willing to "pay any price" feared unlimited risks of conflict with the People's Republic of China. Kennedy opposed the activities of irregular forces sponsored by Chiang Kai-shek that were operating in Laos against the Communists; and so, just weeks after his inauguration, President Kennedy made it clear to Chiang that Taipei's part in the Laotian affair should end.[18] Limited war here also meant limited commitment.

Concern over possible Chinese action persisted despite reports that they were unlikely to move across their borders. Worried that the United States might be frozen over fear of the Chinese Communists pouring into Southeast Asia, Rostow sought to dispel the concern and called for a CIA study. The CIA's appraisal, "The Chances of a Communist Chinese Military Move into Southeast Asia," was sent to him on 11 May 1961. In brief, the report saw such a push as "highly unlikely." It added that, if the continued US presence did not bode an end to communism in Laos or North Vietnam, it would not provoke a Chinese invasion of the region. But this supposed a relatively low level of troop commitment from the United States, and some suggested that expanding hostilities in the South or positioning US troops just south of the demilitarized zone (DMZ) might bring the Chinese across the border. Uncertainty on the issue of Chinese involvement lingered. [19]

Although political considerations affected the course of action in Southeast Asia, political analysis was too imprecise to ensure unambiguous decisions. There was an uncomfortable element of guesswork about it all. Yet the most serious defect may well have been something less well known. The effect of counterinsurgency on the enemy's will to fight depended on simultaneous success in the field and in reforming South Vietnamese politics. And the Kennedy administration interpreted political and psychological results in a damagingly broad and nebulous way. Frequently, the concrete local effects of military actions were evaluated only little, while speculation flourished on the deterrent or psychological power of actions about which little was actually known.

This process disconnected cause from effect, lavishing attention on the latter— which could be speculated about freely. But it shortchanged the former, where assessments depended on hard data. In a memorandum for Secretary of State Rusk, for example, Rostow displayed a tendency to seek solutions for military problems in one location by means of military action in another place, where the psychological impact on the enemy's will to fight seemed easier to judge. He thought the optimum goal of the United States was a more persuasive deterrent position with respect to Laos and Vietnam. Rostow's specific recommendations included capturing Haiphong and taking direct action against Hanoi, underlining his view that a posture aimed more directly against North Vietnam is likely to be more diplomatically persuasive than action in the Mekong Valley. Yet actions conducted in Laos would at least have some effect there; and actions against North Vietnam would not necessarily change conditions in Laos. Specific military results would definitely occur in the field, but the psychological impact of violence by one country against a second to change conditions in a third was fundamentally a matter of guesswork. Nor was Rostow's argument strengthened by his view that counterguerrilla action against the North imposed only a tax at about the same level the Vietcong were imposing in the South. Successful negotiations hinged on something halfway between a threat and a bluff—a possibility that the United States would engage in what Rostow styled direct action on a grand scale if talks failed. But while Rostow and others speculated on how to influence Hanoi, the insurgents in Laos and south Vietnam continued to act. [20]

On 26 July 1961, Robert H. Johnson, member of Policy Planning Council of the State Department told Rostow that the United States "might be able to get away with a higher level of *covert* guerrilla activity in Southern Laos if Khrushchev was determined not to be provoked'' (Johnson's emphasis), suggesting that great power politics affected military decisions even at the low end of the spectrum. Further, memoranda generated by Johnson and others indicated that operations to be undertaken in Laos were intended more to influence the negotiators at Geneva than to achieve practical military results in Laos. And administration personnel put political meanings on military actions even before results were clear. This alone signified that the administration was undercutting its commitment to fight insurgency on its own terms. The action in Laos was persistently viewed as a part of the cold war. Military actions there were meant to change the enemy's estimate of the situation in a general political sense. And this way of thinking affected later measures, for the Kennedy administration began to suspect that Communist advances in Laos might necessitate action directly against North Vietnamese targets such as Hanoi and Haiphong. The administration seemed willing to undertake military operations less to inflict damage on the enemy than to produce indirect political gains. The impulse toward escalated response lay just below the surface.[21]

Late in the Kennedy administration, officials sensed that the counterinsurgency effort was foundering; yet they rarely saw their own actions as part of the problem. Adversary relationships among military officers and civilian advisers, and the competition for influence with the president, consumed energy, attention, and resources. The ''war'' in Washington continued, even as did the one in Vietnam. On 1 February 1963, Presidental Assistant for Far Eastern Affairs Michael V. Forrestal advised President Kennedy about the proper use of air power in Southeast Asia. He focused on issues related to command and control and to interservice rivalry, arguing that they gutted the effect of operations. President Kennedy himself appears to have doubted the effectiveness of the US effort for he told Forrestal to suggest concrete remedies.

At root, Kennedy and Forrestal feared that counterinsurgency was being supplanted by more conventional forms of warfare. Forrestal urged President Kennedy to grill Army Chief of Staff Gen Earle Wheeler (who was to report on a recent visit to South Vietnam) on whether close air support and liaison capabilities in the Farm Gate counterinsurgency program were sufficiently emphasized. Clearly, Forrestal thought not. He saw undue emphasis on ''large-scale operations and air interdiction, which have had . . . bad political and useless military effects.'' Forrestal named ''air support of ground operations'' and ''quick reinforcement of strategic hamlets by [both] ground and air'' as two areas in which US military efforts were faltering badly. He thought these two missions received only low priority from the military, blaming the problem on interservice rivalry. Forrestal was uncertain whether the Army or the Air Force should provide support for these isolated Special Forces camps.[22]

Forrestal specifically argued that Gen Paul D. Harkins in Saigon should report directly to the Joint Chiefs of Staff; but Adm Harry D. Felt, the incumbent CINCPAC, strongly opposed this change, leading Forrestal to suggest that

Ambassador Maxwell Taylor persuade Felt to compromise by creating less interference for Harkins in the tactical area. In day-to-day performance, the US effort seemed riddled with flaws. The Army promoted its own helicopters and light aircraft for liaison and reinforcement missions being carried out by the Air Force; and Forrestal believed that other interservice conflicts caused inadequate liaison with the US Agency for International Development and with Special Forces personnel. Disputes over communications resulted in delays of several hours before camps under attack could get reinforcements. Finally, Forrestal wanted Kennedy to freeze the strength of air units in South Vietnam until the US military decisively distinguished between clear and hold operations on the one hand and hit and withdraw and interdiction operations on the other. The former suited special warfare and counterinsurgency while the latter smacked of conventional techniques.[23]

Civilian aides held many in the military in low esteem, partly due to the discrepancy between the swift turns of their own minds and the far less nimble movement possible within the military system. White House aides and other civilians might legitimately complain if confronted by international resistance from the services, but the military had equal cause to complain when civilians failed to appreciate that all hope of successful outcome required using the military system largely in ways for which it had been designed. The civilians tended to forget their earlier role in deciding the mix of resources in the theater, which itself helped to determine what the US military in Southeast Asia could do. A controversy developed over losses of T-28 aircraft in mid-1964 when McGeorge Bundy claimed that the "commander on the spot" in Vietnam could have gotten jet aircraft for use in Southeast Asia, "Geneva accords or no," an assertion without basis in experience. Indeed, the administration had been reluctant to accede to this kind of military request. Yet Bundy claimed the losses had really resulted from "the fact that the USAF refused to use clearly superior Navy planes at the outset." Such controversies raised the question of how much latitude the administration would allow a commander in the field. Civilian advisers sought to lay the major responsibility for options exercised at the door of the services, thereby mirroring the process of charge and countercharge that beset the military.[24]

The interaction of self-interest, adversary relationship, diffusion of effort, and bureaucratic drives lurked beneath one seemingly discrete problem after another. In fact, frustration was one of the few things all parties shared. By letting their sense of urgency override the counterinsurgency techniques they thought best, civilian officials unintentionally made matters worse by making strategy ambiguous. And the military could find no way to use this ambiguity without opening themselves to charges of parochialism. Symptomatic of this mutual mistrust between military and civilian was the progressive lowering of esteem in which high-ranking military figures were held by civilians and, at times, greater candor—by Secretary McNamara in particular. In addition, civilian officials sometimes attributed views to the military that they had not clearly adopted. Even so, scrutiny of military views were often subjected to considerably more analytical rigor than befell civilian views.

Secretary McNamara's communications with President Johnson betrayed slanted interpretation of military opinions. Reporting to President Johnson on his meeting in Honolulu with Taylor, Sharp, Wheeler, and Westmoreland, McNamara minimized the differences among them and made their views seem more compatible with his own by saying "their strategy for 'victory,' over time, is to break the will of the DRV/VC by denying them victory." Although McNamara did not completely misrepresent what the military believed, neither did he present with full candor the positions held by military men—particularly Adm U.S. Grant Sharp's known desire for more speedy and decisive action in Vietnam. McNamara's remark was especially disingenuous given the limits imposed on the US military. Furthermore, McNamara seemed to imply that the greatest shift in thinking about the war and the worth of fighting it was occurring among the military. In reality, however, military officers usually waited until retirement to dissent openly from how McNamara and others had reported their views to the White House. Thus, military leaders may well have been hawkish while bound to an equivocal strategy.

Not long after McNamara gave his version of military opinion to Johnson, McGeorge Bundy unintentionally revealed an inconsistency. In demurring from Under Secretary of State George Ball's warning that the United States would "double [its] bet and get lost in the rice paddies," Bundy claimed that the United States could "waffle through" its problems. Bundy admitted that there were "serious, ominous implications" to what he styled "our new policy." The "waffling" was not subjected to much scrutiny; nor was its possible damage to military effectiveness much explored by the administration.[25]

Even after bombing the North became routine, some civilians remained testy over relying on professional military advice—perhaps due to their own growing doubts, but also due to impatience with the military for its continuing dissent. On 17 December 1965, McNamara told Johnson that he could ignore JCS resistance to a possible bombing halt over the North. "I can take on the Chiefs," McNamara was recorded as saying. President Johnson was more sympathetic to the need for professional military advice, and he had more respect for the officers' accomplishments. He referred to a number of proposals and asked McNamara: "Is this what you want to explore with the chiefs?" The Secretary responded: "No, I need to know what *you* want. . . . We decide what we want and impose it on them. . . . I know exactly what the arguments of the chiefs are" (emphasis added). Yet it is not clear that McNamara conveyed the real views of the JCS. Moreover, since they were denied an opportunity to influence Johnson directly, the chiefs inevitably became technical managers rather than strategists. And McNamara's questions to President Johnson—what do we want to achieve, how do we want to do it, and how might our methods limit our chances—elementary as they might seem—broke down when the administration seemed uncertain whether the adversary was in Hanoi or the Pentagon.[26]

War as Politics

The ill-concealed contempt running through Secretary McNamara's remarks about the JCS suggested his views that the military services were insensitive to the political dimensions of war, but his view missed the fact that how one assessed a war's politics depended upon how one conceived of the war itself. To some extent, then, the disdain felt toward the armed services came because military men had differed with prominent figures in the administration. As pressure escalated, a new war emerged: new techniques were possible, new hardware available, new units accessible, and new resources expendable. Many in the military hoped escalation would clarify and simplify the conflict; but civilian officials held their ground, hobbled by their own sense of the war's political complexity. The actual making of war thus remained largely an unusually lethal act of grand politics. What was left of counterinsurgency remained rhetorically prominent while declining in practice.

Although military escalation was being considered in 1964 and put into operation soon after, US political objectives remained essentially unchanged. Likewise, President Johnson kept on many of Kennedy's advisers, who maintained their habit of giving primarily political interpretations to military operations in Southeast Asia. They continued to speak of the conflict as essentially political with military overtones, and they proposed escalation whose impact was projected in the international political sphere more than in the actual theater of combat. When Johnson showed interest in stepping up US efforts in Vietnam, civilian officials from the Defense Department suggested a "program of pressure on NVN [North Vietnamese] of rising intensity" and "probes into Laos, including use of US advisers and air resupply." Aerial reconnaissance, including flights over Cambodia and Laos, also seemed useful and reasonable to Defense Department officials. However, some civilian advisers—Michael Forrestal and William Sullivan among them—feared that these measures would be unproductive and might frustrate a diplomatic settlement. Yet to others in the administration, air operations posed less risk of international political embarrassment and less chance of becoming trapped in Southeast Asia than did ground operations. Thus, the desire to hedge the administration's political bets gave preference to one set of military options even when their political effectiveness was unproven.[27]

McGeorge Bundy, recommending escalation against North Vietnam, explicitly stressed the diplomatic and psychological results that would follow. It was almost as if the material effect of destroying military targets was secondary to the psychological effect of deciding to take action at all. The first strike against the North, he advised the president on 25 May 1964, "would be very carefully designed to have more deterrent than destructive impact, as far as possible." On 15 June 1964, he gave the president a list of military options not needing a congressional resolution which might be used against North Vietnam as signs of US political resolve. He urged that such actions be sharply limited—not only to elude congressional control but, more significant, to keep Hanoi's attention off the military effects of the proposed operations and on the political goals behind them. Bundy did not yet speculate on whether there need be any correlation between physical destructiveness and psychological deterrence—whether there was any evidence that the threat of future escalation had more impact than the delivery of immediate damage.[28]

Bundy recommended as most interesting Vietnamese air force action in the Laotian corridor along with small-scale reconnaissance-strike operations. By late August, various contingency plans for limited escalation were in preparation—principally naval harassment, air interdiction in the Laotian panhandle, and fleet movements in the Gulf of Tonkin. Bundy noted in a 31 August 1964 memorandum to the president, "the objective of any of these would be more to heighten morale and to show our strength of purpose than to accomplish anything very specific in a military sense." But the persuasiveness of the specific measures Bundy cited apparently required threatening a naval quarantine of North Vietnam in the indefinite future; thus, the political effect anticipated from one military operation apparently depended on the supposed political effect of still greater military operations not yet undertaken.[29]

The tendency to let political considerations override military ones showed itself forcefully in a National Security Council meeting in the Cabinet Room on 10 February 1965. Seeking reprisals for the Vietcong bombing of an enlisted men's barracks at Qui Nhon, Ambassador Taylor reportedly favored swift action for two largely psychological reasons: to improve morale in South Vietnam and to send a signal of US resolve to the North Vietnamese. Secretary of Defense McNamara advocated moving more forces to Southeast Asia, even though the United States already had overwhelming air power in Southeast Asia and even though the Joint Chiefs reportedly opposed such an increase. But McNamara saw merit in the measure "for political reasons." Thus, concern over political and psychological motivations remained the driving force behind US decisions—even unto military deployments and operations.[30]

Even the US desire to encourage indigenous forces required a commitment of US forces as well, if only as a political symbol. Michael Forrestal urged the United States to keep a low profile while putting more pressure on Hanoi for effective negotiations. Forrestal wanted Asians to carry the main effort in air and cross-border actions in the Laos panhandle, "keeping our own involvement *initially* to a minimum" (emphasis added). These measures were meant to give the Laotians and South Vietnamese "a sense of involvement and responsibility in actions against the North," which existing patrols did not. Forrestal reported to McGeorge Bundy on 22 September 1964 that the United States had already asked Vientiane to use Laotian air forces against some corridor targets. A joint State and Defense Department message to the US embassy in Vientiane on 6 October 1964 authorized US officials to urge Laotian attacks on Vietcong infiltration in the Laos panhandle, excluding the Mu Gia Pass and "any target which Lao will not hit without US air cover or fire support." The initiative was supportedly to be with the Asians, yet it was to be fostered by hints of heavier US support. The real depth of US commitment was to be decided later.[31]

Even before the dramatic bombing of North Vietnam in Rolling Thunder, the trend toward escalation was evident. To an extent not easily pinpointed, it appeared in the fixation on political interpretations of military action. Ironically, this in turn stemmed from a desire for predictability and control. But predictability and control diminished when taking action whose effects were only speculative. Instead of deepening control, such actions seem to have constrained future US policy. In a 24 September 1964 memorandum to John McNaughton, assistant secretary of defense for international security affairs, Forrestal stated that he shared the widespread concern within the administration over political weakness and the psychological problem in dealing with Hanoi. Forrestal advocated marine operations under a broad plan McNaughton had outlined called Operations Plan 34a. But Forrestal did not emphasize their possible military merit—rather that failure to act might suggest weakness. Air strikes "against targets in the Laotian corridor" were not justified for their military effectiveness—indeed, Forrestal intended not to destroy large numbers of targets but to impress Hanoi that we are slowly walking up the ladder. The advantage of air strikes was that they could probably be started more quickly and were more controllable. Even if one could start actions under this requisite control, however, there was no guarantee that their effects would resemble Forrestal's forecasts.[32]

The Continuation of War as Politics

Civilian officials and advisers began with the conviction that the Southeast Asian problem was at root a political one, but they appear to have miscalculated what political meant. They confused the performance of an act with its effect, and they behaved as if the psychological impact of an action could be devastating even when the action itself was not. Officials sometimes wondered if military actions were producing the political results hoped for, but proposals for action were rarely given advance scrutiny for their military operational requirements and other special demands. The emphasis on war as a political act distracted officials from the military features of war. Only when measures were put into execution were officials compelled to respond, even to the unexpected and undesired effects of their own deeds.

Nor could the political judgments about making war have been made meaningful without a true consensus on the character of the war itself. But the executive branch did not commit to one specific version of the war. Even air war against the North was conceived as a means of affecting the ground war in the South. Yet it was to do so more by encouraging Hanoi to stop sending supplies than by direct interdiction. Moreover, this goal could not be practically demonstrated. It seems, then, that a disjunction developed between the war as a theoretical construct and the war as a real combat experience—in the construct, nearly anything was both imaginable and possible; in the reality, nearly everything presented difficulties.

NOTES

1. The themes in the historiography of the Vietnam War are varied. Among the most pertinent for present purposes are: the civilians yielded to the military; the military were dominated by the civilians; the public support for the war was insufficient largely because of the role of the media, especially the electronic media; the war could not be won by the United States and its allies; the war was already won by the United States at the time of Tet 1968; the war was fundamentally political and a counterinsurgency; the war was essentially an invasion by North Vietnam of the presumably separate South Vietnam, conditioned upon the irrelevance of the 1954 Geneva Accords.

2. Robert L. Gallucci, *Neither Peace Nor Honor* (Baltimore: Johns Hopkins University Press, 1975).

3. Memorandum by Walt Rostow to Dean Rusk, "Nuclear Weapons: The Dilemma and Thoughts on Its Resolution," Rostow folders, 11/60–1/61, Staff Memoranda Files, President's Office Files, Kennedy Papers, John F. Kennedy Library, Dorchester, Massachusetts.

4. Memorandum by Chester Bowles to John F. Kennedy, 22 May 1961, Bowles folders, 3/24/59–7/5/61, Special Correspondence Series, President's Office Files, Kennedy Papers.

5. Memorandum by Chester Bowles to John F. Kennedy, 1 December 1962, Bowles folders, 10/11/62–12/30/62, Special Correspondence Series, President's Office Files, Kennedy Papers. Perhaps the deeper issue was not whether there was attention paid to the concerns Bowles identified but whether the attention was knowledgeable.

6. Memorandum by McGeorge Bundy to the president, 4 April 1961, Bundy folder, 2/61–4/61, Staff Memoranda Files, President's Office Files, Kennedy Papers.

7. Memorandum by Walt Rostow to McGeorge Bundy, 30 January 1961, Vietnam folder, 1/61–3/61, Countries File, National Security File, Kennedy Papers.

8. Memorandum of conversation, subject: Laos, 29 April 1961 (Department of State), Laos, vol. 2, 6/61 folder, Countries File, National Security File, Kennedy Papers.

9. Memorandum by Walt Rostow to the president, 23 February 1961, Rostow folders, 11/60–2/61, Staff Memoranda Files, President's Office Files, Kennedy Papers.

10. Walt Rostow, "Counter-Guerrilla Programs," 3 April 1961; State Department, "Internal Warfare and the Security of the Underdeveloped States"; and Edward Lansdale, "Binh Hung: A Counter-Guerrilla Case Study," 1 February 1961, Counter-Insurgency folder, Subjects File, President's Office Files, Kennedy Papers. Also see memorandum by Walt Rostow to the president, 29 July 1961, Southeast Asia General folder, 7/29/61–7/31/61, Regional Security File, Kennedy Papers.

11. Memorandum by Walt Rostow to McGeorge Bundy 30 January 1961. Memorandum by Roswell Gilpatric to the president, 29 March 1961. Vietnam folder, 4/1/61–4/24/61, Countries File, National Security File, Kennedy Papers. Memorandum by President Kennedy to Comdr Alan B. Shepard, Jr., 18 February 1961, JFK Memo folder (Labor-Navy), Departments and Agencies File, President's Office Files, Kennedy Papers. Memorandum by President Kennedy to Secretary Nitze and Admiral McDonald, 7 November 1963, JFK Memo folder (Labor-Navy), Departments and Agencies File, President's Office Files, Kennedy Papers. Memorandum by President Kennedy to McNamara, 15 July 1963, Defense folder, 7/63–11/63, Departments and Agencies File, President's Office Files, Kennedy Papers. Memorandum by President Kennedy to Rostow and Taylor, 7 August 1961, Rostow folder, 6/61–12/61, Staff Memoranda Files, President's Office Files, Kennedy Papers.

12. It is not surprising that there should be institutional lag in an organization of considerable size. The point here is that it became a contributory drag or weight on the conduct of the war as well as a point of distraction to various parties in the executive branch.

13. Memorandum by Robert W. Komer to McGeorge Bundy, 31 July 1962; memorandum by Lyman Lemnitzer to the Special Group (CI), 17 July 1962, "A Summary of U.S. Military Counterinsurgency Accomplishments since 1 January 1961"; and Enclosure E, "Department of the Air Force Counterinsurgency Organization," July 1962, Special Group (CI) Military Organization folder, Meetings and Memoranda File, National Security File, Kennedy Papers.

14. The quotation is from Brig Gen Gilbert L. Pritchard to Maj Gen D. O. Darrow, 6 May 1963. Various documents pertinent to Air Force concerns over Army efforts in special warfare and specifically over the possible exclusion of the Air Force from the effort appear in "Special Air Warfare Center Indoctrination and Information Folder," SAWC-DOP, 1963, Headquarters USAF Historical Research Center, Maxwell AFB, Ala. The suggestion that General LeMay had reservations about a buildup of special warfare forces may be found in transcripts of interviews conducted with LeMay after his retirement.

15. Memorandum by James A. Van Fleet to Elvis J. Stahr, 26 March 1962, Army 1962 folder, Departments of Agencies File, President's Office File, Kennedy Papers.

16. Memorandum by Lyman Lemnitzer to Special Group (CI), 30 January 1962, Special Group Military Training folder, Meetings and Memoranda File, National Security File, Kennedy Papers. This is not to suggest that General Lemnitzer lacked concrete ideas, such as he presented in suggesting medical training of Laotians in a limited twelve-week program as a useful means of giving positive identification to the United States, building a cadre of pro-American Laotians, and developing a potential intelligence infrastructure. The problem was one of relative commitment and proportion of effort. On the proposed medical program, see memorandum by Lyman Lemnitzer to the Special Group (CI), 3 July 1962, Special Group (CI) folder, 7/62–11/63, Meetings and Memoranda File, National Security File, Kennedy Papers.

17. "A Summary of U.S. Military Counterinsurgency Accomplishments Since 1 January 1961," July 1962, Special Group (CI) Military Organization folder, Meetings and Memoranda File, National Security File, Kennedy Papers.

18. Memorandum, "Meeting of Task Force in Laos," 27 February 1961, Laos Security folder, 3/1/61–3/10/61, Countries File, President's Office File, Kennedy Papers.

19. CIA Office of National Estimates, "The Chances of a Chinese Communist Military Move into Southeast Asia," 11 May 1961, Memorandum by Rostow to the president, 12 May 1961, Communist China, Security folder, 1961, Countries File, President's Office File, Kennedy Papers.

20. Memorandum by Walt Rostow to the secretary of state, 13 July 1961, Vietnam folder, 7/5/61–7/13/61, Countries File, National Security File, Kennedy Papers.

21. Memorandum by Robert H. Johnson to Walt Rostow, 26 July 1961, Southeast Asia General folder, 7/25/61–7/28/61, Regional Security File, Kennedy Papers; "General Taylor's Suggestions for Pentagon Planning," 15 July 1961, Southeast Asia Rostow Report (2d Try) folder, Regional Security File, National Security File, Kennedy Papers; memorandum of discussion on Southeast Asia (President Kennedy, Rusk, R. H. Johnson, Taylor, Bundy, Rostow et al.), 28 July 1961, Southeast Asia General folder, 7/29/61–7/31/61, Regional Security File, National Security File, Kennedy Papers.

22. Memorandum by Michael Forrestal to the president, February 1963, Vietnam Security folder, 1961, Countries File, President's Office File, Kennedy Papers.

23. Memorandum by Michael Forrestal to the president, 28 January 1963, Vietnam folder, 1/10/63–1/30/63, Countries File, National Security File, Kennedy Papers.

24. Memorandum by McGeorge Bundy to the president, 12 May 1964, Vietnam Memos, vol. 8 (5/64), Memo 113a, Vietnam Country File, National Security File, Johnson Papers, Lyndon B. Johnson Library, Austin, Texas.

25. Memorandum by McNamara to the president, 21 April 1965; memorandum by McGeorge Bundy to the president, vol. 12 (July 1965), Memo 12b, Aides Files, National Security File, Johnson Papers. Also see U. S. Grant Sharp, *Strategy for Defeat* (San Rafael, Calif.: Presidio Press, 1978), passim. Meetings with Foreign Policy Advisers (21 July 1965), Memo 23a, Meeting Notes Files, Johnson Papers.

26. Meetings with Foreign Policy Advisers (17 December 1965), Memo 41, Meeting Notes Files, Johnson Papers.

27. Cable from Rusk to Henry Cabot Lodge, 6 December 1963, Vietnam Cables, vol. 1 (11/63–12/63), Cable 44, Vietnam Country File, National Security File, Johnson Papers. Memorandum by Michael Forrestal to McGeorge Bundy, 16 April 1964, Vietnam Memos, vol. 7 (4/64), Memo 168, Vietnam Country File, National Security File, Johnson Papers.

28. Memorandum by McGeorge Bundy to the president, 25 May 1964, McGeorge Bundy Luncheons with the President, vol. 1, part 1, Memo 79, Aides Files, National Security File, Johnson Papers.

29. Memorandum for meeting on 15 June 1964, 1800; McGeorge Bundy Luncheons with the President, vol. 1, part 1, Memo 73a, Aides Files, National Security File, Johnson Papers. Memorandum by McGeorge Bundy to the president, vol. 6, Memo 49, Aides Files, National Security File, Johnson Papers. The overemphasis on affecting perceptions with limited uses of force seems particularly curious in retrospect when it is placed against the opportunistic de-escalation contained in Mao's notion of stages in a protracted war. In that scenario, the level and character of warfare (which may be compared to the behavior of the insurgent or revolutionary) depend on the objective character of forces relative to the enemy. This implies a policy of maximum practical use of force available at the time, conditioned only upon the ability to sustain the use of force at the level chosen sufficiently well and long to avoid sustaining major subsequent damage through a counterattack. The use of political force as symbolism is inherent in this exercise of force, too; but it communicates resolve by moving to the highest available capability—not by keeping to the lowest feasible demonstration.

30. National Security Council Meeting folder, 10 February 1965, Memo 15, Meeting Notes File, Johnson Papers.

31. Memorandum by Michael Forrestal to McGeorge Bundy, 22 September 1964, Vietnam Memos, vol. 13 (9/15/64–9/30/64), Memo 258, Vietnam Country File, National Security File, Johnson Papers.

32. Memorandum by Michael Forrestal to Assistant Secretary of Defense John McNaughton, 24 September 1964, Vietnam Memos, vol. 13 (9/15/64–9/30/64) Memo 254a, Vietnam Country File, National Security File, Johnson Papers.

PART TWO

"TWO, THREE . . . MANY VIETNAMS"

At a historical moment both typified and shaped by President Kennedy's explicit determination to counter "wars of national liberation," the ominous prediction by Latin American revolutionary leader and theorist Ernesto "Che" Guevara that the United States would encounter not one but numerous "Vietnams" took on a literal meaning.[1] The general feeling among Kennedy's advisers was that Communists, working in tandem, would seek to multiply the troubles of the United States and its friends around the globe. What gradually transpired in Southeast Asia was an extension of Che's prediction: in addition to wars in many places, the United States faced many wars—and many kinds of war—in one place.

The complexity of the Vietnam conflict was not, in principle, unique. World War II likewise encompassed many kinds of fighting in many places; different strategies for its prosecution were posed among the Allies; innovations in tactics were developed; and technological advances were made. But even when their efforts were channeled in different directions, all nations participating in the war had a broad national vision as to the war's purpose and character. The area of agreement between Allies at times was narrow, perhaps confined to the defeat of a common enemy. Yet each nation's sense of unified purpose in the war survived the diversity both before and after the conflict.[2]

What differed in Vietnam was the complexity of vision—the diffusion of understanding—of the war itself and of how to conduct it. Other problems emerged as well, to be sure, and the outcome came from the interplay of those many difficulties. But the importance of the fragmented way in which the war was understood and prosecuted would be difficult to exaggerate. President Kennedy has often been cited as a symbol of firmness for embracing the "long, slow struggle, with no immediately visible foe." But he could be criticized for the operational approach he permitted toward "another type of war,"[3] which tended to confuse responsiveness with vacillation. One could not say that Vietnam was the same as other wars; but to act as if it were another type altogether, and as if the "old rules" of war could be jettisoned, was both confusing and inaccurate.[4]

Since a clear vision of the war as a whole was absent, the whole enterprise splintered into pursuing its parts, which might seem individually defensible but which might contribute little to an overall strategy. No one measure could fill the whole bill, and each became faulty when extended beyond its own logic. The dizzying complexity of the war continued throughout its course; many kinds of conflict raged at the same time and sometimes even in the same place. In this context, the effort to extend a vision of the war useful in one locale to the entire conflict could only bring conflict with other visions of the war. The experience recalled the case of a World War II corporal (soon to become a private) who asked his company commander which of his contradictory orders he wanted followed first.

The availability of air power in Southeast Asia encouraged rethinking of what kind of ground operations might be successfully conducted, whether some new kinds were possible, whether some traditional ones were outmoded, and how such traditional strengths as mobility and firepower could best be exploited. But lines of thought were many. Ground commanders adopted a restrained and evolutionary approach. They saw air power as a means of enhancing ground operations, while some air officers favored autonomous or independent operations. Some Air Force officers felt that things did not go their way, but their distress paralleled that of Army proponents of the airmobile concept. So too, in defending remote outposts at Khe Sanh and elsewhere the traditional American emphasis on firepower was much in evidence, even though less glamorous matters such as aerial resupply were crucial.

Despite the abundance of air power resources in Vietnam, thinking about how to fight the ground war was not driven primarily by air power—even though conduct of the ground war was definitely altered by it. Thus, although air power altered both the nature of and expectations for ground combat, it did not seem to be a consideration to which the traditional concerns of ground combat might be subordinated. Clearly, one cannot assume that air power will be taken as a revolutionary factor in a future war, no matter how imposing the air assets.

Traditional roles such as search and rescue, reconnaissance and intelligence-gathering, transport and supply, and medical evacuation were executed with special skill and considerable effectiveness in Vietnam. That they did not enjoy the attention accorded to the "high-ticket" bombing programs, whether over the North or elsewhere in Southeast Asia, is telling. Middle-ground roles such as close support and interdiction were seen as important to the ground war in the South. But there were times when air power was used in ways which opened great discrepancies between cost and benefit. Such devotion of resources invites speculation about how the priority accorded various roles could survive their cost as well as how the priority was set in the first place.

An acknowledged need of military forces in conflict is to determine the importance of assigned responsibilities, to establish a hierarchy of importance, and then to act in accordance with the rankings. Considerations born of institutional or professional pride can be detrimental to orderly pursuit of the mission. In Vietnam, failure to maintain clear priorities added to the difficulties of fighting the war and led to its final unraveling.

Technological and tactical innovations in Vietnam were numerous and impressive for many reasons. Among them were defoliation, tactical employment of B-52s, and development of fixed-wing gunships. But there was a tendency to whittle away at the new inventions and use them in unintended ways. This suggested a certain discontent with accepting the war on its own terms and with accepting innovations for the purposes they had been designed to serve. Throughout the war, US decision makers showed an irresistible interest in roles other than actual ground combat and, in compensation, closer to the high-profile methods traditional in air power doctrine.

Using technological innovation and tactical versatility to meet the demands of a war can contribute to military successes; but innovation can be made a creature of doctrine and lose relevance. The process of innovation itself can be corrupted into one of institutional self-interest and self-protection. In this event, innovation may fail; and, if seen as self-interest, the measures may invite negative consequences and lasting hostility.

NOTES

1. Article by Ernesto "Che" Guevara, Havana, Cuba, 16 April 1967, quoted in Daniel James *Che Guevara* (New York: Stein and Day, 1969), 258.

2. This difference of interpretation may be seen in such specialized terms for the conflict as the "Great Patriotic War," "The War of Resistance Against Japanese Aggression," "The Continuation War" [Finland], and "World War II." The terms reflect differences in the comprehending visions of the various warring states, as well as nuances in their senses of the stakes and the critical locus of decision.

3. Quoted in Gen William C. Westmoreland, *A Soldier Reports* (Garden City, N.Y.: Doubleday & Co., Inc., 1976), 39.

4. For one, Harry G. Summers, Jr., *On Strategy: The Vietnam War in Context* (Carlisle Barracks, Pa.: Strategic Studies Institute, US Army War College, 1981), observes how the belief that nuclear weapons made all previous thinking about war obsolete permitted civilian theorists to displace military professionals in developing strategy. However, one may also add that the armed services in the 1950s and 1960s were also driven by their own internal competition and did not react exclusively to civilians.

CHAPTER 4

Rethinking Ground Warfare

Off and on for forty-nine days SLAM [seek, locate, annihilate, and monitor] strikes pummeled the enemy around Con Thien and demonstrated that massed firepower was in itself sufficient to force a besieging enemy to desist, a demonstration that was destined to contribute to my confidence on a later occasion.

Gen William Westmoreland, 1976

It is probable that without helicopters "search and destroy" would not have been possible and, in this sense, the helicopter was one of the major contributions to the failure of strategy.

Sir Robert Thompson, 1970

The air power available to the United States and South Vietnam permitted much thought on how ground operations might be enhanced, modified, or even supplanted; but the thinking was neither clear nor simple. People with different professional backgrounds and priorities saw the potential of air power from different perspectives. Ground officers tended to see air power as a means to *augment* ground combat—not revolutionize it. The Army expressed enthusiasm for air power, but it was enthusiasm for relatively conservative ways of applying aviation to the war. And, although many outside the air arm considered them to be revolutionary, measures proposed by the Air Force really reflected no more than traditional concerns. So the traditional views of the Air Force and the Army came into close comparison and competition. The habitual attachment of the Air Force to autonomous—even independent—air operations clashed with the Army's reluctance to accept that use of air power. Thus the proper character of an air offensive became a constant theme in the argument over how to fight the war in Vietnam.

General Westmoreland, in retrospective explanation of his early military goals as MACV commander, hints at how important these differences were. "From the first," he wrote, "I contemplated eventually moving into Laos to block the infiltration routes of the Ho Chi Minh Trail." His staff prepared plans for this purpose in 1966 and 1967, recommending at least a corps-size force of three divisions. The size of this proposed force left no doubt that Westmoreland had in mind a major operation in conventional land warfare.[1] He seemed to doubt that air power was sufficient to interdict enemy supplies or that interdiction was enough to undermine the enemy's war in the South. Even so, Westmoreland's views in 1964

73

and early 1965 favored some use of air power. When he could not undertake the ground operations he preferred, Westmoreland could see air operations as the "only way to deter the enemy's rebuilding of his sanctuaries." One example was the bombing of Cambodia that President Nixon authorized in the spring of 1969 as an alternative to "ground forays into Cambodia."[2] But Westmoreland substituted air power for ground action only when land operations were out of the question.

For the Army, the basic premise that the war had to be won on the ground stood unassailable. The Army's commitment, first to counterinsurgency and later to large-unit operations, did not support autonomous air operations, nor did it view air power as having a major role apart from supporting the ground war. Gen William DePuy, commander of the First Infantry Division in Vietnam from March 1966 to February 1967 and, later, head of the US Army Training and Doctrine Command (TRADOC), concluded that the Army flailed about "trying to figure out what [counterinsurgency] meant." But he also remembered, "we thought we could do it, and Kennedy and McNamara backed us."[3]

In a message to Maxwell Taylor on 30 December 1964, President Johnson affirmed his own emphasis on the ground war: "I have never felt that this war will be won from the air and it seems to me that what is much more needed and would be more effective is a larger and stronger use of Rangers and Special Forces and Marines and other appropriate military strength on the ground."[4] Although the president approved bombing targets in North Vietnam and elsewhere in Southeast Asia, he never expected air power to be decisive. Yet, what air power might offer remained open to experiment, interpretation, and reevaluation.

Mobility versus Autonomy

In his commentary on the Vietnam conflict, Gen William Momyer suggested that General Westmoreland saw air power primarily as a source of firepower to augment ground artillery, essentially in support of localized ground combat. And while increased firepower and enhanced mobility did affect calculations as to what operations might be conducted safely, the employment of air power did not seem to alter fundamentally Westmoreland's thinking about how to wage war. He still thought "the main task was that of the soldier 'finding and fixing' the enemy." Air power was "a supporting element rather than a dictating consideration."[5] Nevertheless, Westmoreland did value air power as an evolutionary supplement to ground warfare.

To say that Westmoreland was not a revolutionary military thinker is not to slight him. He showed genuine willingness to consider new options and try new tactics. Westmoreland had wanted to join the Army Air Corps after West Point, but a minor vision deficiency prevented this. He saw his second choice, Field Artillery, as temporary, and hoped to transfer into the air arm at the start of World War II. He even began taking commercial flying lessons. Although disappointed by assignment to an artillery unit with the Ninth Infantry, Westmoreland quickly established good working relationships with the commander of the 82d Airborne Division, Maj Gen Matthew B. Ridgway, and with General Taylor, Ridgway's artillery commander. James M. Gavin, a colonel in command of a parachute infantry regiment of the 82d Airborne during the Sicilian campaign, and another Army officer with a reputation for novel thinking were impressed with Westmoreland. After becoming a general, Gavin had Westmoreland transferred to the 82d Airborne as commander of the 504th Parachute Infantry. In Korea, Westmoreland commanded the 187th Airborne Combat Team. After the war, following staff assignments in Washington, Westmoreland took command of the 101st Airborne Division at Fort Campbell, Kentucky. Prior to Vietnam, then, Westmoreland had shown real interest in how the Army might exploit aviation. Because he had attended only the parachute school at Fort Benning, Georgia, and the cooks and bakers school at Schofield Barracks, Hawaii, Westmoreland "was amused when people would accuse me of doing things 'by the book'."[6]

The parameters of Westmoreland's military inventiveness may be described best in his own memoirs. As commander of the 101st Airborne Division, Westmoreland favored training for counterinsurgency, showing special concern for small-unit training and for developing "resourceful small-unit leaders." (He had already criticized the "disease" of oversupervision in the military.) He created a special divisional school, named RECONDO, which he said combined "reconnaissance" and "doughboy" or "commando." In a sense, the neologism itself suggested how the eras of the doughboy and the counterguerrilla fighter were mixed in Westmoreland's thinking.[7]

At the 101st, Westmoreland showed himself to be both a team player and an independent thinker. A case in point was the testing of the "Pentomic Division," which had been designed to meet the threat of nuclear weapons on a European battlefield. Under the concept, infantry and airborne divisions had five battle groups of 1,400 men, combining two levels of command into a single command structure. These could be employed individually or together, presumably enjoying substantial operational independence. Westmoreland later recalled that the 101st approached the testing of the Pentomic Division with the intent to support it. The slogan was: "Our job is not to determine whether it *will* work—it is to *make* it work!" Nonetheless, he criticized "yes-men" who were reluctant to denounce the organization as unsound.

After completing his command of the 101st in 1960, Westmoreland recommended that the Pentomic Division be abolished. Coordination and control were difficult, and he concluded that it would have disastrous effects on the Army's warfighting capacity if applied outside the narrow theoretical framework for which it was designed. He did not oppose change, but he objected to the changes required by the Pentomic Division on the basis that the concept had not been fairly and honestly proven; and the Pentomic Division was displacing a system which, for all its difficulties, had a considerable track record. Westmoreland kept this inclination toward incrementalism during the era of Vietnam.[8]

Perhaps experimental use of helicopters in airborne units came too close in time after Westmoreland's experience with the Pentomic Division for him to view the helicopter without skepticism, but his instinct to accept major changes only after reliable testing would have been sufficient reason for him to reject the more radical notions about airmobility and helicopters. Nor was Westmoreland alone in his thinking. The Army had rarely developed a force structure and operational doctrine on the strength of promise alone.[9] In addition, helicopters and airmobility were largely associated, even in the minds of their advocates, with larger conflicts.

Few Army leaders predicted that helicopters and air mobility would suit wars of national liberation.[10] Gen George Seneff, original commander of the First Aviation Brigade in Vietnam, later said, he "damn near rolled on the floor" when General Abrams informed him that the Utility Tactical Transport Company (the forerunner of the First Aviation Brigade) was to deploy to Vietnam.[11] General Seneff attributed the movement of Army helicopter units to Southeast Asia to "expediency." They could be deployed promptly and they might create a credible allied presence where it had long been lacking. The helicopter gunship units of the Utility Tactical Transport Company, the First Brigade's antecedent, "had the capability of getting back into Pleiku when nothing else could because the roads had been closed for years."[12] But mere transportation was not the point. The helicopters combined mobility to insert and resupply troops, the ability to give prompt fire support, and the chance of removing troops from an extreme threat. Even so, the Army's rotary-wing aviators had to advance their proposals cautiously lest sensitivities among the services threaten acceptance of the helicopter.[13]

In the end, then, General Westmoreland did not turn his back on air power; but he failed to satisfy either the Air Force or the Army about how their air resources should be used. General Westmoreland's understanding of mobility seemed to evolve from his own experience in World War II and Korea; he tended to view mobility as a means of coupling ground and air units for simultaneous efforts. Army aviators were inclined toward something parallel to an independent air campaign— autonomous action by airlifted troopers, bringing firepower with them, not dependent on separate ground units. So Westmoreland saw that air power could be considered a force-multiplier. But airmen, whether in the Air Force or Army, could sometimes see the character of air forces and their effectiveness as justification for autonomous operations. Or, to recall General Momyer's distinction, they could see it as a "dictating consideration."

At the start of the 1960s, the prospect of effective autonomous operations beckoned the proponents of airmobility and encouraged major modifications in tactics and strategy. Lt Gen Harry W. O. Kinnard, commander of the First Cavalry Division from July 1965 to May 1966, thought mobility had made remote outposts defensible and that it invited rapid redeployment of forces. He contrasted the French use of "little Beau Geste forts" for positional warfare in Indochina with the United States' use of the helicopter to begin a fight. The commander no longer needed to think of holding a reserve in a traditional way. "They could be out . . . in the jungles or wherever," General Kinnard noted, "[and you could] pull them out of there and have them fighting someplace [else] in part of an hour or an hour."[14] The helicopter increased the tactical potential of the soldier as the commander gained a convincing ability to supply his men effectively: "I wanted light-weight, fast-stepping infantrymen who can really move and you don't do it by having him carry all that crap around. The helicopter will let you get it into him."[15] In a war where "the name of the game . . . was contact," the helicopter and other air assets altered what was possible and what was thinkable.[16]

At Song Be, helicopters were marshaled in separate areas, flew out "on the deck," and met over Cu Chi. From there, they launched a swift and coordinated attack for which the Vietcong were clearly unprepared. General Seneff commented, "It was an outstanding example of what you can do with . . . an operation [that really differs] from a pattern that you've established in the past." But the advantages of airmobility seem to have been compromised appreciably by the onset of routine. US and South Vietnamese movements became more predictable and easier to counter. General Seneff judged it a "horrifying thing" that the scenario at Song Be was not repeated and that other novel approaches were not developed. Even so, the helicopters provided "tactical dexterity" and, as General Seneff believed, had a liberating effect on General Westmoreland. Seneff argued that because the helicopter redefined lines of communication, supply, and airlift, it helped lessen Westmoreland's concerns about the problems suffered by the French in the early 1950s and about changing the shape of the war.[17]

Army Brig Gen Edwin L. Powell thought his service's aviation "had a huge effect on causing the leadership to think in more mobile terms." Yet, as General Kinnard pointed out, limits remained. "Westy really did not understand the air mobile division, which is no criticism of him." Moreover, as General Powell observed, the highest leaders tended to think of the helicopter as a means to "more direct command influence in the course of the battle"; and so, even as air assets transformed the combat environment, the views of those without a strong aviation background might well prevail in their deployment.[18]

One of the many ironies of this troubled war was that an impressive rotary-wing air force was created in response to circumstances not anticipated by its most ardent proponents and used in ways that fell short of their prescriptions. Yet Westmoreland, although not sold on the purists' views of Army air power and certainly not on interpretations that would have excluded helicopters from air power altogether, proved to be a happy and satisfied customer.

Firepower and Firebases

What air power allowed General Westmoreland to think possible in the ground war was exemplified by the defense of the firebase at Khe Sanh in the first months of 1968. The combat at Khe Sanh and the decision to hold the base were the culmination of procedures developed and used earlier in the war, now writ large and tinged with the special emotion of the Tet offensive. The appreciation of Khe Sanh at the time was inevitably a creature of Tet and of US domestic reaction to it, but its lasting significance comes from its place in a pattern—support for remote bases and outposts. The distinctiveness of Khe Sanh, then, grew partly from transitory circumstances and partly from magnitude; and its intensity sharply illuminated Westmoreland's aspirations for the ground war and his instinct for how air power could serve it.

At the time, the defense of Khe Sanh could not be freed from memories of the French defeat at Dien Bien Phu in 1954. Although the circumstances on the ground at Dien Bien Phu and Khe Sanh differed greatly, similarities were enough to cause extensive comparison. As an Air Force history noted in 1973, "The decision to defend Khe Sanh was made with Dien Bien Phu in mind and the defenses of the Marine base were strengthened accordingly." Yet the position was not held only with local resources nor, perhaps, could it have been. The United States enjoyed two tremendous advantages over its French predecessors—greater firepower and better logistical support, both based largely on air assets. The French had no more than 200 planes per day on which to rely, many of them light observation planes. "In defense of Khe Sanh, the Americans could draw upon a Southeast Asia armada of 2,000 planes and 3,300 helicopters." Moreover, radar direction from ground control facilities permitted accurate bombing in fog or darkness, at least for the Navy and Marine Grumman A-6s.[19]

Westmoreland gave limited thought to another option available to the United States—tactical nuclear weapons. President Johnson called Gen Earle Wheeler, USA, and asked if he might have to decide as to use of nuclear weapons. Learning of this, Westmoreland "considered that I would be imprudent if I failed to acquaint myself with the possibilities in detail." He "established a small secret group to study the subject," but it was swiftly disbanded due to fears in Washington that word would leak out and opinion would be adverse. Westmoreland later judged it a "mistake" to fail to consider this option, especially since "civilian casualties [would have been] minimal" in the sparsely inhabited region. Moreover, he added with irony, "if Washington officials were so intent on 'sending a message' to Hanoi, surely small tactical nuclear weapons would be a way to tell Hanoi something."[20] On the other hand, such contingency planning might as plausibly have assured Hanoi that Washington was running scared. In any event, the option was foreclosed—one of the few forms of firepower to be dismissed almost out of hand.

The drama and magnitude of the effort at Khe Sanh obscured the fact that tactics used there had been developing for years. Well before Khe Sanh, the United States had perfected many techniques born of need and had improvised many others to support large-unit operations. Perhaps even more impressively, methods had been developed that enabled small units to function under heretofore lethal conditions. Westmoreland's confidence about Khe Sanh was clearly bolstered by his earlier experience with B-52 Arc Light strikes in less-publicized operations. In explaining the need for Operation Niagara I—the intelligence-gathering and sensor-planting action before the expected defense of Khe Sanh—Westmoreland cited the value of Arc Light strikes, and of good intelligence, to guarantee "our ability to preempt or blunt . . . a concerted attack."[21] Resupply efforts had also been effective elsewhere. So, if the enemy would stand and fight, he would presumably suffer a heavy toll— one that would totally eclipse allied losses.

Westmoreland was clearly affected by the tremendous aerial firepower that the Seventh Air Force had marshaled in the latter part of 1967 when the enemy was besieging Con Thien. Tactical aircraft and B-52s were utilized in close coordination with naval gunfire and artillery as well as ground fire. The extraordinary volume of fire at Con Thien, and its effect on the enemy, convinced Westmoreland that "massed firepower was *in itself sufficient* to force a besieging enemy to desist, a demonstration that was destined to contribute to my confidence on a later occasion"[22] (Westmoreland's emphasis). In linking Con Thien with Khe Sanh, the general thus suggested how air assets helped him to overcome the troubling memories of the French loss at Dien Bien Phu. If massed firepower by itself could force an enemy to desist or disengage, then it was possible to risk much else. In fact, the risk seemed more apparent than real; if all else failed, firepower could be ordered in quantities sufficient to rescue the situation. But while Westmoreland did not see Khe Sanh as a Dien Bien Phu, he did believe that the North Vietnamese hoped to make it one.[23]

At Khe Sanh as elsewhere, attrition was not meant to be a strategy; and despite the assertions of its detractors, "search and destroy" was not merely attrition. For one thing, the intent was to make the trade-off a distinctly unequal one. To serve this goal, aerial firepower was expected to play an important part, irrespective of the specific platforms for its delivery. Whatever final judgment one makes of the whole process, attrition was not mindless. Efforts to measure progress in the conduct of the war by comparing losses for the enemy and friendly forces reflected the desire to give logic to the war. In his 1968 report on the war, General Westmoreland cited five factors as proof that the tide was running in favor of US and South Vietnamese forces. Four dealt with personnel and force relationships. First was the ratio of enemy to allied casualties (fig. 1); the others dealt with the balance of North Vietnamese and Vietcong forces and the relationship of South Vietnamese fighting strength to that of US and other free world forces. It was an effort to relate past performance to present need and infer what the future had in store.[24] And all wars have aspects of attrition—of costs as well as gains, and of balancing one's own losses against the enemy's. The process becomes discreditable when costs have no evident purpose and when gains are dwarfed by costs. Seen in this light, Khe Sanh offered Westmoreland a prospect he was inclined to relish more than to fear. He saw it as an opportunity to do what he had wanted to do all along. Westmoreland sought favorable contact with the enemy, "attempting to engage the enemy so that America's awesome firepower (everything from M-16 rifles to B-52

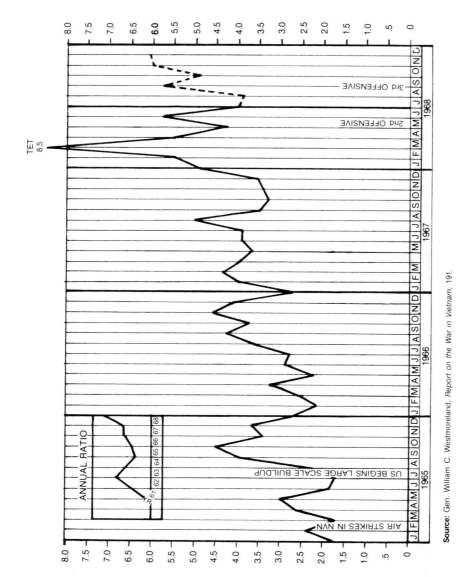

Figure 1. Ratio of Enemy to Allied Casualties.

Source: Gen. William C. Westmoreland, *Report on the War in Vietnam*, 191.

bombers) could be brought to bear. His objective was not to capture a hill or ridge line, but to destroy enemy soldiers and hostile units.''[25]

General DePuy, commander of the First Infantry Division during Operation Cedar Falls in 1967, argued that air strikes and artillery bombardment would have only limited results unless coordinated with action on the ground. He noted that in an area such as the Iron Triangle, cited as a ''notorious VC haven,'' the presence of numerous civilians ''hampered free-fire activities.'' Thus, in General DePuy's view, bombing and artillery had to be used circumspectly. But this restraint negated much of the sweep and shock of a coordinated rain of firepower. General DePuy enthusiastically reported ground advances by Army infantry-engineer bulldozer teams, seeing conditions on the ground enhanced by what was done from the air. He left little doubt, however, that he saw air power as limited when used by itself.[26]

Westmoreland had often failed to force the enemy to engage US forces, so he was eager to exploit the North Vietnamese commitment at Khe Sanh. He expected such a battle to cost few US and South Vietnamese men, whereas allied firepower claimed large numbers of North Vietnamese and Vietcong. (He was later to claim that losses ran 8 to 1 in favor of the United States and South Vietnam.)[27]

Senator J. Strom Thurmond, a persistent advocate of vigorous prosecution of the war, expressed the view that 75 percent of the Vietcong killed in the war had fallen to artillery fire and air assaults, including bombs dropped from B-52s. For Senator Thurmond, as for Westmoreland, the lesson learned was the need to coordinate Army and Air Force efforts. And firepower clearly enhanced the safety of the US fighting man on the ground, whether shot from guns or dropped from aircraft.[28]

At Khe Sanh between mid-January and late March, the aerial firepower was particularly awesome in volume and diversity. There were some 10,000 Air Force fighter strikes, more than 5,000 Navy and 7,000 Marine strikes, and more than 2,500 B-52 strikes—upwards of 24,500 in all. General Westmoreland envisioned, and received, round-the-clock shelling and bombing. Cells of three B-52s left their bases on Guam and in Thailand every three hours, putting B-52s over Khe Sanh every hour and a half. Although the psychological impact of such strikes was deemed great, a Marine Corps history of Khe Sanh's defense suggests that the regimental commander was even more impressed by ground-controlled radar bombing by lesser craft, which better met his pressing needs.[29]

In addition to Arc Light strikes, Mini- and Micro-Arc Lights were available. In the second week of February, for example, a Mini-Arc Light attack was executed against what had been identified as a major North Vietnamese Army (NVA) headquarters. ''Two Marine A-6 Intruders and four F-4B Phantoms unloaded 152 500-pound bombs into the [target] block in concert with the opening volleys of eight artillery batteries (total of 350 artillery rounds).'' ''The target was obliterated,'' but ''whether or not this unusual ambush netted any NVA brass-hats was never ascertained.''[30] Micro-Arc Lights used smaller volumes of ordnance; but they took a mere 10 minutes to put into effect, whereas it took roughly 45 minutes to plan and execute the Mini.[31] Three or four Minis and six to eight Micros were executed on an average night during the prime weeks of the enemy attack. In all, tactical aircraft delivered over 35,000 tons of bombs and rockets, B-52s dropped over 75,000 tons of bombs, and Marine howitzers at the firebase and Army 175-mm guns at Camp Carroll fired more than 100,000 rounds (about 1,500 per day).[32]

With so many kinds of air power—and so much of it—the coordination and control problem was appreciable. During the siege, Westmoreland learned that Maj Gen Norman J. Anderson of the First Marine Air Wing had not been in direct communication with the Army's First Cavalry Division even though Westmoreland had told Anderson to keep close contact. The MACV commander concluded that the Marines were not giving sufficient tactical air support to the Army because overlapping air control systems were causing confusion. Westmoreland then endorsed General Momyer's proposal for a single tactical air control system under Westmoreland's deputy for air (Momyer). In his memoirs, Westmoreland complained that the Marines "made a doctrinal issue of it" with the Joint Chiefs and that Army Chief of Staff Gen Harold Keith Johnson underplayed it "lest a precedent be established that might lead to the Army's losing its helicopters to the Air Force." It was all "exasperating" for Westmoreland, whose attention was riveted on the fight at Khe Sanh while the chiefs debated long-range implications of Momyer's proposal in an environment clean of the scent of napalm and powder.[33]

For the Marines, the matter did include an element of institutional self-protection. They took a largely conservative, traditional approach to the war; and nothing at Khe Sanh seemed so strange or pressing as to unseat their doctrine. This view lasted throughout the war. Gen Wallace M. Greene, Jr., commandant of Marine Corps, defended Marine air support doctrine and its suitability to the Marine effort in Vietnam. Before the Senate Appropriations Committee's Subcommittee on Defense Appropriations on 24 March 1966, he cited the helicopter, whose use by the Army had been seen as a novelty, as standard in Marine Corps operations. He claimed the "vertical assault concept" as a Marine Corps innovation that was combat-proven. In 1965 alone, Marine helicopters flew 200,000 sorties, lifted more than 14,500 tons of cargo, and carried more than 388,000 troops. Given Vietnam's limited rail and road infrastructure, helicopters were all but indispensable for maintaining mobility. Greene maximized the achievement of Marine aviation efforts and minimized their departure from previous Marine practice or doctrine. He acknowledged only that the ratio of rotary to fixed-wing aircraft was higher than it would be if used in an amphibious assault. Rich with reference to Inchon and Guadalcanal, General Greene's testimony cast the mantle of history over his service's special interests in the Vietnam conflict.[34] The Marines could consider changes, but reluctance to "throw the baby out with the bath-water" ensured their preference for gradualism.

Despite problems, the achievement at Khe Sanh was considerable. Of the massive impact of a B-52 drop, Marine Maj Gen Rathvon McC. Tompkins, Third Marine Division commander, said: "It was as if a little part of the world suddenly blew up from no apparent cause."[35] General Westmoreland characterized the whole enterprise as "an awesome display of firepower . . . one of the heaviest and most concentrated in the history of warfare."[36] Air power supported Khe Sanh, permitting General Westmoreland to maintain his sense of the war substantially intact.

Supply, Support, and Security

Outlying bases could not be defended exclusively by massed firepower, even if it was a critical element. Logistical support was also needed to give commanders confidence that the risks of maintaining scattered posts in a "war without fronts" were acceptable. The defense of Khe Sanh showed that this confidence was well placed and that remote bases could be held against great pressure if one had the necessary resources, intelligence, manpower, and purpose.

Abundant as US resources were, they were not infinite; and resupply is accompanied by operating costs and maintenance problems. Major bases such as Tan Son Nhut, Da Nang, and Cam Ranh Bay had only 40 percent of their cargo-loading equipment in good operating order in early 1967. At isolated air strips, dust and sand caused equipment to gum up. Such difficulties continued into 1968, and the demands of Tet and Khe Sanh did nothing to lessen them.[37]

In his official report on the war, General Westmoreland said that a "potentially serious situation" caused by enemy attacks on Khe Sanh was alleviated by "the initiative of the tactical logisticians and the magnificent support provided by the cargo aircraft of the US Air Force and Marines."[38] Westmoreland claimed, credibly, that the enemy had made "every effort to halt supply of the garrison by air" but had failed. But not all US efforts worked with equal effect. On 7 March, enemy antiaircraft increased markedly; 13 US Marine aircraft were fired on and an Air Force C-123 was hit and crashed a few miles east of Khe Sanh.[39] Air and artillery attacks coordinated in Operation Niagara II were thought to have preempted a full-scale ground attack, but they could not protect a landing strip at Khe Sanh. Hence, by the end of March, most supplies for Khe Sanh were being airdropped or brought in by helicopter.[40] Still, even with restraints on what aircraft could be employed, Khe Sanh was supplied well enough to meet the test.

Other factors complicated keeping the "aerial highway" to Khe Sanh open. On the one hand, a wide range of aircraft could be used to keep Khe Sanh supplied; and the broad capabilities of available aircraft—C-130s could deliver 13 tons per sortie; C-123s, 8 tons; and C-7As, 3 tons—were impressive. On the other hand, the steel-mat landing strip could not withstand sustained use; but the variety of aircraft available gave flexibility. When the C-130s began to do serious damage to the landing strip at the firebase, delivery was shifted over to the much lighter de Havilland craft.

Innovations in tactics and technology also helped to keep Khe Sanh resupplied. Speed off-loading (running pallets of supplies off C-130s along guide rails using the forward motion of the aircraft) reduced time on the ground during unloading from

5–10 minutes to as little as 30 seconds. All aircraft coming into Khe Sanh, especially the C-130s, were vulnerable to fire during landing and taxiing; and ground troops had to clear shell fragments and other rubble from the runway between flights. Partly because of these conditions and partly due to periodic poor weather, Brig Gen Burl W. McLaughlin of the 834th Air Division concluded that large quantities of supplies would have to be airdropped.[41]

Thus, difficulties faced at Khe Sanh fostered innovation. One such innovation was a parachute radar guidance system based on principles only recently tested at Pope Air Force Base, North Carolina. Pressed into use, this system added to the ability of cargo aircraft to deliver supplies in bad weather: cargo extraction equipment and refined parachute techniques guaranteed that the materiel dropped would reach its intended customers. (The French had unintentionally supplied enemy troops about as well as they supported their own at Dien Bien Phu.) The accuracy and reliability of aerial delivery at Khe Sanh were new achievements.[42] In other circumstances, the only alternatives would have been continued destruction of the airstrip, a serious interruption in support for the troops, or both.

Supply of Khe Sanh's outposts could be achieved only by helicopter. But rapidly increasing enemy antiaircraft capability made it imperative to provide better support for the rotary-winged ships. In February, the North Vietnamese strengthened their installations until it was agreed that helicopter gunships were sufficient to support the supply ships. As one commentator noted, "the Marines responded by devising what they called the 'Super Gaggle,' a tactical innovation that made its debut in the last week of February. This was simply a formation of supply-carrying helicopters escorted by the usual gunships plus McDonnell-Douglas A-4 Skyhawk attack planes."[43] The helicopters left from an intermediate point at Dong Ha on a schedule that would bring them to their destination just at the time the A-4s hit known and suspected antiaircraft emplacements. Two A-4s laid down a protective smokescreen for the helicopters, while two others battered the North Vietnamese positions.[44] Using napalm and rockets, the A-4s disrupted enemy forces enough to permit transport helicopters (mostly CH-46s) to land their cargo safely and then fly to Chu Lai and Da Nang. The A-4s accompanied the helicopters back to safety and then refueled from KC-130 tankers.[45] In good measure, the support of the central installation at Khe Sanh and its outlying posts exemplified the effort to extend control from large and defensible positions to more precarious sites.

In "marketing" the Vietnam War, military officers often described the same event as both defensive and offensive. On the one hand, for example, they talked of the "defense" of Khe Sanh, the "siege" of Khe Sanh, and the "relief" of Khe Sanh. Such terms suggested that the North Vietnamese had the initiative. But Westmoreland called it an "offensive in place," and said the United States was winning a real victory by grinding down North Vietnamese forces with firepower. The common understanding of an "offensive" as incorporating positive geographical movement was being challenged since air assets might conduct an offensive in one place. Provided the aerial supply lines were genuinely defensible, the more satisfactory term might be "pitched battle." Westmoreland seems to have taken this view.

Such buoyancy of vision could not always be sustained. At Kham Duc, later in 1968, for example, it was harder to claim some sort of victory since the position was ultimately not held. In April 1968, intelligence analysts suspected that the special forces camp at Kham Duc would soon face a Vietcong and North Vietnamese attack. The enemy was known to be building roads in the area, developing the kind of infrastructure General Westmoreland wanted to break with his own ground forces. Since Kham Duc could be a base from which to attack that infrastructure, Westmoreland directed its reinforcement. Lt Gen Robert E. Cushman sent 600 troops plus some artillery and ammunition from the American Division on 10 May. An additional 32 troops and more supplies came on the following day. Including 272 Vietnamese dependents, there were 1,760 people in the camp. Kham Duc's outpost at Nagoc Tavak fell even as the reinforcements were arriving; it had been a bad place to be—surrounded by high terrain held by the enemy, pressured by enemy troops, having only a short airstrip of limited value, and shorn of its utility as a forward base for patrol and reconnaissance. It proved impossible to evacuate Nagoc Tavak by air, to reinforce it sufficiently, or even to attempt further support without still worse losses. The outpost was abandoned and the men moved under fighter aircraft cover for high ground. There they cleared a landing zone for four Marine CH-46 helicopters, which shuttled them to Kham Duc.[46]

Kham Duc itself soon came under pressure. Its seven outposts were successively attacked, one after the other falling despite aerial firepower brought to their support. AC-47 Spooky gunships forced the enemy to disengage long enough to let the defenders escape to the main base at Kham Duc. The closer the enemy came, the tighter the ring encircling Kham Duc—and the more vulnerable US aircraft became. Since B-52 attacks on suspected enemy positions had not stalled their attack, and since the tightening of the ring around Kham Duc made resupply much less feasible, General Cushman recommended that Westmoreland order withdrawal. He did so on 11 May, noting that it lacked the "defensive potential" of Khe Sanh. The geography was against them, intelligence on enemy dispositions was imprecise, and air strikes consequently lacked punch. Meanwhile, resupply by air became ever more tenuous.[47]

The evacuation of Kham Duc averted a massacre. This fact cannot be ignored; but it also showed that air power was not a cure-all and that Westmoreland's hope of blocking the enemy's trail system may have been too grand. Additionally, Kham Duc showed that whatever victory some US forces might have claimed following the successful countering of the Tet offensive, they obviously were not in a position to undertake their own offensive with boundless optimism. The enemy was still a potent force and a genuine reason for concern.

The final lesson of Kham Duc was that supply and firepower could be provided by air; but not against all odds, under every set of adverse circumstances, or in disregard of enemy numbers and intentions. Air power was necessary, if not sufficient, to overcoming the difficult; but it could not accomplish the impossible nor defend the indefensible.

"Secret" Bombing and Hidden Warfare

Air power could augment ground operations and add overwhelming firepower when the enemy chose to stand and fight. But governmental officials sometimes tried to use it as an alternative to ground actions. Important among them was President Richard Nixon. Sharp reaction within the United States to the US "incursion" into Cambodia in 1971 suggested that President Nixon could use ground forces only at considerable cost at home. Bombing, on the other hand, required far fewer men. Also, bombing allowed a narrow definition of "need to know," enhancing the prospects for maintaining security. Security itself was dual-purposed: to avoid compromising the mission and to prevent opponents of the war from interfering. And since the "secret bombing" of Cambodia was no secret either to the Cambodians or to the North Vietnamese and Vietcong, the importance President Nixon and his very closest advisers attached to keeping the circle of debate on bombing policy as narrow as possible is not surprising.

Although this sort of secrecy became nearly an art during the Nixon administration, it began under President Johnson. Under both presidents, the immediate question seemed not whether the bombing had reliable effects but whether any sort of action could be taken at all. At the same time, reports that the B-52 bombings actually were effective gave some cause for hope. Vice President Hubert H. Humphrey told Johnson in January 1966 that his own skepticism had been overcome by what he saw in a trip to Vietnam: the B-52s were doing a "superlative job blasting VC redoubts that haven't been reached for 10 years."[48] But just as pressing—sometimes more so—was the advantage of political circumspection.

Some evidence exists that hopes for security against the enemy in Southeast Asia and against potential political enemies in the United States were intertwined. The matter remains clouded. But to whatever extent it was so, secrecy itself became a measure of bombing effectiveness. Thus the pursuit of secrecy became a preoccupation, deflecting attention from the merits of bombing. The press, and through it the public, assumed target status for the Johnson administration in the campaign for secrecy. In a memorandum for Assistant Secretary of Defense John T. McNaughton on 23 February 1967, Rear Adm W. E. Lemos reported State Department and White House staff approval for B-52 strikes in Laos while using targets in South Vietnam "within the same time frames to serve as press cover."[49] Long after the event, in 1973, a Defense Department report justified the inclusion of inaccurate data into reports and into the computer system's data base, noting that failure to account for all missions adequately would have "almost certainly led to speculation that unreported operations were being conducted."[50]

The National Security Council wanted to minimize public speculation, and so it chose those to be informed about such operations on a strict need-to-know basis.

The determinant of "need" was completion of the operation (if one's knowledge promoted the operation, one had a need to know); rank or formal authority did not count. These measures were defended on traditional grounds of military security, but the Lemos memorandum and the Defense Department's later explanations suggest the linkage between political and military dimensions. At the very least, the unusually tight security gave political cover to the Laotian government so that it might act as if Laos was not absorbed in the war and still had some semblance of neutrality: if the bombing was an official "nonevent," Vientiane did not have to comment on it.[51] Assuming that security as to time and place of a strike would have been observed even if the general existence of the bombing program had been acknowledged, the purpose in preventing general disclosure of the bombing would not likely have been to frustrate the enemy. The general existence of the bombing was obvious enough to them. It was those outside Southeast Asia who literally did not know what they were missing.[52]

Procedures later invoked to keep secret the bombing missions in Cambodia (operations Menu and Patio) followed this principle of narrow control and limited advice, and they deeply troubled Senator Stuart Symington and others in Congress. In special hearings held by the Senate Committee on Armed Services, questions of authority and responsibility abounded, as did questions of fair play in dealings between the administration and Congress over conduct of the war. Symington worried over what effect the special procedures used for the Cambodian bombing would have on the military establishment. He feared that tightening the circle of those with a need to know was leaving even those who knew something not knowing enough. In the Armed Services committee hearings on 9 August 1973, Symington rejected the view of the chairman of the JCS, Adm Thomas H. Moorer, that all officials with a need to know had the requisite information. Symington explained that he had asked the former head of SAC and the former head of SAC's Pacific operations for details of how Menu operations were handled, and that the two descriptions did not coincide. "So it became very clear to me," Symington said, "that this situation, computer bank or no computer bank, was so vague" that confusion and error were possible because of "the way the orders were delivered." He expressed the hope that future orders would be given "in a more definitive form."[53]

The charge that orders for Menu were vague reflected more than worry over operational efficiency—it raised the issues of civilian authority over the military and the integrity of the military chain of command. Secrecy went to the heart of the issue of who was running the war; the question of the worth of the bombing itself fell to second place. Admiral Moorer sought to distinguish between the many civilians responsible for managing the military and the very few civilians with command responsibilities over it. He focused on the president and the secretary of defense executing their intentions through the Joint Chiefs. Admiral Moorer thought this showed that civilian control of the military was "not just an abstract Constitutional principle . . . but an everyday rule governing all of our national military operations.'' He consigned congressional and public relations to the civilians as ''policy matters,'' implying that any displeasure over Menu should be directed at the secretary of defense or the president.[54] He distinguished sharply between two purposes in defense organization—one pertaining to management, the other to command—and argued that highly streamlined command procedures did not contradict an elaborate administrative apparatus.

According to Moorer's interpretation of the National Security Act of 1947 as amended, the service secretaries and chiefs were responsible for ''such things as morale, discipline, promotions, logistic support, readiness, and so on,'' but not for operations—and thus not for command. Moorer spoke of ''another entire chain of command'' stemming from the president and the secretary of defense through the JCS to the unified commanders. The secretaries, and the chiefs in their capacities as senior service officers, were thus out of the chain. Moorer defended this as ''streamlining'' required by ''the advent of nuclear weapons'' and as suited to the size of the US armed forces and their worldwide deployment.[55]

Moorer passed lightly over the charge that reports on US operations had been grossly distorted. He even defended the integrity and organization of the data compiled during the Vietnam War by defining the data's purpose narrowly: the data in the defense computer system was for ''management purposes, not for evaluation of the efficiency of the weapons systems or the degree of effect that the operation had on the enemy.'' In his eyes, this data comprised ''a logistics support document'' but not ''a description of what took place in the war.'' The latter was provided in intelligence summaries, war diaries, and special reports. He noted a Defense Department report on operations in Cambodia and Laos that used operational reports (OPREP-4s) of SAC missions in Menu bombing as the basic input for its automated data base. According to Moorer, the resulting data base was intended only to show the number of hours and missions flown by each aircraft so as to make appropriate allowances for fuel, spare parts, munitions, and other logistical matters.[56] He implied that it made no difference whether targets and routes were reported accurately as long as the numbers came out the same.

This defense of the data base exposed the issue of authority underlying the debate over bombing policy. Senator Symington recognized this. He flatly rejected any interpretation of command that permitted the secretary of the Air Force to be kept in the dark on the use of his bomber force, as had happened to Secretary of the Air Force Robert Seamans during the Menu operations. Having served as the first secretary of the Air Force, Symington bristled over a service's secretary being led to make ''gross misrepresentations and misstatements.'' Symington said he ''would not have touched that job with a 10-foot pole'' if Truman had imposed similar terms of office on him. The senator believed that Menu procedure jeopardized the morale and effectiveness of both civilians and military officers. Senator Harold Hughes speculated that Gen John D. Lavelle, commander, Seventh Air Force, who had been rebuked for concealing his own air strikes against North Vietnam, did so in imitation of Menu bombings. Hughes wondered whether the extreme security measures had not demoralized those who entered false coordinates into reports. He wondered if men had been made to doubt their own integrity—all the way up to misinformed service secretaries and chiefs left sidelined and useless in the dark.[57]

As the US experience in Vietnam approached its end, demoralization of the armed forces and of the US civilian leadership became a matter of genuine concern. To the extent that demoralization was a cost of the bombing, it is fair to ask what was gotten in return. One thing gained by these special security measures was several years of comparative secrecy. Other effects, however, are harder to verify. Bombing did not keep the enemy from undertaking ground operations that the United States was unwilling to counter with ground action of its own, but hopes of dissuading them seemed to have been ill-founded. The use of B-52s in Laos and Cambodia after Johnson left office reflected the combat orientation of Arc Light, Khe Sanh, and Kham Duc less than the psychopolitical hopes of Rolling Thunder.

According to a 1973 Defense Department report, the use of B-52s to bomb military targets in Northern Laos's Plain of Jars had been intended to assist the ground forces of Royal Laotian General Vang Pao by "blunting the anticipated North Vietnamese offensive."[58] Prime Minister Souvanna Phouma had requested this specific support through the US ambassador, who transmitted all further requests for B-52 bombing in the Plain of Jars area. These operations began on 17 February 1970 under the code name Good Look. Their purpose was to counter the North Vietnamese buildup of an estimated 15,000 troops. Specific targets were forwarded by the US ambassador in Vientiane, were subsequently validated by the COMUSMACV and CINCPAC, and were then forwarded to the chairman of the Joint Chiefs. After review by the joint staff, the chairman requested civilian approval at the highest levels. COMUSMACV was given authority to approve missions by B-52s in the Plain of Jars area after 1 January 1972, subject only to cancellation by the secretary of defense.

Prior to the appearance of the North Vietnamese force, which brought on the approval of B-52 bombings, the United States had conducted a B-52 radar reconnaissance mission over the Plain of Jars as part of contingency planning under the name Good Look Alpha. According to the Defense Department report, this reconnaissance effort was repeated in Good Look Bravo "in the hope that Hanoi would perceive the warning that B-52 operations were being considered in the Plain of Jars, and would modify its operations in northern Laos."[59] When this political move failed, the United States undertook bombing to assist Vang Pao directly. A Combat Skyspot radar site was established at Ubon, Thailand, to direct missions and increase their accuracy.[60] These facilities ensured that bombs would hit the intended coordinates, but they could not ensure that bombs would hit profitable targets. In a conventional war, fixed installations stayed put. Some campaigns might be profitable with intelligence that was days or even weeks old and the "timeliness" of military intelligence had one meaning. But in Laos, timeliness meant something else. The enemy was elusive, moving with ease and speed, greatly magnifying the problems of gathering meaningful intelligence; and accurate intelligence could be made worthless in a matter of hours.

After the hearings that focused on the Cambodia bombings, General Westmoreland delicately referred to "the intimation of doubledealing in high places" as one cause of public furor over the matter.[61] He approved the purpose of these bombings, whether before or after the incursion of allied ground forces into Cambodia, but he preferred calling these strikes "unannounced" rather than secret.[62] Westmoreland reasoned that, "barring other forays" into Cambodia, the B-52 strikes gave the only chance to destroy enemy base areas.[63] Yet the ability to locate them precisely and "take them out" was not infinite. Although secondary explosions were reported, suggesting that worthwhile targets had been hit, the problem of knowing exactly what those targets had been, how valuable they were, and how much was left intact remained a knotty one. Westmoreland's sense of the purpose behind the bombings inhibited him from taking a skeptical view of their concrete effects. But the exact dimensions of their effects were matters of judgment and speculation—hidden from critics, hidden in computers, hidden by the jungles.

Half-Told Tales

Although bombing, especially from B-52s, was one approach to dealing with enemy forces in the jungles, other ways of using air power against them also had advocates. Some hoped that a full range of military problems could be countered by using high-intensity weaponry. Others, believing that insurgent forces in jungles had to be dealt with in special ways, favored specialized units and weapons. Again, how one viewed air power depended on how one viewed the war itself. The question was whether air power could make counterinsurgency viable and, if so, precisely how. Measures either proposed or adopted received comparatively little attention as the scale of the war expanded during the mid-1960s; and the stories of actions undertaken became tales only half told, measures given only partial attention, and lessons with no more than fragmentary impact.

For Presidents Kennedy and Johnson, the focus on winning the war on the ground reflected the realization that the Saigon government had to regain control of the countryside while holding the cities. Seeing counterinsurgency as a distinctive form of war, they put some urgency on developing distinctive forces tailored to the special features of the war. At the same time, the mere existence of certain technologies, hardware, and units created drives of their own. Thus, for example, the deployment of airmobile units to Vietnam played to Kennedy's intent to fight a counterinsurgency, even though some others thought the units ill-suited to it.

A distinguished leader in the Korean War, retired Army Gen James A. Van Fleet reviewed his service's counterguerrilla and counterinsurgency capabilities. He was impressed with new air power assets, such as the helicopters, and advocated that the Army take revolutionary steps to deal with insurgencies. In a lengthy letter to Secretary of the Army Elvis J. Stahr, Jr., Van Fleet wondered what value two new conventional divisions authorized for the Army would have in waging the cold war; he described their use in a hot war as "remote." He urged that the manpower be devoted, instead, to special forces, augmented with helicopter airlift capability, "again compensating for lack of numbers and firepower through increased mobility and concentrated shock action." Clearly, the new capability represented by efficient and supportable helicopters caused major rethinking of tactics and even some reconception of the ground effort as a whole. The new "combat task forces" he wanted would be, in essence, large special forces units.[64]

Some Army aviation proponents regarded the US reliance on helicopters as a mixed blessing. Airmobility would allow the swift relocation of forces by leapfrogging them over obstacles on the ground. It would also increase the chance of making contact with the enemy and free US ground forces from the knotty tasks of clearing more road mileage and ground area. "I guess it's really a question of the American way of fighting," Gen Robert R. Williams later thought. Airmobility's image of surgical cleanliness and efficiency had more appeal than conventional movement on the ground. But Williams also recalled a correspondent's insistence that overflights by helicopters were no match for Vietcong presence in villages. Even if one drove the Vietcong away with air power, how long would they stay away unless men on the ground forced them? Given the extraordinary tunnel systems the Vietcong built in many places, it was sometimes even a matter of doubt that they had been driven out at all. "You have to fight it down in the muck and the mud at night, and on a day-to-day basis," General Williams said. "That's not the American way and you are not going to get the American soldier to fight that way." Col Delbert Bristol later expressed similar misgivings. His concern stemmed in large measure from his adherence to the traditional Army interest in occupying territory.

> I still think that the Army exists to seize and hold terrain. To a certain degree you have to stay on the terrain in order to do that, and I think to that degree we may have erred a little bit in our conduct of the Vietnam War. More than a little bit.[65]

Colonel Bristol particularly wondered if taking and holding lines of communication, and controlling critical areas, would have had greater results than did "search and destroy."[66]

If the American temperament had truly precluded this close-quarters approach to the war, then perhaps using more advanced technology was the only alternative to withdrawal. In some sort of mechanized and higher technology war, the helicopters were more suitable. But was the character of the combatants more of a key to suitability than was the war itself? "It was," General Williams suggested, "the best way to go short of reversion to true, massive, dirty, low-down guerrilla warfare."[67] Evidently, to this participant, the "true" way to fight guerrillas was on their own terms. Using higher technology was true to American inclinations, if not fully to the nature of the fight.

Since the helicopter could be viewed as an effective force multiplier, it enabled US leaders to think of keeping as few US personnel as possible in Vietnam despite the widespread belief that a counterinsurgency required an overwhelming numerical advantage over the insurgents. And Army Brig Gen O. Glenn Goodhand, reflecting on the war, thought US forces would not have done as well in Vietnam had they not had helicopters.

> Most people, historians anyway, it seems to me had a theory that to combat insurgency forces it takes something over a dozen men per insurgent with normal transportation means[,] and I think that in Vietnam they brought that ratio down to something like four or five to one, which I think is directly [attributable] to the capability to move the forces around, which would have been totally lacking without the helicopter transport.[68]

Whether what was actually done was sufficient to the tasks at hand was another issue. In essence, the questions were whether air power and firepower could alter a war and whether they could do so to any good purpose. These questions were especially compelling since the French had held more territory with fewer troops and lower technology than used by the United States.

Air power and firepower changed the character of the war in Vietnam, even on the village level. A Vietcong defector and informant named Hai Chua told US Army adviser Stuart A. Herrington, "The government troops did not pose too much of a problem [to the Vietcong] at first, but the Americans with their helicopters and artillery changed the face of the war overnight."[69] Airlifting troops and supporting them with considerable firepower deprived many Vietcong of havens they had enjoyed. Officials in both the United States and Saigon often complained that the war had no "front lines" and no completely safe rear areas, and the same was substantially true for the Vietcong (and to some extent for the NVA) after the introduction of American equipment and tactics. According to the Vietcong defector, the village people grew concerned about associating with the Vietcong as casualties and property damage mounted, even if they hesitated to give allegiance to Saigon.

The swift movement and fire support that air power made possible still needed good intelligence to have a political payoff. Intelligence without a physical capability to exploit it is futile, and mobility and force without intelligence are mindless; but when all elements work in harmony, much can be accomplished. One incident that illustrates this came in early November 1971: A heliborne operation in the Trang Bang district of Hau Nghia Province, with South Vietnamese troops using eight Hueys, descended swiftly into an area carefully charted by intelligence officers who had debriefed prisoners and defectors; in one afternoon, 23 Vietcong were taken—identified by name, house number, and other essential data. These prisoners fingered other Vietcong, and the net of intelligence began to snarl VC operations in the district. This coupling of intelligence with mobility must still be counted as a positive achievement, permitting hits against the enemy while discriminating between real insurgents and mere bystanders.[70]

But the helicopter was no cure-all. Its use for secure movement of troops fell off drastically with the introduction of Soviet-made SA-7 heat-seeking surface-to-air antiaircraft missiles (SAMs). Hand-held and fired from the shoulder, these missiles were said to have "changed overnight the ground rules for use of the helicopter." In essence, the SA-7 challenged at least locally US and South Vietnamese dominance of the air—a hint of what might have been in store had the enemy been equipped to challenge the whole spectrum of air operations.[71] With the SAM challenge, camps that "had to rely solely on an aerial life line" rapidly became less secure.[72] So the improvement of the enemy's defensive technology complicated US difficulties in exploiting technological advantages. As one officer observed of Operation Nathan Hale in 1966, "superabundant mobility" let the US forces come upon the enemy so quickly that they sometimes walked into trouble unawares. "Most of their grief," he said, "came of engaging precipitately while reconnoitering indifferently."[73] The danger was that air power and firepower might go beyond compensating for relative scarcity of manpower, distorting judgment of what was to be accomplished and how.

The air efforts and their impact on the war needed to be put into some perspective. Testifying before Congress in 1967, Gen John P. McConnell, Air Force chief of staff, struggled to find a relevant criterion to judge the effectiveness of air power and its impact on the war. In essence, he accepted the force-multiplier logic of such ground officers as General Goodhand. He characterized the air bases, the aircraft, the men, the bomb tonnages, and the sorties generated as "enormously impressive." He added, "It is so impressive as to make the question 'Why hasn't air power won the Vietnam war?' a natural one."[74] General McConnell concluded that, in a sense, it had. Since the Vietcong and North Vietnamese main force and regular units had lost all major-unit actions in South Vietnam during the preceding year, the aerial firepower employed must have had positive effect. He concluded further that North Vietnamese efforts to supply the war in the South must have been contained, since the frequency of enemy attacks had declined despite an increase in the number of enemy battalions.[75] General McConnell sought to evaluate the effectiveness of air power against specific performance objectives as limited by the political contours of the war rather than against some absolute vision of victory. "The effects of air power," he said, "must be considered in terms of our national objectives."[76] But what he said could really be reduced to the observation that air power had forestalled an enemy victory.

Another way some analysts supported claims of air power's effectiveness, and one which proved to have continuing appeal, was to cite its apparent ability to alter the calculus of military force on the ground. The abundance of tactical air activity made it possible to "concentrate force against an enemy in terrain where the advantage has in the past almost always been with the guerrilla."[77] In 1966, for example, US Air Force, Navy, and Marine aviation flew 124,000 attack sorties in South Vietnam, a large proportion of them in direct support of ground forces. And the Army's helicopter aviation was an important part of the air power mix. Taken together, General McConnell concluded that these facts showed that air power had thus "*consistently enabled* the allied forces in Vietnam to defeat enemy units with considerably *less than half the 10–1 advantage* some authorities believe is needed to deal with guerrilla forces and small units in jungle warfare" (emphasis added).[78] As McConnell apparently saw it, air power was not really asked to produce an absolute victory by fighting the sort of war that airmen had been preparing for. Instead, it was asked to do something less; and in the process, it at least provided a means for conducting some sort of action aimed at the enemy while supposedly helping to limit US manpower levels.

In a war where predictability and clarity were in short supply, air power could not ensure a string of victories—but it could be depended on with some confidence to avert the prospect of genuine defeat. And in a war where the commitment of manpower was regulated to meet both domestic and international pressures, air power reduced the number of men needed for operations. Seen in its best light, then, McConnell's argument hinged on the notion of substitution—what would it have been like *without* air power? But even this standard had its ambiguities. The positive interpretation was that air power had at least enabled the United States to persist in a war that was as confused as it was confusing—one that lacked clarity of direction and simplicity of focus. The negative interpretation was the same.

NOTES

1. Gen William C. Westmoreland, *A Soldier Reports* (Garden City, N.Y.: Doubleday & Co., 1976), 148. Westmoreland also said that one of his purposes in wanting to hold Khe Sanh was to use it as a staging base for a future ground attack against the Ho Chi Minh Trail (see page 198).

2. Ibid., 389.

3. Quoted in Ward Just, *Military Men* (New York: Alfred A. Knopf, 1970), 200.

4. Quoted in Robert L. Gallucci, *Neither Peace Nor Honor, The Politics of American Military Policy in Viet-Nam* (Baltimore: Johns Hopkins University Press, 1975), 52.

5. Gen William W. Momyer, USAF (Ret.), *Air Power in Three Wars,* (n.p., 1978), 80.

6. Westmoreland, *A Soldier Reports,* 15–32. References to oversupervision appear on pages 18 and 31.

7. Ibid. The direct quotation is on page 17. Although never a student at either, Westmoreland did serve as an instructor at the Army Command and General Staff College and at the Army War College.

8. Ibid., 37–38.

9. In this particular, the Army appears to differ somewhat from the Air Force which, as suggested in chapter 1 of this study, has traditionally been more likely to embrace an idea or a weapon for its potential and prospects even before it has been tested or proved.

10. See, for example, interview with Gen Robert R. Williams, USA, conducted by Col Ralph J. Powell and Lt Col Philip E. Courts, 1977, US Army Military History Research Institute, Carlisle Barracks, Pa., Oral History Series, The History of Army Aviation, 60–62. Also, chapter 2 of the present study includes material pertinent to this issue, most of which will not be repeated here.

11. Gen George P. Seneff, USA, interviewed by Lt Col Ronald K. Andersen, US Army Military History Institute, Carlisle Barracks, Pa., Oral History Series, The History of Army Aviation, 37.

12. Ibid.

13. See chapter 2 of this study competing service views on the helicopter and its implications. Here, attention will be limited to the impact of these air assets (and thinking about them) on the ground war in Southeast Asia.

14. Lt Gen Harry W. O. Kinnard, interviewed by Col Glenn Smith and Col August Cianciolo, 31 March 1977, US Army Military History Institute, Carlisle Barracks, Pa., Oral History Series, The History of Army Aviation, 25, 27.

15. Ibid., 32–33.

16. Ibid., 24.

17. General Seneff interview, 42, 55, 57.

18. Brig Gen Edwin L. Powell, interviewed by Cols Bryce R. Kramer and Ralph J. Powell, US Army Military History Institute, Carlisle Barracks, Pa., Oral History Series, The History of Army Aviation, 29. Interview with General Kinnard, 2.

19. Bernard C. Nalty, *Air Power and the Fight for Khe Sanh* (Washington, D.C.: Office of Air Force History, 1973), 19.

20. Westmoreland, *A Soldier Reports,* 338.

21. Nalty, *Air Power and the Fight for Khe Sanh,* 90.

22. Westmoreland, *A Soldier Reports,* 204.

23. Lyndon Baines Johnson, *The Vantage Point: Perspectives of the Presidency* (London: Weidenteld and Nicolson, 1971), 381. George Herring, *America's Longest War: The United States and Vietnam, 1950–1975* (New York: John Wiley & Sons, 1979), 185. Herring paints a somewhat different picture of the key players. Here, General Westmoreland has a much gloomier and tense aspect.

24. Gen William C. Westmoreland, *Report on the War in Vietnam (as of 30 June 1968),* sec. 2, "Report on Operations in South Vietnam, January 1964–June 1968" (Washington, D.C.: Government Printing Office, 1968), 189.

25. Nalty, *Air Power and the Fight for Khe Sanh,* 21.

26. Quoted in Bernard Rogers, *Cedar Falls—Junction City: A Turning Point* (Washington, D.C.: Department of the Army, 1974), 78.

27. Westmoreland, *Report on the War in Vietnam,* sec. 2, 191.

28. Senate, Committee on Armed Services and Subcommittee on Department of Defense, Committee on Appropriations, *Hearings, Military Procurement Authorizations for Fiscal Year 1968,* 90th Cong., 1st sess., testimony of Gen Harold K. Johnson, 31 January 1967, 577.

29. Willard Pearson, *The War in the Northern Provinces* (Washington, D.C.: Department of the Army, 1975), 71–72; Westmoreland, *A Soldier Reports,* 339; Moyers S. Shore II, *The Battle for Khe Sanh* (Washington, D.C.: Headquarters US Marine Corps, 1969), 103–4.

30. Shore, *The Battle for Khe Sanh,* 110.

31. Ibid., 110–11.

32. Westmoreland, *A Soldier Reports,* 339.

33. Ibid., 343–44.

34. Senate, Committee on Armed Services and the Subcommittee on Defense Appropriations, Committee on Appropriations, *Hearings, Military Procurement Authorizations for Fiscal Year 1967,* 89th Cong., 2d sess., testimony of Gen Wallace M. Greene, Jr., 24 March 1966, 671–72. Westmoreland noted that the Marines not only were reluctant to engage in joint operation with the Air Force but also were resistant to the helicopter gunship "so that often he almost had to force them to accept US Army support." Westmoreland, *A Soldier Reports,* 165.

35. Westmoreland, *A Soldier Reports,* 413.

36. Ibid., 412. Peter B. Mersky and Norman Polmar, *The Naval Air War in Vietnam* (Annapolis, Md.: The Nautical and Aviation Publishing Company of America, 1981), 141. Mersky and Polmar suggest that the B-52 Arc Light strikes were ultimately the single most critical element in the firepower delivered, concluding that they "finally evidently broke the enemy's resistance."

37. Brig Gen William Moore, "Tactical Airlift in Southeast Asia," 18 May 1967, K-Div-834-SU-RE, USAF Collection, US Air Force Historical Research Collection (USAFHRC), Maxwell AFB, Ala., 2; 834th Air Division, "Tactical Airlift Support for Khe Sahn," 21 January–8 April 1968, K-Div-834-SU-RE, USAF Collection, USAFHRC, declassified 31 December 1976.

38. Westmoreland, *Report on the War in Vietnam,* sec. 2, 182.

39. Ibid., 185.

40. Ibid., 185–86.

41. Nalty, *Air Power and the Fight for Khe Sanh,* 20.

42. Middleton et al., *Air War—Vietnam* (Indianapolis: The Bobbs-Merrill Co., 1978), 170.

43. Ibid., 44–45.

44. Ibid., 56.

45. Mersky and Polmar, *The Naval Air War in Vietnam,* 139–40.

46. Alan L. Gropman, *Airpower and the Airlift Evacuation of Kham Duc* (Maxwell AFB, Ala.: Airpower Research Institute, 1979), 3–8.

47. Ibid., 9–11. Also see Westmoreland, *Report on the War in Vietnam,* 167–68. The erosion of the US–South Vietnamese position at Kham Duc followed a sequence somewhat reminiscent of the fall of outposts and the encircling of Dien Bien Phu, as recounted by Bernard Fall, *Hell in a Very Small Place: Siege of Dien Bien Phu* (Philadelphia: J. B. Lippincott Co., 1967).

48. Meeting in Cabinet Room, January 17, 1966; Meetings with Foreign Policy Advisers, Memo 41, Meeting Notes File, Johnson Papers.

49. Senate, *Bombing in Cambodia: Hearings before the Committee on Armed Services,* 93d Cong., 1st sess., 30 July 1973, 418–19. Memorandum by Adm W. E. Lemos to Assistant Secretary of Defense John McNaughton, 23 February 1967.

50. Senate, Committee on Armed Services, *Hearings, Bombing in Cambodia,* 487–88.

51. Ibid., 489.

52. Ibid., 486–89. The conclusion that the kind of secrecy observed over the Menu bombing was aimed at domestic US critics is supported, at least inferentially, by the fact that senators and congressmen were apparently advised of the activities privately and with great selectivity. For example, Senators John Stennis and Richard Russell, regarded as "hawks," were informed, as was House minority leader Gerald Ford; but the Senate majority leader Mike Mansfield, a known critic of the war, was not.

53. Senate, Committee on Armed Services, *Hearings, Bombing in Cambodia,* 402–3.

54. Ibid., 380–81.

55. Ibid., 422.

56. Ibid., 418, testimony of Adm Thomas Moorer, August 1973.

57. Senate, Committee on Armed Services, *Hearings, Bombing in Cambodia,* testimony of Admiral Moorer, August 1973, 465.

58. Ibid.; written testimony of Under Secretary of Defense William Clements, "Department of Defense Report on Selected Air and Ground Operations in Cambodia and Laos," 10 September 1973, 489.

59. Senate, Committee on Armed Services, *Hearings, Bombing in Cambodia,* 465.

60. Ibid.

61. Westmoreland, *A Soldier Reports,* 389.

62. Ibid., 183.

63. Ibid., 389.

64. James A. Van Fleet to Elvis J. Stahr, Jr., letter, 26 March 1962, Army 1962 folder, Departments and Agencies Files, President's Office File, Kennedy Papers, John F. Kennedy Library, Dorchester, Mass.

65. Col Delbert Bristol, USA, interviewed by Col Ralph J. Powell and Lt Col Ronald K. Andersen, US Army Military History Institute, Carlisle Barracks, Pa., Oral History Series, The History of Army Aviation, 69.

66. Ibid., 70.

67. General Williams interview, 66.

68. Brig Gen O. Glenn Goodhand, USA, interviewed by Col Bryce R. Kramer and Lt Col Ronald K. Andersen, 9 May 1978, US Army Military History Institute, Oral History Series, The History of Army Aviation, 78.

69. Stuart A. Herrington, *Silence Was A Weapon, The Vietnam War In The Villages* (Novato, Calif.: Presidio Press, 1982), 30.

70. Ibid., 104–5.

71. Ibid., 115.

72. Allan W. Sandstrum, "Three Companies at Dak To," in John Albright et al., *Seven Firefights in Vietnam* (Washington, D.C.: Office of the Chief of Military History, United States Army, 1970), 85.

73. S. L. A. Marshall, *The Fields of Bamboo, Three Battles Just Beyond the South China Sea* (New York: The Dial Press, 1971), 167–68.

74. Senate, Committee on Armed Services and Subcommittee on Department of Defense, Committee on Appropriations, *Hearings, Military Procurement Authorizations for Fiscal Year 1968*, statement by Gen John P. McConnell, 2 February 1967, 815.

75. Ibid., 816–17.

76. Ibid., 816.

77. Ibid.

78. Ibid.

CHAPTER 5

Problems in the Performance of Traditional Roles

Within the Department of Defense, emotion overcame logic on discussions of the role and importance of air power and the specific missions of air power in Vietnam. Somehow the bombing of North Vietnam became the symbol of the importance of air power, which was both tragic and illogical. Advocates of air power should have been first to point out the fallacies in this line of reasoning, but instead were, in many cases, persons espousing it most vehemently. Air power was playing a vital role in the war—in transport between theaters and within the theater, in search-and-rescue, in reconnaissance and intelligence gathering and in close air support of ground forces. Air power enthusiasts strangely said little of these impressive military achievements.

Phil F. Goulding, 1970

Wheeler: We should decrease by every pound we can to stop the movement of supplies. In interdiction, you start at the beginning and go all the way through to finally stopping it in country. . . .
President: We really pay a price—if we are not getting a payoff.
Rusk: [Bombing] ought to directly help our troops and break the will of the other fellow. My own priority would be to concentrate on operational connections in the South.

Earle Wheeler, Lyndon Johnson,
and Dean Rusk, 1966

The relative importance of various military missions in Vietnam was as difficult to gauge as the missions were essential. Priority given these missions varied according to how different men and institutions viewed the war and its evolution. Disagreements over how to fight the war, even among the highest policymakers, deprived the military services of a standard by which to judge the effectiveness of their operations. Without a firm criterion, it was hard to know when and how a mission fit into the war as a whole. Efficient operation might be possible, but the payoff could remain uncertain. But efficiency, as well as effectiveness, was jeopardized by the lack of agreed criteria for evaluating it. Efficiency requires economy in the application of force, comparing cost to outcome. But since the desired outcome in Vietnam was often elusive and unclear, calculating its cost was frustrating or even impossible. Moreover, to the extent that standards derived from the political and military situation inside Vietnam failed to hold sway, standards rooted in the general interests of the US defense community rose to greater eminence. So, for example, if one could not test the cost of an operation by its effect on the "politico-military economy" of Vietnam, the cost could still be compared to the US capacity to afford it, almost without reference to any logic for expending effort and resources at all. In turn, efficiency was reduced to sheer accomplishment of a designated mission. Confusion over the war and the US national purpose within it ensured contingency in its prosecution. Actions might be simple and clear, but their meaning was indeterminate and ambiguous.

This was an inescapable consequence of the failure to set clear strategy. Lacking a firm and comprehensible standard against which its effect could be tested, even the most efficiently managed tactical operation took on an appalling potential for irrelevance. Without a measure of merit at the strategic level, how could one even talk of the "success" of a mission in any sense larger than flying a particular route and dropping a specified tonnage? The practical consequences of this deficiency were serious. The rise of simple mission accomplishment over demonstrable effectiveness and genuine efficiency as a standard for carrying on the war afforded no way of distinguishing between persistence in meeting one's objectives and mere pride, whose preservation overshadowed political results as the real object of actions undertaken.

Too much uncertainty, too much subtlety, too much of what strategic thinker Homer Lea called "intangible complexity"—these things seem unbearable to most people and particularly so to professionals seeking to do their jobs. And so the absence of some plausible strategic guidance created a void—an "uncertainty factor"—which simply could not continue. Certainty and commitment must come from somewhere, whether the source is appropriate or not. So, as the Vietnam War seemed to lack the broad and cohesive logic that clear purpose affords, so did standards more suited to lower levels of operational execution become dominant at higher levels within the services. The forest was lost while the trees were tended. Problems thus lay in wait even in performing traditional military roles in Vietnam—which roles to emphasize, which ways to pursue them, and how far they should be pressed. Gauging how far the military *could* go in Vietnam, whether judged by technical capability or rules of engagement, was never the real problem. But deciding how far it *should* go remained a perpetual source of disagreement and disarray.

The relative worth accorded to such roles as reconnaissance, airlift, search and rescue, close air support, and interdiction thus fell to the special judgments of different people whose priorities were far from identical. Despite its importance, no single or comprehensive standard of worth was forthcoming; and those institutional traditions and service practices which had been tested in the past all but inevitably substituted for some other norm that might have been set for the specific circumstances in Vietnam. The apparent value of various air missions was governed by considerations that predated the Vietnam War and did not necessarily conform to it. Yet they grew stronger during the war for lack of a comprehensive alternative criterion. Personal heroism, technical skill, and similar concerns thus took on ever more power and meaning even as the greater goal to which they should have been devoted remained unclear; and the standards used to appraise air power varied according to the background and priorities of the different participants.

Persistence and Pride

Gen William C. Westmoreland always considered the interdiction effort important—indeed, one of the most important and potentially most profitable uses of air power in the war. Nevertheless, during the discussions in 1964 that led to the regular bombing of North Vietnam in Rolling Thunder, Westmoreland expressed some concern that the way the North Vietnamese might react would depend on how interdiction was attempted. For the North Vietnamese to desist the United States had to "demonstrate *within South Vietnam* that the insurgency was bound to fail" (emphasis added).[1] Evidently, Westmoreland meant that the war was to be fought and decided on the ground, albeit with substantial air support. In his memoirs, he expressed the view that "we could better use our air power to that end by supporting ARVN operations and by hitting the enemy's infiltration route through Laos."[2] He seemed optimistic that air power could succeed in interdiction closer to the ground combat zone.

But the general's hopes sometimes ran ahead of existing capabilities. Even where targets were fixed, they could be devilish to destroy. The experience at the Thanh Hoa and Paul Doumer bridges exemplified some of the problems encountered in using air power against targets in the enemy infrastructure to interdict supply.

> The Doumer Bridge, on the outskirts of Hanoi, served four of five key rail-lines—its destruction would cut these rail-lines and National Route 1 between Hanoi and Haiphong, and also between Hanoi and Southeast and Southwest China. The Thanh Hoa Bridge, some 70 miles south of Hanoi, served to supply men and materiel for battle areas in Laos and South Vietnam.[3]

The attacks against these two bridges, which were at the remote end of interdiction, absorbed much more effort than Westmoreland and other ground force commanders wanted. There were both tactical and conceptual difficulties. On the tactical level, there was danger in approaching an increasingly well-defended target, eventually replete with heavy point defenses including surface-to-air missiles (SAMs), antiaircraft artillery (AAA), and fighter-interceptor cover. Over the years, as US Navy and Air Force efforts against the Thanh Hoa Bridge mounted, so did the losses. In the earliest attacks, the bridge was weakly defended; an F-100 flak suppressor and an RF-101 were lost in the first attack, three F-105s were lost in the second, and one F-105 was lost in the third. None were lost in the fourth. (All were Air Force missions, operating principally out of Thailand.) By May 1966, the defenses around the Thanh Hoa Bridge—an obvious chokepoint—had hardened with increased SAM sites and a greater number of MiGs in the area. Nonetheless, due to effective use of surprise and deception, all aircraft and crews came through an attack on 30 May safely. In a follow-up assault on 31 May, a C-130 departed its base never to be seen again and one of the F-4 aircraft sent on a diversionary attack was lost.[4]

Strikes deep into North Vietnam were halted in 1968 when President Johnson announced his decision not to seek reelection and his intention to concentrate on seeking a peace agreement. The bombing halt symbolized the earnestness of his desire for a negotiated settlement. And these peace talks went on into the early years of the Nixon presidency. Meanwhile, the North Vietnamese rebuilt elements of their infrastructure that had been damaged during Rolling Thunder. The spans of the Paul Doumer Bridge that had been destroyed by US Air Force F-105s on 18 December 1967 again stretched across the Red River. The Thanh Hoa Bridge suffered direct hits from Navy Walleye television-guided glide bombs on 12 March 1967 but came through the attack structurally sound, partly because the yield of the ordnance was no match for this remarkably "over-engineered" span. The approaches to and defenses of the bridge were repeatedly savaged, however. After Johnson's bombing halt, these facilities were restored. When President Nixon suspended negotiations on 8 May 1972, he authorized Operation Linebacker I, again attacking major installations deep within North Vietnam. Despite the proliferation of North Vietnamese AAA and SAM sites, the US attacks had great effect. Sophisticated electronic countermeasures undercut the effectiveness of North Vietnamese emplacements, and Wild Weasel F-105s helped to make the environment as uncomfortable for the defenders as possible. Also, in the years since 1967, new guided munitions had been developed, notably laser- and optically-guided bombs, making it possible to throw 2,000-pound explosives at a target with great accuracy. The Air Force F-4s dropped the spans of the Thanh Hoa Bridge in a single strike. So, too, the Paul Doumer Bridge was once again smashed. Success was sweet—or, perhaps, bittersweet, in light of the costs sustained in the 1960s.

The bridges could be destroyed. Finally, efficient means of striking such targets and destroying them without risking high losses in aircraft and crews became available. Now it seemed possible to deny the enemy such assets in a decisive way. But keeping these bridges out of the enemy's war system required periodic attacks to frustrate repairs and prevent completion of antiaircraft installations. The eventual success of the US attacks depended in part upon the development of effective "smart munitions," including electro-optically guided bombs (EOGB) and laser guided bombs (LGB). For example, in Project Carolina Moon, US planes dropped mass-focus weapons from C-130s into the Song Ma River. These bombs were to detonate when sensors indicated that they had floated beneath the bridge; but they failed to detonate, and the mission produced no positive results. Given the losses over the years and the difficulty of permanently taking out these two bridges, one must ask whether the eventual victory was not a Pyrrhic one.

The lessons from the assault on the Thanh Hoa Bridge fall into two analytically separable categories—human and technical. Among the key human lessons suggested is that an unqualified "can do" attitude can cause trouble when it hits the "reinforced concrete wall" of a target ill-suited to available weapons and munitions. Was it truly more professional to persist in the attack after the munitions had been found wanting? Admittedly, the great bulk of the ordnance dropped—plain iron bombs—was aimed at destroying the rails, roads, and approach areas in the vicinity of the bridge more than the bridge itself; but the cost of reducing the flow of rail shipment was considerable, especially since the effects were temporary. On the technical side, once smart munitions were available, the reduction of the bridge proceeded in a reasonably expeditious manner. Still, this optimistic assessment must be wrapped in caution, since destroying the bridge hinged partly upon the relative advantage in air superiority enjoyed by the attacking aircraft as against the enemy's overall defensive systems. In fact, the increase in defensive capability placed a further premium on a "one-shot kill" offensive tactical capability, creating more pressure for even more sophisticated ordnance.

But the technological lesson suggested by the final outcome in the story of the bridges should not obscure the overwhelming concerns over human choice and behavior—notably related to the cost in lives and equipment as well as to an ironic tax on institutional pride. Parallel to the story of US resolve was the resolve of the North Vietnamese to resist. Parallel to damage was repair, and the imposition of "tax" on the enemy went along with Hanoi's evident willingness to pay it. It was almost enough to invite a cynical speculation over just which party had shown itself readier to "pay any price, bear any burden"; and it justified wonder over precisely what "signals" were sent by such expenditures of lives and equipment. For short-duration interruptions in the North Vietnamese capacity to send supplies south, the cost was high. For suggesting that the United States would spend high for a relatively low return, the cost may have been even higher.

Although General Westmoreland had reservations about what benefits would come from bombing North Vietnam, he appears to have supported bombing the trail systems used to supply the NVA and Vietcong, including B-52 strikes. High-ranking US officials generally tended to claim great benefit from disruption wrought by B-52s and other aircraft on the trail system, but certain Southeast Asian observers gave a less-sanguine report. Predictable results from interdiction became elusive in the specific context of the Southeast Asian war. Brig Gen Soutchay Vongsavanh, Royal Laotian Army, writing in 1981, concluded that, "despite the full weight of American bombing operations, Ho Chi Minh Trail truck traffic increased day by day and the NVA continued to improve the road network, keeping passages open and making roads suitable for high-speed traffic."[5] The Sihanouk Trail through Cambodia was also improved during the same time. Over the long run, the interdiction effort produced certain unintended negative results. Apart from the enemy's ability to repair and even improve its trail system, the US air effort was said to have compelled the NVA to disperse and multiply the routes it used through the panhandle. The bombing definitely changed trail traffic; less clear was how sharply infiltration had been cut.

Infiltration and logistic support for Communist forces in South Vietnam had to go through Laos. The question was how far west through the panhandle they spread,

103

much as later movement of US and ARVN troops into Cambodia made it prudent for Communist forces to move farther into that country. Evidently, some Laotians thought air strikes made the Communist forces press their supply system into the Bolovens and Mekong region where US military air operations were restricted because of the proximity to heavier concentrations of civilian population.[6] In this way, then, persistence in the interdiction campaign complicated matters for allies of the United States; and this outcome raises the question whether the United States might have enjoyed greater success overall by bombing the trail system less. Less bombing might have resulted in less dispersal of enemy ground forces. In one sense, the enemy governed escalation in the war by moving the trail system; in another sense, though, the United States governed it by encouraging the movement.

The difficulties with the interdiction effort that General Vongsavanh observed apparently intensified after the coup staged by Gen Lon Nol against Prince Sihanouk in Cambodia in 1970. Thereafter, US air efforts intensified, Vongsavanh noted, and the trail defenders increased their antiaircraft fire in response. Despite its intensity, the Laotian general asserted that the air effort was largely futile. Craters could be filled, and bypasses could be cut. Trees blasted into barriers could be swiftly cleared.[7] And despite the US air effort, the effort of Cambodian government ground forces to exploit it seemed, in Vongsavanh's opinion, diffident at best. A Cambodian colonel who had 300 men with him in Laos called for air strikes on purported Khmer Rouge headquarters and supply depots in Cambodia; but the colonel's men did not actually clash with the enemy. Vongsavanh noted that, "although the Cambodian colonel often said he planned to send the troops into Cambodia, he never did."[8] If the US leaders believed that B-52 and tacair strikes took on value only when they could be exploited on the ground, then of what value were they under circumstances such as these?

In addition to the question of gains from conducting various operations, there remained the problem of calculating losses, including nonquantifiable ones. The nagging questions about what effect air power was having under varying political and geographical circumstances even suggested that confidence in air power itself was hurt by the inconclusive effort to accomplish tasks that sounded simple in the abstract but were knotty in the concrete. Senate committee hearings in 1973 on the unannounced bombing of targets in Cambodia during 1969 reflected this interest in the state of US forces and procedures. Some Congressional figures revealed deep concern that the command and control system appeared to have been circumvented, and gave thought to possible remedies. Military leaders focused on what they described as the successful outcome of the bombing effort, coded Menu, and justified such strikes as a means of relieving pressure on ground forces. Talk of success did not satisfactorily show what air power's real contribution had been to improvement of conditions in Cambodia. In a 20 November 1969 memorandum to the secretary of defense, Chairman of the Joint Chiefs Gen Earle E. Wheeler proclaimed the Menu bombing in Cambodia "one of the most significant contributions of the war by B-52s." Wheeler minimized the difficulties resulting from making damage assessments 48 to 72 hours after the strikes and expressed confidence that reports by aircrews of secondary explosions indicated that significant targets had been hit. He also pointed to indications that in the wake of these attacks enemy operations had been reduced in targeted base areas 350, 351, 352, and 353, and had been dispersed over a wider area on the periphery of the zones of attack. Unlike some later critics of the Menu strikes, Wheeler expressed no concern that they had merely forced enemy activity farther into Cambodia. He did recommend additional attacks on base area 740, however, where enemy troops were reported to have grouped. Cover sorties over South Vietnam would be recorded to provide credible diversions for the press; but it was also necessary to estimate risks in Cambodia and Laos. Wheeler believed that these strikes would inflict little damage on the Cambodian people and recommended that strikes be continued "as long as the threat persists."[9] When finally approved, this program of bombing was undertaken to degrade the enemy's capability to organize for effective operations.

Such strikes were not clearly strategic in that they did not cut off supplies at the source. But the strikes surely were intended as a kind of interdiction. Nor were they precisely tactical support. They were preemptive strikes against an enemy undertaken in hopes of hitting him in place. But the results were hard to gauge. How could one judge "significant contribution" to the war effort? Despite uncertainty as to material effects of the bombing, there was a special significance to how the operation was conducted and to the circumstances surrounding it. Menu was conducted with an unaccustomed secrecy, eluding the almost routine compromise of security that occurred throughout the war. Further, these missions delivered extraordinary volumes of ordnance rapidly and with a minimal investment of manpower—two factors that also contributed to secrecy, since only the pilot and navigator needed to know the actual target. In such ways, then, the potential significance derived from the political flexibility of the military means chosen rather than from whether those means accomplished identifiable military purposes.

This, in any case, was the general interpretation given to the Menu bombing by Senator Stuart Symington. He considered any discussion of the justification for and effectiveness of the program to be a "separate and distinct subject from the serious questions concerning command and control and official deception" raised by the way Menu was carried out. Symington thought the operation did more harm than good, since the North Vietnamese had apparently responded to Menu by widening their geographic zone of control in Cambodia. He also thought the credibility of the Department of Defense had been badly damaged as high officials unwittingly but repeatedly had given false information to Congress and the press. Parenthetically but acidly, Symington suggested that the Menu operation could not have been completely successful in any event, "since we subsequently had to send ground troops into Cambodia."[10]

The effort to use bombing effectively raised problems even when controversy was less focused, suggesting how hard it was to make gains permanent. Bridges bombed successfully might be replaced by temporary ones that would require repeated subsequent strikes. And these strikes must be carried out while antiaircraft capabilities increased. This in itself was not new to air warfare, but projecting its cost was elusive. Surely, interdiction did impose penalties on Hanoi. Although it could not absolutely seal off South Vietnam from infiltration, interdiction could require a greater investment of North Vietnamese resources to supply Vietcong and NVA units in the South. In addition, the North Vietnamese had to divert greater resources into AAA installations and other efforts to disrupt the US interdiction program. Hanoi certainly sustained added costs because of the US interdiction effort, but it is hard to fix that cost.

At the same time, the cost to the US manifestly rose. Yet it remained difficult to quantify the dimensions of benefit purchased by the interdiction effort. As the campaign grew into a prolonged one, the investment needed to undertake it mounted. To ensure that attacking aircraft might hit their targets with some measure of safety, other aircraft were assigned to suppress enemy defenses and draw fire. Designated Wild Weasels, these missions and the men who flew them displayed a treasure of courage and raw nerve. Yet they also constituted another layer of cost to the United States. So, too, the growing demand for accurate delivery of ordnance sharpened the search for "smart munitions," guided to their targets by such technologies as electro-optical and thermal sensors. Here, too, the achievement was nothing short of brilliant. But the tax to pay for it was both literal and figurative—again, the cost of the war to the United States rose. Against this background, it is fair to ask whether the US interdiction program imposed more of a "tax" on North Vietnam than on the United States itself.

Intelligence and Reconnaissance

The nature and frequency of reconnaissance operations in Southeast Asia varied greatly. Reconnaissance was undertaken on the ground, from the air, and with air and ground units in combination. But one broad assertion can be made. The great bulk of the reconnaissance efforts relied heavily on Army and Air Force air assets, perhaps especially so when ground reconnaissance teams were small and might need added firepower and other support. Not intended primarily as combat units, ground reconnaissance teams obviously needed help when they faced an unexpected fight. Air forces might give them an edge or at least a way out of serious trouble.

The whole sequence of conducting reconnaissance, gathering data, and transforming it into usable intelligence was a complex matter. Air reconnaissance might be conducted through high-resolution photography or it might be undertaken close to the ground by human eyesight from slow-moving aircraft. Ground reconnaissance teams might work substantially on their own or with considerable aid from air assets. So, too, the sources of intelligence varied from human contacts through signals to photography. In a way, the word "intelligence" may best be reserved for the usable version of the data collected from various sources, processed

106

at an intelligence center to answer high-priority questions, and transmitted in timely fashion. In a way, what qualified as real intelligence depended on who needed to know what.

In his history of military intelligence activities in Vietnam during 1965, 1966, and 1967, Maj Gen Joseph A. McChristian, Westmoreland's J-2 (assistant chief of staff for intelligence) at MACV, outlined the perceived intelligence requirements and the forces needed to meet them. He emphasized the need for detailed information about the enemy—the kind obtainable only through frequent close-quarters contact on the ground. McChristian believed that the Vietcong had central organization and direction, but he did not assume that regional and local resistance would end even if the US forces found and destroyed that central source. General McChristian wanted to "know the enemy"—and fight him—across the full spectrum. The principle he sought to fulfill was "centralized guidance and decentralized operations."[11] The movement of enemy troop units and the development of supply and base areas were clearly matters of importance to the higher authorities at MACV; but neutralizing the Vietcong infrastructure, McChristian suggested, could be accomplished only by establishing close familiarity with the people, village by village. Army doctrine specified that their intelligence personnel in the field should conform to the special character of the war at hand, so General McChristian placed great emphasis on getting qualified personnel into the field.[12]

At the same time, those field personnel required support, sometimes from the air. In addition, large ground units conducting operations often needed information and support that exceeded the capacity and responsibilities of US military intelligence personnel in the villages. Air power of various kinds, including some from the Air Force, helped to serve the needs of intelligence operatives engaged against the Vietcong, whether in a particular district on a long-term basis or in supporting specific US operations. Each Army brigade, division, or field force (or corps) had its own regular intelligence detachment. To each field force was added an aviation company equipped with OV-1 Mohawk aircraft, the exact numbers being determined according to terrain features in the area of operation.[13] The Mohawk was capable of performing tactical aerial reconnaissance, although it shared this role with the Air Force's RF-101, RF-4C, RB-57, and RC-47 aircraft. One example of how the OV-1 could be used—and how well it could interact with Air Force assets—came in Operation Tiger Hound, which began in December 1965. On a scale then new to the war, US forces went after Communist forces infiltrating through Laos. The Mohawks were equipped with infrared and side-looking radar and were used at night, often in conjunction with Air Force C-130 flareships. In the war more generally, aerial reconnaissance was conducted under a joint air-ground operations system agreed upon by the Army and Air Force in October 1965, combining aspects of the Air Force's tactical air control system and the Army's air-ground operation system. General McChristian praised Air Force Brig Gens Rockly

Triantafellu and Jammie M. Philpott for their close and enthusiastic cooperation which made it a true joint effort.[14]

Interservice cooperation in the aerial reconnaissance program solved only one part of the problem. Another critical consideration was the worth of the images provided, whether through optics (photography), infrared, or radar. MACV nominated targets for reconnaissance through a monthly plan that included some 750 specified subjects and through daily target requests amounting to about 1,200 per month during the mid-to-late 1960s. The aircraft used to fill a great many of these requests, however, served more than MACV. The 460th Tactical Reconnaissance Wing of the Seventh Air Force was responsible to CINCPAC; MACV was, in effect, a subscriber rather than "executive agent." The film from any given sortie might thus contain little of interest to MACV, although it might be highly valuable for other consumers. But the intelligence could also suggest better use of ground forces. "In fact," General McChristian observed, "the characteristics of the high-performance aircraft used on photo missions permitted tremendous area coverage and raised doubts about the economic feasibility of point targets nominated by ground units."[15] Photo missions by high-performance craft thus put the requests of ground units into a larger perspective. To gain the most from intelligence, the ground forces had to become more aware of how the aerial surveillance and reconnaissance system worked and how it could be used to improve ground operations. General McChristian allowed that this learning process, a major task for the 1st Military Intelligence Battalion Air Reconnaissance Support (MIBARS), took some time. But he asserted that it was aggressively advanced by Army intelligence personnel.[16]

The final judgment on such reconnaissance efforts will vary, according to the beholder. For his part, General McChristian saw degrees of intraservice dedication and interservice cooperation that were above the norm for the war in Vietnam. Still, the "effectiveness" of the reconnaissance depended on how people took advantage of it rather than on formal cooperation. Effectiveness depended on the uses to which the information was put, on how well it was processed, and on the assumptions and methodologies guiding the analysts. If ground commanders asked for too much information, they might be overwhelmed—weakened by their own inability to process what they had requested. In such a case, it was not aerial reconnaissance that was at fault.[17] It was a failure in the "human software" to cope with problems and the data describing them—not a failure in data or the means for gathering it. Moreover, the extensive effort required to make the intelligence worthwhile cost money and manpower. Nothing came cheap.[18]

That the services had to overcome difficulties to work together effectively became clear when the Air Force prepared a pamphlet on "gruntisms" to inform its personnel about Army terminology, to make for effective contact between ground controllers and fixed-wing gunships and between ground personnel and forward air controllers (FACs).[19] Air Force personnel frequently briefed the direct air support centers (DASCs) so they would be aware of the capabilities of available air power.[20]

Yet, some observers considered the DASCs neither fish nor fowl—neither fully Army nor fully Air Force, and so neither as influential nor effective as might have been imagined. Perhaps the observers were wrong, but differences over the DASCs continued. On top of such difficulties, the language-barrier between the bulk of US and South Vietnamese military personnel complicated problems stemming from differences in background and experience.

Visual surveillance held promise of more timely information than that gained through photoreconnaissance, and it was undertaken by all US services as well as by the Vietnamese Air Force (VNAF). Helicopters supported the effort to locate and acquire targets and to provide real-time reports on Vietcong and North Vietnamese army activity; this effort was concentrated at the division level. Army, Air Force, and Marine 0-1 Birddogs formed the "backbone" of the visual reconnaissance force. Air Force 0-1s performing the forward air control role were also effectively undertaking visual surveillance. Under operational control of the tactical air control center (through the DASCs), the Air Force FACs gave accurate and timely information about real conditions on the ground. Timeliness of information, nonetheless, was a somewhat relative notion, depending on how quickly the intelligence had to be used and on what targets had to be hit. For example, ground commanders often saw B-52s as a weapon to be used principally against fixed positions. They were less than certain that they could be used against moving enemy units. Still, even with respect to B-52 operations, the intelligence provided by FACs gave the only opportunity of using the bombers to reshape the ground war—instead of just the terrain.[21]

The potential of air power in reconnaissance and intelligence was affected by restrictions on the use of American aircraft in low-level surveillance for "time-sensitive tactical photography." Because ground patrols led by ARVN soldiers failed to provide much useful information on Vietcong sites along the Laotian border, CINCPAC wanted advance authorization for US advisers to accompany these patrols. High-altitude photography could compensate for weaknesses in the patrol efforts only to the extent of identifying "static installations" and lines of communication. Tactical support, which was arguably more significant for counterguerrilla efforts, went begging.[22] At nearly the same time, officials in Washington viewed the situation along the border of Laos and Vietnam with caution. Michael Forrestal wrote in December 1963, "Actually we have had little or no hard intelligence since October of last year on the use of Laos as a corridor into South Vietnam." He knew that infiltration was taking place, through Cambodia and elsewhere; yet his comment confirmed the concern over shortcomings in intelligence, even if he could not offer an operational remedy.[23]

The mission requirements of intelligence and surveillance put great demands on hardware as well as manpower, and there was significant interaction between mission and aircraft design in an effort to carry out policy as fully as possible. The OV-1, for example, had been specifically designed for tactical reconnaissance in support of battlefield operations. It performed a wide range of missions. The OV-

1A was a rocket-carrying reconnaissance aircraft, although the armed reconnaissance mission did become a matter of interservice contention. The OV-1B had side-looking airborne radar (SLAR) for electronic surveillance; some 107 were operating in Vietnam by 1 July 1969. As the war developed, work proceeded on an aircraft conceived for the special needs of a counterinsurgency. Particular emphasis was given to maximizing visibility from the air. The result was the North American OV-10 Bronco, a propeller-driven, twin-engine craft with twin tail booms. The Bronco's gun pods and rockets armed it for troop suppression and reconnaissance. Production of the OV-10 for the Air Force and the Marines began in 1966; the first Broncos arrived in South Vietnam in 1968. Designed also to handle medical evacuation and light-transport tasks, the OV-10s remained primarily attack and reconnaissance craft. One example was a special Navy light-attack squadron (designated VAL-4, nicknamed the ''Black Ponies'') of OV-10As, which gave cover for river convoys along the Mekong River as well as supporting ground operations.[24]

Aerial surveillance personnel worked in tandem with those collecting information on the ground. Interest in ground reconnaissance into certain parts of Laos and Cambodia adjacent to South Vietnam where the enemy might concentrate and establish bases intensified. Air power became an indispensable element in support of this role. By early 1965, US military and civilian officials substantially agreed that the corridor of southern Laos was being used as an infiltration and resupply route; and the Military Assistance Command Vietnam Studies and Operations Group (MACSOG) was authorized to conduct cross-border intelligence collection and interdiction operations (effective 20 September 1965). First known as Shining Brass, later as Prairie Fire, the operations included such missions as taking prisoners and emplacing sensors; conducting area, point, and strip reconnaissance; and, more rarely, engaging in reconnaissance in larger units of platoon strength. South Vietnamese soldiers under advice and command of US Special Forces personnel conducted the activities. They had use of trooplift and gunship helicopters as well as support from tacair. The South Vietnamese assumed complete control over ground reconnaissance operations after February 1971, and the program was renamed Phu Dung. US tacair strikes nonetheless continued at a roughly constant annualized rate; the annualized rate of gunship sorties doubled. Authority for continued US aerial fire support lasted until March 1972.[25]

The quantity of effort continued to be high, although the quality of results remained uncertain during the period of South Vietnamese control. The number of enemy prisoners reported as being taken for interrogation and the number of intelligence reports filed declined markedly from the rates of previous years. Yet the number of sorties flown to deliver firepower was sustained—even increased at times. Although aerial firepower had a rather skimpy payoff in intelligence for the South Vietnamese, continued air operations facilitated the extraction of Americans from the region. Even as air power had been used earlier to insert and extract US personnel during actual ground operations, so did aerial firepower later sustain an impression of continued involvement (see table 1).[26]

TABLE 1

Missions, Sorties, and Results of Shining Brass, Prairie Fire, and Phu Dung[27]

	1965	1966	1967	1968	1969	1970	1971 to April 1972
Missions							
Reconnaissance team............	7	105	187	271	404	422	183
Platoon...........................	0	12	71	56	48	16	13
Multiplatoon	0	0	0	0	0	3	0
Total...........................	7	117	258	327	452	441	196
Helicopter gunship sorties.........	*	130	329	287	689	1,116	993
Tacair Sorties	155	405	1,157	635	1,106	1,419	623
Enemy Prisoners....................	*	12	10	1	0	3	0
Intelligence Report	21	371	774	410	748	553	175

*Unknown.

As long as US personnel were involved in border area intelligence-gathering, customary US concerns on proper administration of military operations affected the execution of missions in the field. Traditional ideas about efficiency and effective control encouraged measures that tended to inhibit responsiveness, even though the desire to support units in the field was sincere. In large part, the problem was that "responsiveness" was a relative notion; it was a function of the urgency of the situation, which in turn depended on diverse factors such as the amount and kind of firepower organic to a unit operating in the field, possible restrictions on aerial firepower due to security and policy considerations, time required for clearance of requests for air strikes, and other circumstances. John Meyer, a former Army special forces officer, recalled that during Prairie Fire reconnaissance operations in Laos in 1969–70, it took "anywhere from 2 hours to sometimes a day and a half before we could get extracted." But when in an emergency the Prairie Fire team on the ground called for support, Meyer recalled, "every asset in the air was directed to our air support," including both Air Force and Army craft. His impression was that this urgent investment of resources was crucial to the team's survival since in Meyer's estimation the enemy was usually contacted in company or even battalion strength. Moreover, North Vietnamese or Pathet Lao trackers were specially assigned to track down the US and South Vietnamese teams.[28] Given the resulting shortness of time between a drop and first contact with the enemy under these circumstances, "responsiveness" needed to be nearly instantaneous; yet such immediate reaction was rarely feasible. In many instances, US teams had to be prepared to hold on for five hours before they got support. But the ground team could not request support in advance even when it was convinced it would make contact with the enemy. "In reality we knew we were going to be contacted," Meyer explained.[29] But in theory the operation was intended for reconnaissance and not combat; hence, the ground rules controlling air support suited political and administrative desires more neatly than they matched the wishes of those in the fields.

Reconnaissance operations across the border into Cambodia, conducted regularly from 1967 through 1972, could not have been carried out or supported effectively without air assets. Operations under the code name Daniel Boone were first authorized on 22 May 1967 in response to requests from MACSOG. Over the years, these operations came to be referred to as Salem House (the program formally authorized to succeed Daniel Boone). Reconnaissance teams consisted of 12 men, of whom, at first, no more than three were to be special forces personnel. They sought information on enemy forces and facilities in the area, gathering evidence of hard-surface roads and even concrete-reinforced bunkers in some places. They were also responsible for bomb damage assessment in connection with the originally secret bombing of Cambodia by B-52s. The teams were authorized the use of five helicopter flights each month for infiltration, although they were not to penetrate beyond a depth of ten kilometers into Cambodia. Tacair strikes were permitted in areas of South Vietnam and Laos adjacent to Cambodia, but they were not conducted in Cambodia itself until after 20 April 1970, when the South Vietnamese assumed complete operational control and manning of the ground operations. The code name was then changed to Thot Not. And, while there were restrictions on the use of tacair, helicopter gunship sorties into Cambodia were a part of the plan from its inception.[30]

The basic purpose of Salem House remained constant, but some modifications in procedure appeared over time. In October 1967, US civilian authorities relaxed their original restriction, which had limited operations to Northeastern Cambodia, to permit operations along the entire Cambodia–South Vietnam border up to a depth of 20 kilometers. In December 1967, with the concurrence of the State Department, the Defense Department authorized using FACs to control helicopters and to conduct reconnaissance of landing sites for teams operating under Salem House. After 30 June 1970, trooplift helicopters were manned only by South Vietnamese. But a fundamental change in manning did not come until 30 April 1972, when ground reconnaissance responsibilities devolved totally upon the South Vietnamese as part of President Nixon's program of "Vietnamization." All US involvement with the cross-border operations ended, and MACSOG was deactivated.[31]

In assessing the success of Salem House operations, various standards suggest themselves—as the number of enemy prisoners captured (24 in 6 years) or the number (2,158) and quality of intelligence reports generated, for example. Salem

House cannot be judged by the increase or decrease in enemy activity in the region; nor can it be judged by the nature of that activity, since Salem House was not a combat program. Moreover, the tactical objective of acquiring information was met—however well or ill the data gained were later used. In this sense, Army and Air Force aviation definitely added something. Yet, since aerial firepower was kept under comparative restraint, the discipline and effectiveness of these reconnaissance operations depended heavily on the character of Special Forces volunteers on the ground. In fact, reconnaissance operations conducted after transfer to South Vietnamese control showed an inverse relationship between tactical air and gunship sorties generated on the one hand and intelligence reports produced on the other. From a high of 607 reports in 1969, when 398 gunship sorties and no tacair missions were flown, the number of intelligence reports fell to 485 in 1970, despite 1,548 gunship sorties and 1,239 tactical air sorties. And this decline came despite an increase in the total number of ground reconnaissance missions from 454 in 1969 to 577 in 1970. The ratio of air support sorties and ground reconnaissance missions undertaken to intelligence reports generated was not so disproportionate during 1971 and 1972, but the results for the effort expended under Thot Not were still worse by a considerable margin than in any year under Daniel Boone and Salem House. Perhaps the policy demands of "Vietnamization" required these dramatic increases in gunship sorties, especially tactical air; but Daniel Boone and Salem House, which produced comparable or superior intelligence results with less firepower than that used under Thot Not, could not be used to prove it (see table 2).[32] Such assessments do not form a conclusive measure of merit, but they do seem to offer a measure of effort.

TABLE 2

Missions, Sorties, and Results of Daniel Boone, Salem House, and Thot Not[33]

	1967	1968	1969	1970	1971 to April 1972
Missions					
Reconnaissance team...........	99	287	454	558	437
Platoon...........................	0	0	0	16	27
Multiplatoon	0	0	0	3	9
Total...........................	99	287	454	577	468
Helicopter gunship sorties.........	67	359	398	1,548	568
Tacair sorties*	34	48	0	1,239	659
Enemy prisoners captured.........	2	3	4	9	6
Intelligence reports	297	373	607	485	396

*Sorties against targets in Republic of Vietnam (RVN) or Laos areas contiguous to Cambodia but none known to be in Cambodia until after 20 April 1970.

Air power was by no means an unmixed blessing in its reconnaissance role in Southeast Asia, as was painfully clear to US teams confronting enemy units that had been attracted to a drop zone by the sound of approaching helicopters. Even in such cases, however, the degree of danger resulted from how air power was used more than whether it was used at all. Much that was done could not have been undertaken without air power except at the cost of intolerable risk; but some of the cost and risk might have been reduced if air power had been used more aptly. Air power was a medicine but not a cure-all, and it had to be used in the right cases.

Search, Rescue, and Evacuation

Air power did produce results that were more immediately gratifying than those in intelligence and reconnaissance. Notably, traditional US concern to limit personnel losses gave renewed impetus to search and rescue missions and to evacuation missions; and this impulse was strengthened by the special political sensitivities surrounding US conduct in the war. In addition, special operations were conducted to recover lost US personnel. Air power inevitably played a dominant role in these interrelated efforts.

Medical evacuation was enhanced by the use of helicopters to an extent far surpassing that in previous wars. In an official history of medical support in Vietnam, the Army claimed a vast improvement. One index to measure the level of effectiveness in the medical support effort is the ratio of deaths to total casualties. On this basis, Vietnam appears in a statistically positive light. Some 29.3 percent of those wounded in World War II died, and 26.3 percent in Korea. The comparable figure for deaths as a percentage of hits in Vietnam was 19.0 percent. Similarly, the ratio of killed in action (KIA) to wounded in action (WIA) suggested that enhanced evacuation capabilities had a marked effect in Vietnam, though aided, to be sure, by advances in medical treatment. The figure in Vietnam was 1:5.6, while it had been 1:4.1 in Korea and 1:3.1 in World War II. Even if the old index—the mortality rate among those admitted to hospitals—is used, the record of medical support in Vietnam was still an improvement over Korea. Some 2.6 percent of those admitted to hospitals in Vietnam died compared to 2.5 percent for Korea, indicating that the widespread use of helicopters in Vietnam brought to the hospitals wounded who would have died en route during previous wars. The 133,447 wounded admitted to medical treatment facilities in Vietnam from January 1965 through December 1972 (some 97,659 of them to hospitals) indicates, at least partially, the contribution made by advanced evacuation techniques.[34]

Because of the special concern to keep casualties as low as possible, and because of the relatively dispersed nature of combat activities, Vietnam needed an evacuation system that matched the dispersed operations. The helicopter proved well suited to in-country support of widely deployed US forces; some 116 air ambulances were available at the height of combat operations in 1968. The helicopter provided heretofore unavailable flexibility in medical evacuation.

Medical personnel could assess the condition of the wounded en route to a medical facility and divert flights to alternate hospitals if the original destination had an unacceptable backlog.[35]

Likewise, the expedient use of other available aircraft afforded extra support. Guided by recollections of experience in World War II and Korea, the US Army and Air Force cooperated in evacuating personnel via returning assault or cargo aircraft. This method would have proved unsatisfactory if used as a firm principle rather than a welcome opportunity, especially when operations intensified; but there was often some correlation between locations where resupply was urgent and where requirements for medical support were most pressing. In-country medical flights were scheduled regularly by 1967, their number growing to 188 annually by the end of 1969. Rapid and flexible helicopter evacuation combined with regularly scheduled movement of wounded troops helped to save lives.[36]

Initially, evacuation out-of-country was provided to US forces by the Air Force Far East Medical Regulating Office (FEJMRO) at Camp Zama, Japan; but in July 1966, a branch office was located in Vietnam in response to heavier traffic. C-141 Starlifters used to carry troops to Vietnam could be reconfigured rapidly to evacuate patients out-of-country; they could carry as many as 80 litter patients, 121 ambulatory patients, or a combination of 36 litter and 54 ambulatory patients.[37] At first, the C-141s were flown to Clark Air Base in the Philippines, from which they were routed either to Hawaii, Japan, the Ryukyus, or the continental United States. Later, in the summer of 1966, additional hospital facilities were opened in Japan to treat those who could be returned to duty within 60 days. The requirements imposed on the Air Force for out-of-country medical evacuation varied in accordance with the level of US troop commitment in Vietnam and the intensity of combat operations; but they were met. Combining in-country and out-of-country aeromedical evacuation to save lives and help the wounded was a redeeming mercy in a most difficult war.[38]

The deep, traditional respect for human life among the US military that bolstered air evacuation extended into the efforts of the Air Force Aerospace Rescue and Recovery Service (ARRS) to rescue downed aircrews. The mission of ARRS derived not only from this moral concern for the sanctity of life, but also from the practical need to save individuals whose experience could not be duplicated quickly and enhance the morale of aircrews.[39] Fighter pilots cost more time, effort, and manpower to train than did ground personnel; so an unemotional cost-benefit analysis suggested priority for aircrews over "grunts," even though the greater difficulty in replacing them posed the chance of operational strains. Also, the HH-43 used by the Air Force cost more to procure than an Army UH-1 and so represented a higher cost-benefit risk; and this perspective seemed even sharper when the aircraft involved were the HH-3 and the HH-53. The use of resources, then, had many practical dimensions; and success depended on harnessing the emotions.

In the earlier stages of US involvement in the war, air evacuation was slow to develop. For one thing, US personnel operating in Vietnam were supposedly restricted to training the South Vietnamese and thus, in theory, were unlikely to be shot down. The political sensitivity of this issue, coupled with political and military differences as to where US rescue units should be located, put constraints on the rescue program.[40] Moreover, the Air Force needed time to match its equipment and training to the wartime environment in Southeast Asia. The commitment and enthusiasm of rescue teams sent to Southeast Asia remained notably high; but the problems were complex, the dangers manifest.

Earl Tilford summarized the work of ARRS in an official Air Force history: "As a team, the search and rescue task force triumphed over nature and the enemy to save hundreds of aircrew members down in the jungles of Vietnam, Laos, and Cambodia."[41] But rescue teams also supported friendly personnel—notably during the Tet offensive of 1968 when thousands of lives were saved, as in the evacuation of the Citadel at Hue.[42] Later, the United States began to combine rescue with special unconventional actions; in particular, the raid on the North Vietnamese prisoner-of-war camp at Son Tay reflected a wish for bold use of these capabilities.[43] The Air Force rescue program progressed from the days of Farm Gate, expanding as US involvement in the war intensified and responding to the growing consciousness that US personnel held as prisoners of war constituted a serious political liability to the US government.

The accomplishments of Air Force search and rescue (SAR) depended in part on extensive adaptation and adjustment as well as changes in tactics and hardware during the course of the war. The stresses on Air Force personnel and equipment varied, partly, according to the theater of operations; for example, operating over coastal waters off South Vietnam versus operating over North Vietnamese territory. And the US Air Force air-sea rescue service had added need to coordinate closely with Navy personnel. Meanwhile, the Air Force use of helicopters for rescue and airlift was brought to a state of high art. Throughout the war, aircraft available for search and rescue kept changing both in technical characteristics and in sheer numbers. In 1965, for example, some six HH-43F helicopters were handling the bulk of the air rescue mission. As the mission diversified in subsequent years, the number and kind of SAR craft did, too. The recital of evolutions in aircraft during the war—from HH-43B through HH-43F, HH-3C, HH-3E, and HH-53B/C— suggests adaptability. In addition, the importance attached to the mission may well have helped to overcome customary institutional drags. The adaptation and the skillful execution had a genuine payoff: Air Force rescue teams saved nearly 1,000 lives in 1967 alone. The cost of running search and rescue operations could be high, but successes could be dramatic.

Naval search and rescue efforts also followed an evolutionary course. The helicopter first played a relatively limited rescue role for naval aviators—that of standing in wait to assist aviators whose planes failed at sea. Later, they sought downed pilots on land where the enemy was active. The earliest efforts were not always successful, as when Lt Charles F. Klusmann was shot down by Pathet Lao forces while on a reconnaissance mission over Laos in June 1964. A helicopter sent to pick him up was forced out of the area by hostile fire. Other stories, such as that of Lt Comdr Harvey A. Eikel, who was rescued despite being encircled by the enemy after ejecting from his photoreconnaissance aircraft, had happier endings. These early efforts underscored the increasing importance of SAR to secure the safety of the pilots as valuable military assets and to enhance their effectiveness by boosting morale.[44]

During the early stages of the 1965 buildup of US forces, the Air Force held primary responsibility for search and rescue efforts over water, relying principally on HU-16 Albatross amphibious helicopters out of Da Nang. The Navy had a limited involvement, namely a roving destroyer that operated in conjunction with A-1 Skyraiders. But by April 1965 a second Navy SAR station, consisting of comparatively small Kaman UH-2A/B Seasprite helicopters aboard a destroyer, was at work. Reaction time was shortened markedly. Toward the end of the year, Sikorsky SH-3 Sea Kings were operating from carriers, adding range, reliability, and payload to the search and rescue effort. Modifications in equipment and procedure were undertaken throughout the war, including the addition of armor and machine guns to the Seasprites as well as regular coordination of search and rescue patrols by A-1 or successor aircraft. The search and rescue effort became a combined, though not always tightly coordinated, effort of the services. For example, US Air Force HH-3Es also operated off Navy destroyers. Whatever differences in procedure existed, the search and rescue effort enjoyed one source of unity—the extreme importance attached to the extraction of air crews from hostile surroundings. The stories of individual heroism in the SAR effort are numerous, but it is harder to judge the tasks to which the courage and effort were put. In some cases, the prompt daring of a helicopter pilot saved the day, as well as a downed pilot; but in others, the toll of losses rose without material return.[45]

In search and rescue operations as in other aspects of the war, an increasingly hostile operational environment continued to raise the "cost of doing business"; and the means required to achieve mission effectiveness multiplied. Before the Senate Armed Services and Appropriations Committees on 30 January 1967, Dr John S. Foster, Jr., director of research and engineering in the Defense Department, testified to this effect. He noted that improvements in air defenses over North Vietnam must be anticipated. Search and rescue operations would thus require quick reaction in suppression weapons, navigation, identification, secure communications, and rescue techniques. Foster even raised the prospect that the enemy would introduce advanced air defense weapons into South Vietnam, threatening US air advantages below the DMZ.[46] Experience validated Foster's concerns, at least with respect to the generally greater threat encountered in the war's later stages; thus weapons for rescue helicopters, and coordination of tactical air strikes to assist rescue operations, often seemed imperative.[47]

Search and rescue form an important and impressive part of the less-heralded story of air power in Vietnam. Improvements in aircraft and reconsiderations of their employment yielded results that included a dramatic reduction in lives lost. But the story generates its own concerns, such as the difficulty in establishing relationships between the costs of an operation and the rewards to be reaped from its success.

Supporting Ground Combat Forces

According to some estimates, Air Force tactical aviation was called in to support only 10 percent of ground battles in South Vietnam. Half of all ground contacts with the enemy were too short—less than twenty minutes—to call in strikes from the Air Force. Also, from the Army's point of view, helicopter gunships gave them the advantage of ready firepower. Many Air Force analysts thought airplanes should have been used more extensively, but Army ground commanders were prone to view these Air Force assets as most beneficial in an extended contact involving larger numbers. Behind this difference in perception lay a difference in vision of the war and how best to fight it.

Operation Attleboro (September–November 1966) demonstrated the usefulness of extensive aerial support for a large-scale operation. Some 22,000 US and allied troops were ultimately involved in this action, which began on 19 October in Tay Ninh Province (War Zone C). To support the operation, 1,600 close air sorties dropped 12,000 tons of ordnance. (About 225 sorties were flown by B-52s, which released 4,000 tons of bombs. Some 3,300 sorties by cargo aircraft transported 11,500 passengers and 8,900 tons of cargo between 18 October and 26 November. Later, military intelligence reports claimed 2,130 enemy dead, and attributed 1,000 of the deaths to air strikes.)[48] In an Army history of these activities, Gen Bernard Rogers gave high marks to Army–Air Force cooperation.[49] Speaking of Operation Cedar Falls (January 1967 in the Iron Triangle) and Operation Junction City (February–May 1967 in War Zone C), General Rogers applauded what he considered the "short reaction time" required to get support for the ground forces, praising especially the dedication of the FACs. The "ability to lay down cluster bomb unit runs within thirty meters of friendly forces in order to cause the enemy to break contact" also inspired General Rogers's enthusiasm.[50] That the FACs were performing in an exceptional manner seemed evident. How effectively the air strikes were applied depended to some extent on perspective—on what one viewed as the best use of such resources.

On some occasions during Operation Junction City in 1967, the tactical air support provided by the Air Force clearly assisted ground combat units by providing heavy volumes of ordnance with great accuracy. The task of reenforcing isolated units would have been harder, their casualties would have been greater, and the daring of the plans approved would have been diminished without confidence that aerial fire support could be brought in on time and on target. At Prek Klok, for example, Capt Donald S. Ulm called for fire support when Company B, 1st Battalion, 16th Infantry, was hit by a combination of grenades, rockets, 60-mm mortar rounds, and small arms fire. After sustaining fire over a period of hours, the company was relieved. In his history of the operation, General Rogers asserted that credit for breaking the enemy's attack and forcing him to break contact "had to go to the fifty-four sorties of the Tactical Air Command and the intensive artillery fire."[51] As it was, the unit suffered 25 dead and 29 wounded.

Apparently, Army officers' satisfaction with the close tactical air support provided by the Air Force depended somewhat on when those officers served in Vietnam and on the circumstances under which they saw combat. This notion is supported by a postwar survey conducted by Brig Gen Douglas Kinnard. Some 60 percent of the Army general officers who responded to Kinnard's inquiry rated cooperation with the Air Force as "outstanding," while only 2 percent styled it "unsatisfactory."[52] Air strikes were widely regarded as valuable, but this sentiment was tinged by substantial opinion that they were "not vital." Some 15 percent of respondents dismissed them as "not worth the effort." (The ambivalence concerning air strikes was paralleled by doubts about ground-based fire support: while 57 percent of the Army star-rank respondents rated it as "about right," a substantial minority of 30 percent called it excessive.)[53] Arc Light operations, however, were very well thought of, particularly among generals whose experience with them came during periods of enemy large-unit activity. One respondent specifically suggested that the Arc Light effort was unimportant earlier in the war but "decisive" when the NVA were pressing on toward Hue in 1972.[54] Kinnard summarized the views he gathered:

> Whatever their lack of effectiveness earlier, when the enemy was employing guerrilla tactics, there was no question of the effectiveness of American airpower against the conventional mode the North Vietnamese had now adopted [1972 Easter Offensive]. It had a vulnerable logistics tail: tanks and artillery needed petrol and ammunition. Again these large weapons systems were themselves vulnerable to air and ground weapons.[55]

In essence, Kinnard recognized that the apparent effectiveness of different forms of firepower depended on the apparent nature of the war itself. For the enemy to employ "conventional forces against American airpower without any airpower to counter" could well prove impossible.[56] At the same time, however, an implicit question lingered. What was the limit of air power's usefulness if the enemy chose to avoid conventional warfare or was prevented from ascending to that level? Such questions help to reveal that much of the difficulty in assessing US air power in various roles is human more than technical. The impressive dedication and courage of the airmen who carried out the missions incline one to praise what they did. Yet the praise due their personal character would not extend to the missions themselves if they were conceptually flawed. The distinction between efficiency and effectiveness has been applied to the overall interdiction effort and to the bombing of North Vietnam; it must also be brought to the assessment of the full range of air operations.

NOTES

1. Gen William C. Westmoreland, *A Soldier Reports* (Garden City, N.Y.: Doubleday, 1976), 110; Lyndon Baines Johnson, *The Vantage Point* (London: Weidenfeld and Nicolson, 1971), 240.

2. Westmoreland, 110.

3. *Air War—Vietnam,* Introduction by Drew Middleton (Indianapolis: Bobbs-Merrill Co., Inc., 1978), 6, and passim.

4. Ibid.

5. Brig Gen Southchay Vongsavanh, Royal Laotian Army, *RLG Military Operations and Activities in the Laotian Panhandle* (Washington, D.C.: US Army Center of Military History, 1981), 53.

6. Ibid., 52.

7. Ibid., 27.

8. Ibid., 33.

9. Senate, *Bombing in Cambodia: Hearings before the Committee on Armed Services,* testimony of Gen Earle G. Wheeler, 93d Cong., 1st sess., 30 July 1973, 151–53.

10. Ibid., 180. This last point concerning the threat to revise the command and control structure was clear to Adm Thomas Moorer, who specifically sought to block such thinking in his own testimony to the Armed Services Committee concerning the Menu bombing (see page 422).

11. Maj Gen Joseph A. McChristian, *The Role of Military Intelligence, 1965–1967* (Washington, D.C.: Department of the Army, 1974), 10–13, quotation on page 11.

12. Ibid.

13. Ibid., 14.

14. Ibid., 96.

15. Ibid., 98.

16. Ibid., 99–100.

17. Ibid., 7–8.

18. Ibid., 57.

19. Jack S. Ballard, *Development and Employment of Fixed-Wing Gunships* (Washington, D.C.: Office of Air Force History, 1982), 66–67.

20. Ibid.

21. Ibid., 102, 120, 137; Peter B. Mersky and Norman Polmar, *The Naval Air War in Vietnam* (Annapolis, Md.: The Nautical and Aviation Publication Company of America, 1981), 131–32.

22. Telegram from CINCPAC for the Secretary of State, 5 December 1963, Vietnam Cables vol. 1 (11/63–12/63), Cable 8, Vietnam Country File, National Security File, Johnson Papers.

23. Memorandum for the president from Michael Forrestal, 11 December 1963, Vietnam Memos vol. 1 (11/63–12/63), Vietnam Country File, National Security File, Johnson Papers.

24. Mersky and Polmar, *The Naval Air War in Vietnam,* 147–50.

25. Senate, *Bombing in Cambodia: Hearings before the Committee on Armed Services,* 93d Cong., 1st sess., 9 August 1973, 492–93; "Department of Defense Report on Selected Air and Ground Operations in Cambodia and Laos" (10 September 1973), provided by Under Secretary of Defense William Clements.

26. Ibid.

27. Ibid.

28. Senate, *Bombing in Cambodia: Hearings before the Committee on Armed Services,* 93d Cong., 1st sess., 7 August 1973, 256.

29. Ibid., 261.

30. Ibid., 493–94, concerning bomb damage assessment, see page 239.

31. Ibid., 493–94.

32. Ibid.

33. Ibid.

34. Spurgeon Neal, *Medical Support of the U.S. Army in Vietnam* (Washington, D.C.: Department of the Army, 1975), 50–51.

35. Ibid., 70.

36. Ibid., 71–72.

37. Ibid., 74–75. Navy medical evacuation sorties were also numerous, peaking in 1968 when some 42,000 helicopter missions were flown with some 67,000 persons rescued. See Mersky and Polmar, *The Naval Air War in Vietnam*, 163.

38. Neal, *Medical Support of the U.S. Army in Vietnam*, 76–77.

39. Earl H. Tilford, Jr., *Search and Rescue in Southeast Asia, 1961–1975* (Washington, D.C.: Office of Air Force History, 1980), 2–3.

40. Ibid., 37.

41. Ibid., 156.

42. Ibid., 97.

43. Ibid., 103ff; Benjamin F. Schemmer, *The Raid* (New York: Harper & Row, 1976).

44. Mersky and Polmar, *The Naval Air War in Vietnam*, 11–12.

45. Ibid., 113–20.

46. Senate, *Military Procurement Authorizations for Fiscal Year 1968: Hearings before the Committee on Armed Services and the Subcommittee on Department of Defense of the Appropriations Committee*, 90th Cong., 1st sess., testimony of Dr John S. Foster, Jr., 30 January 1967, 449.

47. See, for example, the dangerous circumstances surrounding the rescue of a pilot who ejected and landed a mere 60 yards offshore from Communist installations in North Vietnam in 1968, in Mersky and Polmar, *The Naval Air War in Vietnam*, 145.

48. Bernard William Rogers, *Cedar Falls-Junction City: A Turning Point* (Washington, D.C.: Department of the Army, 1974), 11–12.

49. Ibid.

50. Ibid. Some will detect irony in an approval of measures to *break* contact with the enemy in a war in which a major complaint was the same enemy's elusiveness.

51. Ibid., 115.

52. Douglas Kinnard, *The War Managers* (Hanover, N.H.: University Press of New England, 1977), 63.

53. Ibid., 47ff.

54. Ibid., 48–49.

55. Ibid., 149–50.

56. Ibid., 150.

CHAPTER 6

The Limits of Innovation

I don't think any unbiased Air Force officer visualizes B-52s finding and dropping weapons on a small guerrilla troop concentration in the jungles of Indo-China—or some other area of concern in the local war problem. I not only think it illogical, but feel that it would be a pure mal-employment of such an expensive force when we can do the job better and more economically with tactical air forces.

Gen Otto P. Weyland, USAF, 1957

A defoliant capable of enhancing visibility along the Laotian-Cambodian border and on key roads and waterways would be extremely useful in compromising the enemy's ability to infiltrate arms, equipment, and personnel and to stage ambushes.

W. H. Godel, Advanced Research
Projects Agency, 1961

Innovation, flexibility, and versatility are part of the vocabulary of virtue in the United States—praiseworthy qualities whose possession and exploitation enhance the prospects for success in whatever one chooses to do. The experience in Southeast Asia, however, gives reason for pause and reconsideration of this unspoken creed. Innovation proved quite possible—but not in all circumstances, not for all purposes, and not always to positive effect. In fact, in some cases, innovation may have brought more harm than good, more risk than opportunity. The difficulty lay largely in calling correctly where innovation turned into excess, where the effort to transcend old operational limits and restraints foundered on its own complexity and cost, and where innovation became an expression of preference about the war one wished to fight rather than an appropriate adaptation to the conflict that was actually in progress. Whether tactical or technological, innovation did not assure respect for local conditions of warfare because there was no sure way of preventing adaptation and initiative from becoming distortions and caricatures of the war at hand. In addition, any solution attempted could in turn generate new problems; thus, the risk was that these problems would fan out in geometric fashion from a common but quickly forgettable point of origin. Each new problem could then call attention in its own right, potentially distracting interest from the broader goal to which the original solution had been devoted.

The Kennedy administration, given its vision of the war as fundamentally an insurgency, strongly supported efforts either to create new weapons and devices or to develop new tactical applications of existing weapons to counter the enemy.

Specific advocacy for such programs fell to the Vietnam Combat Development and Test Center, a subsection of the Defense Department's Advanced Research Projects Agency (ARPA). The center developed and improved fragmentation weapons and studied the effects of chemical and biological agents. It tested experimental defoliants, studied terminal guidance beacons, and considered improved shoulder weapons. In addition, the center tested short takeoff and landing aircraft (notably the Caribou) "for suitability in Vietnamese conditions" and advanced numerous other measures. In a progress report from the Vietnam Combat Development and Test Center, Deputy Director William H. Godel claimed that the purpose of these measures was to "bring [South] Vietnamese troops out of their Beau Geste forts and into active pursuit of the enemy." Godel did not estimate how sophisticated the South Vietnamese would need to be to use the new US-grown tactics and weapons effectively and sharpen their combat flexibility and aggressiveness.

While ARPA sought "higher technology" solutions to South Vietnam's ills, an occasional voice cast doubt on the pertinence of such solutions in Southeast Asia. After spending three weeks in South Vietnam, William J. Jorden of the State Department's Policy Planning Council recommended to Gen Maxwell Taylor various "low technology" measures. Jorden believed that most of the Vietcong problem in South Vietnam was local in origin, and he thought that the problem had to be dealt with on a local and low-level basis. He favored junk operations along the coast, riverine operations by the South Vietnamese, "small, special forces units" to make hit-and-run strikes against guerrilla substations along the infiltration routes and "a few hard-hitting strikes" at their main bases "by tough, special forces outfits." Indicative of Jorden's concern about meeting local conditions was his suggestion that "some kind of light uniform" was better than US fatigues and that "light sneakers are preferred to heavy boots." He noted that some Vietnamese preferred to go with no shoes at all, much like the Vietcong in the paddies. Requirements would vary from the mountains to the delta, but the guiding principle would be ease of operation as judged against local conditions. Jorden was no Luddite seeking to turn back the technological clock (he recommended, for example, that the light uniforms be made of synthetics), but he warned against allowing an alien set of technocratic values to warp the conduct of war. Using technology to keep the fight at the lower end of the spectrum was a challenge, since technological innovations created strong pressures to change the nature of the conflict.[1]

Nonetheless, the Advanced Research Projects Agency continued to develop devices to use in Vietnam, shifting its focus as the war seemed to change. In Senate hearings in 1967, for example, Secretary of Defense Robert S. McNamara cited new high-frequency radios, battlefield flares, devices permitting helicopters to lay smoke screens, and many other inventions among ARPA's accomplishments. Other research went to improving the speed of helicopters and developing prototype airborne weapons for antitank action. Also, ARPA promoted the use of CH-54 "flying crane" helicopters to move heavy Army equipment over otherwise impassable terrain. To this extent, although experimentation took place, much of ARPA's research aimed at improving the large ground units and at using air power to support a conventional war.[2]

Even a small sampling of the tactical and technological innovations pursued during the long course of the conflict in Southeast Asia suggests questions about the interplay between assumptions and preferences on the one hand and actual behavior and performance on the other. Fixed-wing gunships reflected long-standing reliance on firepower, as well as a wish to reduce the guerrilla's traditional advantage in night operations. The way defoliation and crop-destruction efforts changed suggested an inclination to see the war on a larger scale, as well as a way to overcome natural hazards such as jungle growth. The US military, adapting transport aircraft and bombers to meet these tactical needs, similarly showed signs of long-standing traditional thinking and of responsiveness to present problems. Together, these efforts at innovation explored the demilitarized zone (DMZ) between brilliance and self-indulgence.

Fixed-Wing Gunships: Square Pegs, Varied Holes, and the Penknife of Innovation

Although the Air Force's official history praises individuals who advocated the fixed-wing gunships as proof of the enduring importance of the human element in an era of advanced technology, the need for their extraordinary persistence reflects the underlying diffidence within the service to the significance of what these individuals were championing. The fixed-wing gunship was not fully accepted as a weapon until after it had clearly demonstrated its capability to secure positions on the ground in Vietnam. It was not unusual for a strategic system to win strong support as a mere design concept, and enthusiastic gunship supporters sought the kind of ample support that made development more prompt and deployment more likely. But, unlike strategic weapons, support systems were rarely the darlings of the air power community; they tended to win few loyal proponents at the conceptual stage or in preliminary development.

Even more, the interest which some Air Force shops developed in these gunships centered on their potential contribution to interdiction more than on support of friendly forces in ground engagements. In a sense, the "square peg" of the gunship as a weapon system was whittled by technological and tactical innovation in an effort to fill varied mission "holes." Air Force Lt Col Gilmore Craig MacDonald, who had suggested firing weapons from the sides of aircraft as early as 1942, revived the proposal on "Transverse Firing of Rockets and Guns" before a Tactical Air Command (TAC) panel on 14 September 1961, adding a supplementary annex on 19 September. The proposal seemed suitable to Kennedy's emphasis on counterinsurgency, but it went nowhere within the Tactical Air Command. Ralph Flexman of Bell Aerosystems, while serving on a reserve tour of duty at Eglin AFB, Florida, late in 1961, met MacDonald and learned of his proposal. Flexman eventually submitted this proposal to Dr Gordon A. Eckstrand of the Behavioral Sciences Laboratory at Wright-Patterson AFB, Ohio. Although not exactly an "end run" around established procedures and bureaucracy, Flexman's action hints at bureaucratic indifference to what proved, in the end, to be one of the more profitable technological adaptations during the war. The drive came from individuals more than institutions, and it succeeded by swimming against the tide within the service.[3]

The importance of individual persistence in developing the gunships showed itself in the efforts of Capt John C. Simmons. On 26 April 1963, he forwarded Flexman's proposal to the Aerospace Medical Research Laboratory (AMRL) and the offices at Wright-Patterson AFB that dealt with limited war and counterinsurgency. The proposal was also forwarded to Aeronautical Systems Division's (ASD) review boards, composed of experts in weapons and ballistics, which expressed strong doubts. Captain Simmons then attempted to "sidestep local flight-support requirements," as an official history phrased it, and requested that the US Army Laboratory at Fort Rucker, Alabama, test the dispersal pattern for guns fired from the side of aircraft. Although Simmons's supervisors reminded him that weaponry was not his expertise, he kept seeking ways to get funds and authority for live-fire tests and finally won some interest in the office of the deputy for engineering, ASD. After a series of tests with a T-28 and then a C-131, advocates of gunships won a more favorable hearing; a full test plan appeared to be in the offing.[4]

In an official Air Force history, Jack S. Ballard has characterized gunship progress as "crablike." Key personnel were called to other duties deemed more important by their superiors, and the gunship program was consequently slowed. A few test flights were finally made in the summer of 1964, a year after Simmons and others first gave evidence that the proposal might have merit. Rescuing the project from limbo was again largely the work of an individual—Capt Ronald W. Terry— whose experience in Vietnam led him to see merit in the idea. Captain Terry supported a side-firing C-47 in Vietnam, seeing it as an independently operating forward unit to hold off an enemy on the ground while added defensive measures were taken. Moreover, the C-47 gunship seemed better able to meet the needs of ground units than were fighter aircraft brought in by forward air controllers (FACs)—particularly in bad weather.[5] In November 1964, Gen Curtis E. LeMay approved combat testing of the C-47 in Vietnam. However, in an interview in 1972, he showed little enthusiasm for it. "It's not a very good platform and you can't carry the load," he said. "You don't have the range, staying capacity, or anything else. They're too vulnerable both on the ground and in the air."[6] That this criticism sometimes applied to fighter aircraft and FAC aircraft (or Army helicopters) was not mentioned; and the suspicion about the side-firing C-47 may have been the reciprocal of the emphasis on fast planes and heavy firepower that was so strong in the 1950s. Gen Walter C. Sweeney, Jr., head of the Tactical Air Command, opposed the gunship because it was too vulnerable. He also objected to using a

126

slower and less-powerful aircraft armed with guns because it might weaken the Air Force's case against Army helicopters in providing fire support for ground operations. Ironically, despite these objections and General Sweeney's claim that gunships might set precedent which would be "disastrous in some future conflict" by favoring slow and vulnerable aircraft in a high-threat environment, TAC was charged with using the gunships in combat.[7] In the end, as Vice Chief of Staff Gen John McConnell told General Sweeney, the gunships were really justified for a role in counterinsurgency.[8] But mixed feelings about gunships lingered. Apprehension over a possible war in Europe especially disfavored the gunships, but the vision of Vietnam as a special kind of war militated in favor. The fate of the gunships thus depended, in a sense, on which war was considered more pressing—the one in progress or the one yet to be fought.

In the war actually being fought in Southeast Asia, the special effectiveness of the gunships in night operations soon proved to be a persuasive selling point. According to Captain Terry, these operations proved so effective that saving forts or hamlets at night "was the only thing we ever got to do." The first night missions were conducted on 23 December 1964 when a gunship on airborne alert was sent toward Thanh Yend, which was under heavy Vietcong attack, and another gunship was sent to aid Trung Hung. In the latter village, defenders testified that the Vietcong broke off the attack as soon as the gunship opened fire. Hope rose that the night need not belong to the Vietcong after all and that areas designated safe by Saigon might really become so. The addition of firepower delivered from the fixed-wing gunships seemed to be telling; flares alone, which had been used throughout 1963 and 1964, no longer seemed to deter the Vietcong. Operations at Ngai Giao on 28 December 1964 and in the Bong Son area on 8 February 1965 gave more evidence that gunships were changing the balance on the ground. At Bong Son, some 20,500 rounds were fired and about 300 Vietcong were killed. Now convinced of the value of the new system, the Air Force hierarchy in July 1965 approved sending a squadron of gunships to Vietnam on a permanent basis with deployment to be completed in November of the same year. From inception to deployment, the task had taken about four years and had depended on luck and on the persistence of a few committed individuals. Whether this was a long or a short time for introducing a new system is a matter of perspective and judgment.[9]

Despite this early success with gunships in support of ground combat, attention soon shifted to using them to interdict Vietcong supply lines, particularly if the gunships' night capabilities could be enhanced. It would seem that using gunships in interdiction was what some learned from the support of Trung Hung and Ngai Giao. To maximize the gunships' night capability, the Air Force initiated Project Red Sea to test the use of forward looking infrared (FLIR) systems on the FC-47 aircraft. Although these systems were judged inadequate since they did not distinguish such features as village perimeters, the search for ways to enhance the interdiction role continued.[10] The persistence was justified by the fact that some 80 percent of Vietcong supplies was estimated to flow at night.[11] But it also suggested that the US command structure considered attacking enemy sources of supplies more advantageous than direct fire support of ground operations. US ground forces might thus be helped more by interrupting the flow of enemy materiel at distant targets than by close support of the ground forces in combat.

Despite the interest in using the gunships, now designated as AC-47, to enhance interdiction, their primary contribution for some time remained direct support of ground forces. Seventh Air Force's Operations Order 411-65 specified the mission: "to respond with flares and firepower in support of hamlets under night attack, supplement strike aircraft in defense of friendly forces, and provide long endurance escort for convoys." Testifying before the Senate Armed Services and Appropriations committees in 1967, General McConnell, Air Force chief of staff, justified Special Air Warfare Center units in Southeast Asia largely by the persistence of guerrilla and small-unit threats; the side-firing AC-47 gunships provided support even for remote outposts. As General McConnell observed, Southeast Asia had become a place "where subversion insurgency continues to spread,"[12] inviting special ways to counter it. Although much fighting in Vietnam had to be conventional, some did not. In addition to their support mission, the AC-47s were used in search and rescue, forward air control, and reconnaissance. Also, late in December 1965, AC-47s began flying perilous armed reconnaissance over southern Laos, attacking targets along the Ho Chi Minh Trail system in the "Steel Tiger" area.[13]

In many ways, changes in the gunship program during combat employment in Southeast Asia played to the interest in interdiction—and, in effect, to a more conventional vision of the war. The limitations of the C-47 aircraft as an operational platform, which had brought some Air Force personnel to oppose the gunship, later led to improving the platforms once the gunship program was approved. The search to enhance or replace the AC-47—whether with the AC-119 favored by Secretary of the Air Force Harold Brown or the AC-130 advanced by the Air Staff—stemmed first from genuine concerns with respect to night operations, volume of fire, survivability of the aircraft, and similar pertinent matters. But arguments for improved gunships also showed a shift in the relative weight of site defense and interdiction. For example, the Air Staff justified AC-130s, which it wanted deployed to Southeast Asia, by saying their specified mission would be around-the-clock interdiction of enemy supply routes through Laos. This role for the AC-130 clouded the priority initially given to using the gunships in the direct support of ground forces.[14]

In February 1968, Secretary of the Air Force Harold Brown requested Secretary of Defense McNamara's approval for an AC-119 G/K force to go along with the AC-130, thus accepting two roles for gunships. Brown wrote, "I see a clear distinction between the more localized support and protective role of the AC-119 aircraft and the predominantly search-and-destroy concept envisioned for the AC-130."[15] But the two basic roles did not win equal enthusiasm among Air Force officers. For example, Seventh Air Force Operations Order 543-69 (July 1968) gave clear priority to interdiction. At the top of the list of missions was "night interdiction and armed reconnaissance to destroy wheeled and tracked vehicular traffic on roads and sampans on waterways." Close support of friendly installations ranked third, after night interdiction of targets that were bombed and then hit with suppressive fire. The fifth-ranked mission, after search and rescue support, was "offset firing in support of troops in contact by use of aircraft radar and ground beacons." The actual employment of AC-130s was diverse. Indeed, some AC-130 missions differed little in fundamental purpose and character from those of the AC-47s. Overall, the Operations Order represented a different mix of roles and difference in emphasis, justifying the gunships mostly in roles other than that which had given birth to the program.[16] Also, although the AC-119 was given "close fire support of friendly troops in contact with the enemy" as its primary role, this was not the basis for endorsement when it received combat evaluation in November 1969 through February 1970. The evaluators concluded that the aircraft effectively supported Pacific Air Forces (PACAF) because "it was capable of destroying trucks and attacking targets as assigned."[17] Again, the interdiction effort persistently came to mind.

The continued operation of the gunships enlivened the internal debate in the Air Force, even while it raised hope for improving the interdiction effort. For one thing, those who saw jet-powered aircraft as the key to the interdiction doubted that propeller-driven gunships were effective. The Joint Chiefs of Staff (JCS) informed the commander in chief, Pacific (CINCPAC) in December 1967 that a JCS study had shown propeller-driven craft to be nine times as effective as jet aircraft per sortie in killing trucks and watercraft, but the proponents of jet aircraft did not view that evidence as conclusive. Instead they pointed to loss rates for the propeller craft four times greater than for jet aircraft as evidence that the propeller craft were ineffective. Just beneath the surface was continuing disagreement over force structure and service roles, and how they should be fulfilled. To some, the slower aircraft implied greater priority to ground action and, thus, the possibility of subordination to the ground effort and ground commanders. The faster aircraft implied somewhat more autonomous air operations. Complicating matters further was the growing need to use F-4 aircraft to suppress antiaircraft fire directed against the AC-130s, thus seeming to subordinate the jet aircraft still further to seemingly outmoded types.[18] The development of improved systems for the AC-130, under the name Surprise Package, sharpened the quarrel. TAC, the Air Staff, and the JCS urged that improvements for gunships be introduced gradually, while Secretary of the Air Force Robert Seamans and Secretary of Defense Melvin Laird urged rapid development of a full Surprise Package gunship force.[19] There was pressure for quick results; but the challenge was to avoid taking steps that damaged doctrine and the service's interests over the long run.

The "larger" demand of interdiction became an irrespressible theme in the use of fixed-wing gunships; and matters of force structure, doctrine, and institutional priorities dogged the gunship program throughout its lifetime. But in a clear emergency, gunship operations temporarily reverted to the focus on fire support for friendly ground forces. During the Tet offensive of 1968, for example, the gunships contributed enormous and well-placed firepower in a combined effort with B-52s, tactical aircraft, and Army helicopters to spoil enemy attacks around the country. AC-47s around Da Nang were credited with reducing the intensity and frequency of the expected attacks.

Even those cool to such estimates of effectiveness based on the principle of "subtraction"—namely, that things would have been even worse without the gunships—could be impressed by the defense of outlying camps, such as the Civilian Irregular Defense Group (CIDG) and Military Assistance Command Vietnam (MACV) compound at Duc Lap in Quang Duc Province. On 23 August 1968, the North Vietnamese and Vietcong opened an assault with rocket and mortar fire. Army helicopters responded within 30 minutes, soon followed by two AC-47s. Officers on the ground said the rain of firepower strengthened their resolve, after especially difficult going in the early phases of the attack. The gunships fired some 761,044 rounds and dropped 1,162 flares. Although it would be too much to argue that air power "won the day," resisting a dedicated foe without the massive aerial firepower brought to Duc Lap's defense would have been unpleasant to contemplate.[20]

The withdrawal from Ngoc Tavak, a forward outpost of the Kham Duc base, depended on AC-47 Spooky gunships and also harked back to the original purpose of the gunships. On 10 May 1968, Ngoc Tavak was attacked by enemy forces, first with heavy artillery and mortar fire and then with a ground assault. With only two 105-mm howitzers and four mortars, the Americans soon fired their 100 remaining rounds. The last two days before the camp was evacuated, firepower came from the AC-47s and from tactical fighter sorties controlled by FACs. This helped to keep the US and South Vietnamese CIDG forces from being overrun, although it could not give positive control over a numerous and aggressive enemy. The US forces and the South Vietnamese CIDG consequently moved to high ground and hacked out a landing zone for Marine CH-46 helicopters. Two CH-46s had been destroyed on the landing strip at Ngoc Tavak earlier on the same day, victims of the enemy's superior ground-based firepower.[21] Whatever debates may persist over the role of gunships in aspects of interdiction, their contributions to site defense cannot be overlooked, even if the practical burdens of using them cannot be minimized.

Such advantageous use of gunships had a price—the great effort expended to manage a busy, complicated enterprise. Gen William Momyer later said of the defense against the North Vietnamese Easter Offensive of 1972 that An Loc "would have been lost without the day and night support flown by fighters and the AC-130 and AC-119 gunships." But managing the high volume of aircraft in a small area was a complicated enterprise. "Even though there were sufficient FACs to control the strikes," Momyer noted, "only so many aircraft could be controlled at a time. Both terrain and the compactness of the area to be defended set some limits on the uses of air power."[22]

Often this kind of direct support seemed to have more obvious results than did the kind of operations from which gunship assets were diverted. In mid-1969, for example, AC-130s were diverted from Commando Hunt interdiction action and AC-47s were diverted from operations in South Vietnam. They were then sent to counter North Vietnamese and Pathet Lao attacks on Lima Site bases used by friendly forces in northern Laos. The gunships gave effective fire support, which ground and air observers agreed did much to frustrate the enemy's advance. One could not say precisely how many enemy attackers equaled one gunship, nor could one state exactly the threshold of gunship fire support beneath which friendly morale would disintegrate. But observers agreed that both considerations were present during this use of the gunships.[23]

Nonetheless, as the Air Force official history of the gunship program puts it, "since their truck-killing could be verified quite closely, the gunship crews found the usual absence of specifics from their attacks to aid troops somewhat demoralizing"—a rather ironic effect given the positive impact the gunships had on the morale of the ground forces.[24]

In the early 1970s, debate over the effectiveness of gunships in interdiction intensified. At the same time, reports of their worth for site defense continued unabated and unchallenged. In April 1971, the Air Staff informed Air Force commanders in Southeast Asia that official Washington had grown more concerned over bomb damage assessment (BDA) of the interdiction effort. "AC-130 BDA is the hottest thing in the theater this moment," their message stated.

> Seventh Air Force is really concerned about the validity of the BDA reported by the AC-130 gunships in their truck killing operation. They stated all aircraft BDA for this hunting season indicates over 20,000 trucks destroyed or damaged to date, and if intelligence figures are correct, North Vietnam should be out of rolling stock. The trucks continue to roll however.[25]

At the same time, US claims for the value of the gunships in night fire support—during Lam Son 719, for example—were generally beyond controversy.[26]

The weakness of the "truck count" as a standard of gunship operational effectiveness in interdiction can be seen in the discrepancy between the honest judgments made in combat and the results of tests conducted both in Vietnam and in Florida. On 12 May 1971, a test was run on orders from Seventh Air Force Commander Gen Lucius D. Clay, Jr., at Tan Son Nhut Air Base; a direct hit from an AC-130 left a truck immediately operable, while several others could be used after only limited repair. The results clearly suggested that the mounting truck-kill figures were much too high, even though the discrepancy did not stem from deliberate falsification. Similar tests at Hurlburt Field, Florida, in the autumn of 1971 showed that a 105-mm M102 cannon could take out a truck with a single shot while the 40-mm gun could not. But these results came too late to be of much use as Vietnamization proceeded and US commitments were narrowed.[27] The meaning of "truck count" numbers remains clouded, a disturbing side effect of the passion to quantify military performance.[28]

An impressionistic representation of gunship innovations underscores the divergence between interdiction and support. Figure 2 offers an image of gunship operations, suggesting that roles closely associated with support of ground operations were convincing as to effectiveness and minimal as to controversy while roles leaning toward interdiction and the ''larger'' vision of war sparked questions as to effectiveness and dispute as to results.

One of the many ironies of the Vietnam War is that the missions which sparked the gunship program in the first place were those that gave doubtful results but had greater attractiveness for various policy, doctrinal, and institutional reasons. Thus, one is led to speculate that the technical and tactical virtuosity of US personnel permitted—perhaps even encouraged—modifications which, rather than perfecting the initial innovation, changed its purpose—indeed, may even have undercut it.

War and the Environment

Although the concept of an ''operational environment'' has usually implied restraints and limitations within which armed forces must operate, innovative uses of air power let various US officials in and out of uniform see at least the physical environment of Vietnam malleable. If counterinsurgency could alter the political environment and dry up the ''sea of the people'' in which the guerrilla fish swam, might not the jungles actually be thinned—even bared—to strip concealment from the enemy? And if this could not be done everywhere, might it not be done at least selectively?

The practical goals were simple enough to state and to understand. By using air resources and US chemical and mechanical know-how, US and South Vietnamese troops would be able to operate in places that otherwise might have been too dangerous. So, too, South Vietnamese roads and rail lines of communication might be made safer. In the event of a fight, the cost to friendly forces might be contained. Yet the pursuit of these goals gradually became less clear and less practical. Persistence in doubtful measures owed something to pride, as well as to a reluctance to accept Vietnam on its own terms. Defoliation undertaken in Operation Ranch Hand, for example, reflected not only the practical goals of the US program. It also showed a predisposition in favor of technology (suggested in the advertising slogan ''Better Living Through Chemistry,'' which was eventually used by antiwar activists as a mockery of defoliation and napalm). During the course of the defoliation effort, divergence grew between the use of defoliation for defense of friendly sites, presumably deterring the enemy by opening clear lines of fire, and its use in such efforts as crop destruction to deny the enemy essential resources. In a sense, this latter emphasis in Ranch Hand paralleled the assignment of gunships to interdiction, altering the original purpose of an innovation.

The personnel, tactics, and special equipment needed for large-scale spraying in Vietnam were being developed in the United States during the 1950s. In June 1959, an experiment at Camp Drum, New York, proved that herbicides could clear a

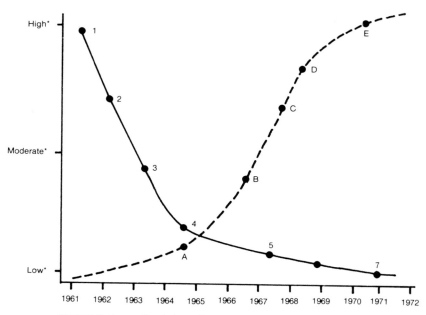

*Factor of Controversy, Complexity, and Doubt about Effects

(1) Proposals by MacDonald and Flexman, (2) Advancement of proposal by Simons, (3) Testing by Terry, (4) Gunship successes at Ngai Giao and Bong Son, (5) Fire-support successes during Tet 1968, (6) Lima Site Support, (7) Night fire support during Lam Son 719.

(A) Steel Tiger armed reconnaissance, (B) JCS studies of jet versus propeller aircraft effectiveness, (C) Harold Brown statement on AC-130 interdiction role, (D) PACAF evaluation and concern in DOD, (E) BDA tests under Clay.

The figure suggests a decline in assuredness that interdiction, in general, would succeed, as doubt was compounded by the increasing complexity of the effort.

Figure 2. Impressionistic Representation of Decreasing Doubt/ Difficulty of Gunship Fire-Support Role ——— and Increasing Doubt/Difficulty of Gunship Interdiction Role – – – .

wooded area to facilitate military operations. Meanwhile, the Special Aerial Spray Flight (SASF) of the Tactical Air Command at Langley AFB, Virginia, had been flying repeated missions, spraying insecticides. The first crews and equipment for the defoliation effort in Vietnam came from this latter program.

The unit's origins go back to the 1940s. Although not really a stable military unit or organization in the normal sense, SASF ran 1,200 insecticide missions at 69 government installations in the 15 years after World War II. The group also participated in chemical and biological warfare research at Camp Detrick, Maryland, in 1951. At a conference at Langley in 1960, little mention was made of roles other than insecticide application; and within a year, this task became a major one.[29]

By July 1961, the desire to restrict enemy movements had generated much more detailed interest in defoliation. By August, the first test runs were undertaken in Vietnam, and President Ngo Dinh Diem personally chose the target area for the second mission. To destroy Vietcong crops, Diem said he was willing to use virtually any chemicals, even those under the restrictive categories of chemical, biological, and radiological (CBR) weapons. Defoliation to improve combat conditions on the ground seemed less interesting to Diem than crop denial. In October, a meeting was held—attended by the secretaries of state and defense—to discuss a memorandum written principally by Under Secretary of State Alexis Johnson; among the supplementary recommendations was large-scale defoliation of Vietnamese jungles, even before any possible large-scale US troop commitments. At a National Security Council meeting the following day, President Kennedy apparently deferred a decision on that proposal. But the Combat Development and Test Center established in Vietnam with US assistance and management had already been testing defoliation and, by 23 September, had plans for a large operational program. Its goals were to strip the border areas along Cambodia, Laos, and North Vietnam to "remove protective cover" from Vietcong reinforcements, to defoliate Zone D in the Mekong Delta where the Vietcong had numerous bases, to destroy the manioc groves that the Vietcong used for food, and to destroy the mangrove swamps where the Vietcong hid. Taken together, the two phases of the program would have defoliated 31,250 square miles of jungle—about half the land area of South Vietnam—as well as 1,125 square miles of mangrove swamps and 312 square miles of manioc groves. It was not intended as a substitute for ground combat but as a means of helping ARVN forces fight more effectively. The overwhelming bulk of the effort was meant to enhance the effectiveness of friendly ground forces rather than to achieve crop denial.[30]

By 3 November 1961, the Joint Chiefs of Staff had recommended a more modest proposal to Secretary McNamara who, although officially uncertain whether he would authorize defoliation, directed the Air Force to provide aircraft and chemicals for this purpose on a priority basis. Within a week of McNamara's order, William Bundy, acting assistant secretary of defense for internal security affairs, summarized benefits and disadvantages of the program. He discriminated between defoliation, which the United States might undertake, and crop denial, which would be handled by the Vietnamese. Supporting the proposal, Deputy Secretary of Defense Roswell Gilpatric said the program showed discrimination in target selection and in means of execution. Along with Secretary of State Dean Rusk, Gilpatric had concerns about where defoliation would be undertaken; he recommended that it begin with a modest phase limited to the areas along major roads. President Kennedy approved the joint recommendation on 30 November 1961. And so, within five months, the modest basis for what became an extensive, incremental, and escalatory program of defoliation and crop destruction was established.[31]

As soon as experimental Ranch Hand missions began (early in 1962), Defense Department officials sought word of their effectiveness. So did the State Department and members of the mission in Saigon. US Ambassador to Saigon Frederick E. Nolting, Jr., thought the program had reduced the number of ambushes; but McNamara concentrated on the effect of spraying on plant growth, from which he inferred effects on operations. McNamara was not happy with the results reported to him during meetings in mid-February; PACAF Commander Maj Gen Emmett E. O'Donnell, Jr., referred to the spray program as "a blooper from start to finish."[32] McNamara's own objection, however, was more specific; he wanted proof that the measures were more than scientific experiments and that they really had military payoffs.

On 10 March 1962, after reports that Ranch Hand's results were mixed and would likely remain so, TAC formally asked Air Force headquarters to reevaluate the program and return as many C-123s as possible to TAC in the United States. PACAF demurred, suggesting that the C-123s would offset a possible Army encroachment in troop transport in Southeast Asia. TAC renewed its request on 20 March, claiming the craft and crews would give TAC an effective "sublimited warfare" capability as well as assets for disaster control and insect spraying.[33] The resistance to Ranch Hand was evidently genuine, even though dispensing insecticide was hardly TAC's first priority. PACAF's demurral left no doubt that Ranch Hand had become an issue in interservice politics and in negotiations behind the visible war, even if only obliquely, through the Army's Caribous. In the end, TAC's complaints were unsuccessful.

By the end of November 1962, Secretary McNamara had recommended and President Kennedy had approved delegating joint authority to the commander, US Military Assistance Command Vietnam (COMUSMACV) and the ambassador to approve future defoliation operations other than crop destruction. The stated goals were "to clear fields of fire to inhibit surprise attack by the Vietcong" and to apply defoliants "in areas wherein attainment of a military objective would be significantly eased."[34] In short, the principal intent was to make ground action by US and South Vietnamese personnel safer and more effective. The restraints on crop destruction at this stage reflected the Kennedy administration's general preference to fight the conflict largely as a ground war at the lowest feasible level.

The ground forces evidently thought more highly of Ranch Hand than did some in the Air Force. In September 1963, a MACV team directed by Lt Col Peter G. Olenchuk concluded that defoliation was effective both technically and militarily and that crop destruction could also be worthwhile. General Paul D. Harkins, the COMUSMACV, and Ambassador Henry Cabot Lodge agreed with the team's findings, although Lodge did not endorse full-scale programs in both areas. The growing acceptance of Ranch Hand culminated in July 1964 with the unit's designation as Detachment 1 of the 315th Troop Carrier Group; it was thus permanently assigned to Southeast Asia and no longer on temporary status. As the US commitment in Vietnam expanded, Ranch Hand's capabilities and operations expanded; that its status was strengthened on the advent of the major buildup of US ground forces in Vietnam is hardly surprising, given the concern for the safety of US forces.[35]

Even so, defoliation was not undertaken only for its direct military effects on ground combat operations. Like so much else in the war, defoliation was also judged for its presumed political and psychological benefits. The need to keep the railroads operating in South Vietnam, for example, was partly a matter of psychological warfare. This goal invited experimentation with chemical agents and burning to increase visibility along the railroad routes and reduce the danger of Vietcong attacks. But these efforts were plagued by difficulties such as timing chemical applications against weather patterns and the onset of the rainy season. Moreover, the desire to restrict the application of chemicals to a narrow corridor favored using ground spraying systems rather than aircraft, since the latter were more suitable for area spraying.[36] On the other hand, Air Force operational interests in defoliation gravitated toward treating larger areas where combat seemed likely.

Gradually, Ranch Hand was enlisted in something akin to an interdiction effort rather than site defense. In December 1965, for example, Ranch Hand operations were extended into parts of southern and eastern Laos to clear, at least partially, areas through which the Ho Chi Minh Trail system passed. When consulted on the matter in January 1965, Ambassador William Sullivan in Vientiane suggested that the plan was a bottomless pit because of the vastness of the jungle area. But interest grew. By November 1965, Gen William C. Westmoreland and Adm U. S. Grant Sharp, commander in chief, Pacific, supported it and the secretaries of defense and state agreed. Ambassador Sullivan finally acceded, perhaps because B-52 strikes there were already transforming the military situation in Laos. He might also have hoped to make the best of a bad business. In May 1966, Westmoreland and Sharp also won approval to include crop destruction (itself a kind of interdiction); but crop destruction never became a massive venture in Laos (fig. 3).[37]

As the defoliation effort grew, so did doubt over the program's effectiveness. The matter came up in congressional hearings in 1967 at the same time spraying in Southeast Asia peaked. Assuring Congress that defoliation was effective, Air Force Chief of Staff Gen John McConnell admitted that "it takes quite an effort though." General McConnell told Senator A. S. "Mike" Monroney that he found nothing

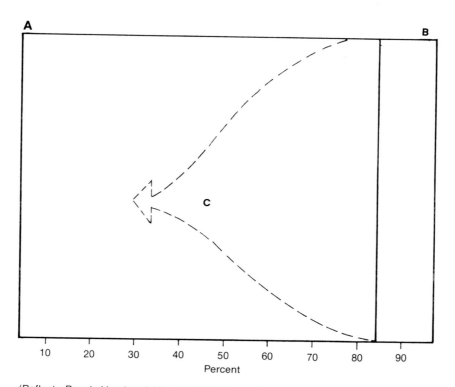

(Reflects Ranch Hand activities in 1967, the peak year, when 1,687,758 acres were affected.)

A. 85 percent of sprayed area was assigned to defoliation
B. 15 percent of sprayed area was assigned to crop destruction
C. Gray area of uncertainty on how much of defoliation was for interdictory efforts rather than site support or preparation for ground-combat operations

Percentage estimates taken from William A. Buckingham, **Operation Ranch Hand, The Air Force and Herbicides in Southeast Asia 1961-1971** (Washington, D.C.: Office of Air Force History, 1982), 119.

Figure 3. Representation of Area of Uncertainty on "Interdictory" versus "Support" Role of Defoliation.

wrong with the defoliation program as then designed, adding that he did not "think there [was] anything we need to do that we are not doing except just more of it." Given the limits on US military resources, the general emphasized that only small areas of jungle could be cleared. Moreover, the effort had to be continued to prevent the cover from growing back, which it tended to do rapidly.[38] In short, defoliation was within technical reach, but its effectiveness hinged on substantial investment of resources on a continuing basis. Every benefit would come at great cost, causing eddies of pressure on other aspects of the war effort.

In January 1968, Ambassador Ellsworth Bunker in Saigon ordered a full-scale review of the defoliation and crop destruction programs. To facilitate the review, he created a committee, the Herbicide Policy Review Committee, composed of members from the US embassy, the US Agency for International Development (USAID), MACV, and the Joint US Public Affairs Office (JUSPAO). The committee concluded that many US lives had been saved, partly because defoliation had substantially improved target sighting and had enhanced the security of friendly positions. But the number of lives saved was considered to be "undeterminable."[39]

Defoliation was hard to evaluate, Ambassador Bunker's report notwithstanding.[40] The criteria for determining effectiveness shifted in subtle but crucial ways over the lifetime of the program. Initially, the intent was to secure railroad and communications lines; at its culmination, the primary goal had become to reduce probable US casualties. Securing the South Vietnamese government and its agencies yielded to the aim of limiting US losses. Although Ranch Hand was not just a holding action, especially for the personnel conducting it, higher authorities' sense of where defoliation fit into the broader picture lost the tone of dynamism and initiative—a development related to the division of focus between ground-support and interdiction roles.

Meanwhile, the costs of defoliation remained extraordinarily difficult to calculate. Ambassador Bunker's Herbicide Policy Review Committee saw that the programs had negative psychological, social, and economic consequences. But the long-term human costs as well as possible financial burdens if US personnel were sickened by chemical agents were not part of Ambassador Bunker's estimate—nor could they have been. They were unknown costs of unexpected problems coming from partially tested measures. In addition, technical problems of defoliation came as something of a shock to many, including some at the high-policy levels—the discovery that seasons mattered, that plants could revive, and many other defoliation problems. Thus, what some had presumed to be a one-shot affair became a continuing burden. It was something like bombing north of the DMZ where, it was argued, bombing could not be stopped once it was started without creating a negative psychological impression. So did defoliation become a self-sustaining requirement that demanded continual reinforcement. Plausible in concept, defoliation and crop destruction faltered in execution. Even short-term cost-effectiveness was hard to gauge, given the need for repeated chemical applications. Nor was there much sense of the longer term implications. Only the future can reveal the final human cost.

Tactical Innovation and the B-52

One of the knottiest cases of innovation in the war appeared in the use of B-52s to support the ground war—one which entailed some technological adaptation of the aircraft but an even greater tactical adaptation and shift in mind-set by military and civilian officials.

The United States had considered using bomber aircraft in prosecuting the ground war before the 1960s. During the Vietminh siege at Dien Bien Phu in 1954, for example, Brig Gen Joseph D. C. Caldera, commander of the Far East Air Forces Bomber Command (Provisional), proposed a large-scale B-29 raid to relieve the French garrison. But Robert McClintock, chargé d'affaires at the US embassy in Saigon, said there were "no true B-29 targets" in the area, assenting to the raid only if no other way to deliver the "required tonnage" on roads and enemy supply areas was available. French leaders, notably Gen Henri Navarre, doubted that ordnance could be dropped on the Vietminh without hitting the French defenders. They preferred an assault on the Vietminh supply base at Tuan Giao.[41] But skepticism was widespread, perhaps contributing to delay.

After the French collapse in the area, Gen Nathan Twining ordered a report on the lessons of the Indochina War. According to the report, prepared by Gen Albert G. Hewitt and transmitted to the secretary of defense on 6 April 1954, French tactical air planners could not develop suitable targets in the "monsoon mountain mass" of North Vietnam. Apparently unable to locate enemy columns effectively, the French got only marginal results from interdiction missions.[42] A study from the Air Force planning staff indicated that bombing in such a war, especially by B-29 bombers, was hampered by several factors. Notable were the lack of information on preferred targets, the complex and fluctuating character of ground operations, and the unpredictable attitude of the local population.[43] The French experience against the Vietminh and the US experience in support of the French had left a legacy of doubt that air power would be effective, especially bombing missions by strategic aircraft.

During the 1960s, however, General Westmoreland showed confidence in the likely efficacy of B-52s. He specifically requested strikes against zones identified as Vietcong base areas. "Earlier attacks by tactical bombers had proven relatively ineffective," Westmoreland recalled, "so deeply had the Vietcong dug in and dispersed their installations."[44] On 14 May 1965, in a memorandum to Admiral Sharp, General Westmoreland specified that MACV needed more than tactical aviation to hit the targets desired—huts, tunnels, trenches, and foxholes. Taken together they constituted important operational bases. But their concealment and primitiveness largely insulated them from the effects of available tacair ordnance. He cited Operation Black Virgin One, conducted on 15 April 1965 against what was regarded as the Vietcong headquarters, known as Central Office South Vietnam (COSVN). Westmoreland called its effects magnificent but limited. Ordnance could be delivered only in a spotty, irregular, inconsistent fashion. Moreover, it took 443 sorties to deliver 900 tons of ordnance over the 12-square kilometer area. Clearly pointing toward the B-52s, he added: "If an attack could have been launched in which the bombs were evenly distributed, the results would have been far more effective."[45]

Westmoreland's proposal suggested that Vietcong base areas had assumed the practical status of strategic targets, even though this terminology was not used. The delivery system to be used and the tonnages required contributed to that impression. At the same time, Secretary McNamara's desire to win the war by actions taken mostly in the South inclined him to use the B-52s as Westmoreland had requested and Sharp had approved. Thus, despite the deep concern of some military leaders over diverting sizable chunks of the nation's strategic nuclear forces to a largely tactical role in a merely regional conflict, the basis for Arc Light bombing was established. The first strike occurred on June 18, and patrols brought back enthusiastic reports. Westmoreland said the B-52s "wedded surprise with devastating power."[46]

The opinions of the efficacy of B-52s used in support of ground operations varied according to time and conditions, including the precision with which areas were targeted and the expectations as to results. Commenting on Operation Cedar Falls in 1967, 1st Infantry Division Commander Gen William DePuy concluded that bombing and artillery fire had "certainly disrupted VC activity" in the Iron Triangle, "a notorious VC haven," but, he added, the "B-52 strikes and artillery bombardment could not be exploited with ground troops" since there were "simply no access routes, air or ground, into the heart of the Triangle."[47] Underlying DePuy's remarks was the view that bombing, including that by B-52s, must be closely tied to ground operations to assure results. Failing that, the efforts must necessarily be inconclusive.

The tactical innovation of using B-52s in very close support of friendly positions and troop concentrations originated rather inadvertently when B-52s flown out of U Tapao, Thailand, on 12 November 1967 dropped bombs within a previously established 3-kilometer safety zone. This strike was but one in a massive application of firepower orchestrated under Gen William Momyer's "SLAM" concept (for seeking, locating, annihilating, and monitoring the enemy). General Westmoreland believed that this free power, along with the tenacity of the Marines, had broken the back of the enemy's siege even as early as October. "Off and on for forty-nine days," Westmoreland recounted in his memoirs, "SLAM strikes pummeled the enemy around Con Thien and demonstrated that massed firepower was in itself sufficient to force a besieging enemy to desist, a demonstration that was destined to contribute to my confidence on a later occasion." Air power's sufficiency in extremis depended on adopting the narrower safety zone suggested by the mission of 12 November. Marine defenders some 1.4 kilometers from the strike's point of impact watched a tremendous array of secondary explosions. Apparently, the enemy had held positions within the wider safety zone set for B-52 drops up to this time. The Marines did not feel endangered by this friendly ordnance.[48]

Even if the B-52 operations at Con Thien were something of a lucky accident, they set a precedent for improving support of ground forces. But the precedent could not be made a policy without resolving numerous technical questions, some of which could only be answered by further innovations. On 8 January 1968, SAC personnel and representatives of the III Marine Amphibious Force discussed the potential benefits that could be derived from the Con Thien action. At first, Air Force personnel were loath to discard the 3-kilometer safety limit, so the Marines called for tests and suggested using additional radar beacons. The basic ground direction for the B-52s came from Combat Skyspot installations. A van-mounted computer furnished flight information to the plane according to data on wind velocity, temperature, the ballistic characteristics of the ordnance, and other considerations. Course corrections and a countdown were initiated from the ground. These procedures provided important control for B-52s as well as for attack planes and fighter-bombers. Without this all-weather capability, such tasks as defending Khe Sanh would have been significantly complicated; and the president and General Westmoreland might not have been as willing to commit to Khe Sanh's defense.[49]

After giving the idea more thought, Air Force Gen Selmon Wells, commander of the 3d Air Division on Guam, concluded that additional beacons would merely complicate the Combat Skyspot mission. He felt they would be highly vulnerable to enemy attack. Finally, a B-52 from U Tapao carrying 108 500-pound bombs ran a test mission on 26 February, guided by Skyspot. The delivery was precise and the equipment operated well. The following day, four missions were run close to the defenders at Khe Sanh. During March, 44 close-support sorties were run. These B-52 missions were taking on the appearance of routine.[50]

Khe Sanh also showed how an innovation intended for one purpose could produce discernible benefit in other areas. The bombing, meant as heavy firepower to hostile combatants, also altered the local environment in a way that helped the defenders. What some described as a scene of desolation was simply a combat area stripped of concealment; and this clearing side effect was at least marginally useful.[51]

Judgments of the effectiveness and appropriateness of B-52s in Vietnam reflected, among other things, the fact that preparations before they were used varied greatly. Merely dropping bombs might offer a brief sense of assurance to the ground forces, but real results meant hitting enemy facilities, resources, and concentrations. In Southeast Asia, this truism fostered an extensive effort to gain added intelligence through sensors coupled with other electronic systems. The success with B-52s at Khe Sanh was hard to repeat where appropriate technical preparation was scant. One place where the B-52 strikes clearly did not frustrate enemy attacks was at Kham Duc. On 11 May 1968, several hundred tons of bombs were dropped on suspected enemy positions between the forward base at Ngoc Tavak and Kham Duc itself. But the enemy was apparently little hindered. The missing ingredient may well have been precise electronic intelligence and guidance such as had been enjoyed at Khe Sanh.[52]

The following morning, B-52 strikes were renewed in an attempt to reduce enemy pressure on Kham Duc. These strikes had become particularly critical, since Spooky AC-47 gunship attacks and fighter support supplied through the I Corps Direct Air Support Center (IDASC) had failed to save the seven outposts ringing the main base. The B-52 bombing took place an hour before fog had lifted; the several hundred tons dropped did little, if anything, to diminish the vigor of the enemy's ground attack.[53] North Vietnamese regiments came at the camp at 0935 and although the assault was blunted by small-arms fire, point-blank artillery fire, and tactical fighter air strikes, the launching of a new attack at the opposite end of the compound showed that enemy forces could still threaten encirclement.[54]

By the time ordnance could be delivered with accuracy, the proximity of the enemy forces to Kham Duc made the use of air power extremely costly. An Army CH-47 helicopter, sent to begin evacuation, was shot down, blocking the runway. A bulldozer sent to push the hulk from the runway was disabled, its operator killed; and an Air Force A-1E fighter that had been dropping napalm and cluster bomb units was shot down. After the runway was cleared, a heavily loaded C-130 landed. But its main wing fuel tank was damaged by ground fire, one of its tires was punctured, and Vietnamese civilians and CIDG personnel mobbed it before it was unloaded. The C-130 could not take off and was moved off the runway.

By now, neither MACV nor those in the camp doubted the importance of tactical air support. But extracting military and civilian personnel came at the cost of seven US aircraft: the CH-47 and A-1E, Marine CH-46, one US Air Force O-2, one Army UH-1C, and two C-130s. Some 120 US Air Force and 16 Marine fighter sorties were flown on 12 May, as were a C-130 ammunition airdrop and numerous Army helicopter gunship sorties. Some 1,500 of the 1,760 persons at Kham Duc on 10 May were safely removed on 12 May, but the cost and the urgency of the action made it no cause for unqualified elation.[55]

The B-52s may have proven more useful in attacks on the camp at Kham Duc after the enemy occupied it. On 13 May, some 6,000 bombs were dropped within 500 yards of the runway; and on one of the 10 missions flown by B-52s that day, an observer spotted 78 secondary explosions. Kham Duc did not prove the irrelevance of the B-52 in tactical support, and the B-52s became more useful as the accuracy of their drops rose. But Kham Duc did show the need for precision in applying support, whatever the yield of firepower.[56]

The great expectations of aerial firepower that had been encouraged by the success of Khe Sanh evidently survived the frustration of Kham Duc. Randolph Harrison, an Army officer in the Daniel Boone-Salem House reconnaissance operations into the Cambodian border area, recalled that he "had been told that B-52 strikes will annihilate anyone down there." He had no reason to be skeptical, and assumed that ground operations after a B-52 strike would go easily. "We were told that we would go in and pick some of these guys up [enemy prisoners], if there was anybody still alive out there they would be so stunned that all you will have to do is walk over and lead him by the arm to the helicopter."[57] This optimism made light of such potential problems as accuracy in targeting and the depth to which the enemy had dug in. It also added to the risks. Harrison recalled that after one B-52 strike, the first reconnaissance mission that he saw run into Cambodia suffered at least 10 dead out of an estimated 13 US and South Vietnamese soldiers. Only his reluctance to sound emotional kept him from saying they had been "slaughtered."[58] Apparently, confusion was considerable; arguments about the best landing zones ensued on the intercoms. After the teams cleared the helicopters, they came under heavy automatic weapons fire before they could get from the landing zone to the tree line. Helicopters sent in to get survivors also took heavy fire. All of this happened despite the B-52 strike. Despite poor trade-off between dangers incurred and results achieved, the major decided to send additional teams immediately into the same area. According to Harrison, some of the men designated for the new team objected. In fact, they so insisted upon their customary prerogative of specifying their own landing zone that they were threatened with arrest. Customary procedure seems to have been altered when the B-52s came into play.[59]

Testifying before the Senate Committee on Armed Services in 1973, Harrison gave no indication that he and other junior officers had been cautioned that the effectiveness of B-52 strikes depended upon the accuracy of targeting information and the security of the operation. A well-delivered strike on hard-surface roads, reinforced bunkers, and base-camp shelters had obvious results, as did a timely strike on a troop concentration. Moreover, when B-52 strikes began in Cambodia in 1969, it was against the backdrop of highly successful use of B-52s in tactical support of Con Thien and Khe Sanh in 1967 and 1968. These cases, especially Khe Sanh, also argued for the critical importance of excellent intelligence and highly accurate guidance. When the B-52s first struck in Cambodia, it was a surprise to most US forces as well as to the enemy; there had been no advance preparations to ensure an effective drop. But effectiveness seems to have depended on this element of surprise. If a B-52 strike hit the enemy, its effect was "devastating." But if it did not destroy them, the effect was "the same as taking a beehive the size of a basketball and poking it with a stick, they were mad."[60]

Even against falsely high expectations, however, operators on the ground tended to support B-52 operations. Typical of many reactions was that of Thomas J. Marzullo, formerly an Army sergeant in special operations. Testifying before the Senate Committee on Armed Services, he said that even if the bombing did not directly take high toll on the enemy, it made life more difficult by forcing them to disperse supply bases and make their movements more secretive. But critics of the war, such as William Shawcross, argued that this was achieved at the expense of widening the zone of combat deeper into Cambodia. More often than not, even in Marzullo's experience, the B-52s had mostly killed "a few monkeys and some birds and tore up a lot of vegetation." This gave a tinge of resignation to his general thought that the program was "definitely helpful."[61]

Although uninformed of B-52 strikes in Cambodia, Air Force Lt Gerald Joseph Greven, stationed at the Special Forces camp at An Loc, saw overflights of B-52s in May 1969, followed by large flashes on the horizon. Greven and his commander were the only Air Force FACs in the area. Since neither knew about the apparent strike, Greven set out in his O-1 the following morning to investigate. He later testified that it was "visually the most destructive raid I had ever witnessed." In an area of about one square mile, "numerous base camps and staging areas had obviously been destroyed as the materials scattered in the tree tops indicated." Although he saw no bodies, Greven thought the strike had been an effective one.[62]

Reliance on aerial firepower, including that delivered by B-52s, was judged according to differing perspectives. During the North Vietnamese Army's Nguyen Hue offensive in 1972, Army Brig Gen John R. McGiffert called the B-52 force "the most effective weapon we have been able to muster" and asserted that the threat of bomber strikes "forces the enemy to break up his ground elements into small units and makes it difficult to mass forces for an attack."[63] Such firepower helped to frustrate enemy assaults in April and May. Some on the ground thought the well-trained provincial militia could overcome the enemy without the air strikes, but this was not attempted. Instead, the ARVN 25th Division's commander chose to bomb the enemy at Trung Lap in Hau Nghia Province. The ensuing air strikes came in for some 36 hours, all but obliterating the village. According to US personnel on the scene, the destruction of some 50 percent of the village—including the almost total disappearance of one of its hamlets—played into the hands of the Communists. Still, somewhat later in the year, those who had ached over what they saw as excessive destruction at Trung Lap were themselves calling in both tactical air strikes and B-52 Arc Light strikes. The point, then, was not to eliminate air strikes but to determine when they were genuinely necessary.[64]

Augmentation of ground operations with air power made sense. Substitution of air power for manpower was another matter entirely; it could invite as many problems as it handled, and some of the new difficulties could be every bit as lethal to the overall war effort. There was even some reason to think that excessive dependence on air power had a demoralizing effect; for example, there was a marked rise in morale when troops, militia or regular, defeated the enemy without benefit of tactical air strikes or gunships. Local militia units inflicted a stinging defeat on North Vietnamese Army (NVA) attackers. This fight led to a three-week series of battles culminating in the enemy's withdrawal. Although there was much that air power could do, there were some things that might still best be done by men; for example, inspiring troops to fight with dedication and persistence.[65]

Despite the long-standing concern to preserve the B-52's integrity as a credible strategic weapon system, it proved possible to use the bomber in Southeast Asia in tactical support of ground units with some success if preparations were appropriate. In areas where preparations were sparse and where strikes were undertaken with little or no ground exploitation, results were ambiguous. Comprehensive assessment of the most effective and worthwhile uses of B-52s in Southeast Asia remains a contentious issue.

Ground Alternatives for Clearing and Interdiction

Limitations and occasional false steps in innovative uses of air power cannot be appreciated fairly if they are isolated from achievements and failures among innovations in other areas. True, there were real problems with trying to use air power tactics and technologies to compensate for ground war deficiencies; but not all of the innovations attempted in ground warfare succeeded either.

For example, one alternative to chemical defoliation in clearing areas of heavy growth was plowing. Between 1965 and the early 1970s, the Army Corps of Engineers bulldozed some 3,000 square kilometers in Vietnam, clearing trees and undergrowth that could have been used as cover by the enemy. Equipped with sharp Rome plow blades (named after the manufacturer in Rome, Georgia), US tractors cut and stripped vegetation. Along roads, for example, they cut swaths from 1,000 to 2,000 feet wide. Forest areas and some agricultural areas were also affected, including at least some water control structures such as dikes. Tractors and Rome plows had clear and immediate results. Chemical-spraying from aircraft was a more intricate process.[66]

In retrospect, Gen Donn A. Starry, USA, gave high marks to the use of Rome plows in Operation Cedar Falls, which was undertaken in January 1967 in III Corps and the first multidivisional operation planned for the war. The operation aimed at sealing the area, splitting it in half, searching it, and destroying base camps and enemy forces. But that last objective proved particularly hard to achieve. Because fighting was light, little could be said about defeating enemy forces. The focus fell on some 500,000 pages of enemy documents captured and on the intelligence thus gained, as well as on the physical destruction of enemy installations. During the Cedar Falls effort, 54 bulldozers with 4 Rome plows and some tanks equipped with blades cleared about 9 square kilometers of jungle. In the process, they uncovered many tunnel entrances and camp facilities.[67] General DePuy, commander of the 1st Infantry Division, praised the "infantry-engineer bulldozer teams [for] pushing back the jungle from roads which can now be used for rapid repenetration of the area" and for destroying base camps and creating landing zones.[68]

Notwithstanding the effort in Operation Cedar Falls, major land-clearing activities awaited the arrival of the US Army's 169th Engineer Battalion in May 1967. Land-clearing teams from the battalion, each of which was comprised of eight Rome plows and two conventional bulldozers, participated in a search-and-destroy mission with a security force consisting of a mechanized infantry company (less one of its rifle platoons) and a tank platoon. A search group composed of one infantry platoon and one engineer squad checked out tunnels and other installations.

After desired information was obtained, these facilities were destroyed. Other operations put greater emphasis on conducting search-and-clear operations around the area being worked by the land-clearing teams, beginning after cutting had begun and after an initial base area had been secured. Land-clearing teams also shared in the securing of roads, which had been a goal for chemical defoliation by aerial spraying. But the land-clearing operations had limitations. Although immediate in their effect (unlike defoliation), these operations were slow. In addition, land-clearing teams used forces for their own security—forces that would otherwise have been available for direct action against insurgent guerrillas.[69]

Notwithstanding the difficulties entailed in the plowing and clearing program, claims have appeared that by early 1970, Rome plow cutting, sensors, and automatic ambush devices were effectively denying the enemy the use of trails along the border between South Vietnam and Cambodia. Cutting the trails appeared to be an attainable substitute for sealing the borders in an absolute sense that had not seemed possible.[70] The actual effectiveness of the venture, however, must have depended on many variables, including the nature of the traffic to be blocked and the ease with which alternative routes might be established. General Starry claimed that "the extensive system of Rome plow cuts and the presence of cavalry and airmobile forces in late 1969 enabled free world forces to choke off enemy supply lines and neutralize bases in War Zone C."[71]

This was no small claim since the only available proof was the absence of major enemy action, which could also have stemmed from temporary shift of enemy attentions. The difficulty in determining effectiveness was thus not confined to air operations.

Rather ironically, the quickening interest in armor operations and Rome plow cutting recalled the earlier work on the so-called McNamara line—an effort to harness new technology to create a new shield along the DMZ. At a meeting at Clark AB in the Philippines in September 1966, Lt Gen Alfred D. Starbird informed Westmoreland that Department of Defense scientists had convinced Secretary McNamara that a largely electronic barrier would stymie the enemy. Their plan, called Project Jason, incorporated electronic sensors, barbed wire, mines, and fortified combat bases to form a fortified line that was to extend from the sea to Laos. Calling the idea "highly theoretical," General Westmoreland later remarked that he "got the impression that some people promoting it, if not McNamara himself, saw it as a cure for infiltration that would justify stopping the bombing of North Vietnam." The general noted that no such plan could assure success without men to cover the line, a fact which "raised the specter of tying down a battalion every mile or so in conventional defense."[72] In fact, the plan was stunted by its own cost even before it was off the drawing board; and although it was partially constructed, hopes for what it would do were never high in the professional communities.

Such interest as there was in developing the McNamara line derived from the enduring concern to restrict infiltration of men and supplies into South Vietnam and from a continuing search—perhaps even a struggle—for methods to achieve it. The high-tech solution embodied in Project Jason emerged only after other measures proved lacking. For example, late in December 1964 and into early 1965 Army Gen Harold Johnson wanted to form an international force to perform interdiction along the DMZ.[73] When such proposals died, technological substitutes such as Project Jason advanced in priority. General Johnson suspected that it was meant to "be an alternate for the bombing" of the North, although he himself thought it would be a mistake to make the substitution. In August 1967, before the Preparedness Investigating Subcommittee of the Senate Committee on Armed Services, Johnson likened reliance on an electronic "wall" to "closing the window and leaving the door open." Moreover, General Johnson accurately predicted that costs would soar and the effectiveness of the system would be doubtful.[74]

Isolating South Vietnam from infiltration was by no means the private desire of Secretary McNamara and his team of civilian theorists. The generals renewed their own proposals after large increases in US troop strength seemed to open new options. Lt Gen Harry Kinnard wanted an area completely cleared, sealing the northern border of South Vietnam clear across Laos. Failing entry into Laos, the border zone should continue all the way down the western boundary of South Vietnam. Recalling McNamara's line, he said, "What I had in mind was to do the same kind of thing except more so, you know, bands of concertina, barbed wire, mines, claymores, the whole nine yards, and then really patrol this thing. I wanted, . . . watch towers and search lights, dogs, and . . . flying helicopters up and down there."[75]

Westmoreland's own aspirations included moving into Laos to block the Ho Chi Minh Trail. His staff prepared plans for such an operation in 1966 and 1967. Ambassador Lodge supported the proposal, as did his successor in Saigon, Ellsworth Bunker. According to Westmoreland, however, President Johnson "was so beset by war critics" by 1968, when forces sufficient to the undertaking were available, that he was unwilling to take a step that could be interpreted as broadening the war.[76] And since action into Laos was not allowed, US forces sought to cut off the flow of supplies and men toward the border areas by other measures; armor operations and Rome plow cutting were in the ascendant.

Shaped by numerous competing interests and constraints, the interdiction undertaken by ground forces permitted some satisfaction over the immediate results in limited areas—in a sense, a confusion of efficient local operation with effective strategic results. More broadly, though, the greater questions about these particular efforts on the ground stemmed from how some elements of air power were to be used in their support. For example, it was at least a little puzzling that praise should come to advancing armor units for securing landing zones that had been cleared by Rome plows on the basis that this benefited airmobile units. After all, these units had first been touted for swiftness of response, suddenness in attack, and versatility. In the end, precisely what ground interdiction added up to was moot.

Self-Sustaining Change

Although an abundance of public testimony to the versatility and adaptability of the US Armed Forces in Vietnam exists, officials did not emphasize the negative side. Innovations often depended upon expensive and relatively complicated systems that could have been highly vulnerable if the United States had not enjoyed control of the air over the South and even over Southeast Asia as a whole. Innovations rippled out, seeming to multiply—and adding new challenges. One example appeared in testimony by Commandant of the Marine Corps Gen Wallace M. Greene, Jr., before the Senate Committee on Armed Services and the Defense Appropriations Subcommittee of the Appropriations Committee on 24 March 1967. He spoke proudly of the construction of expeditionary airfields made of aluminum matting spread out over level sand. Yet, he acknowledged, in largely friendly questioning by Senator Richard Russell, that the aluminum matting was often badly worn by the shock of landings and the blast effect of jet-assisted take-off (JATO).

The solution favored by Marine Corps officials included strengthening the materials used in construction and installing catapults and arresting gear, much along lines customary on aircraft carriers. At Khe Sanh, the vulnerability of even a strengthened metal strip provided some cause to speculate about the limited operational utility of such systems. Moreover, to make the expeditionary airfields workable and to make the aircraft using them mission-capable, pressures were created on other elements of air power. When the Chu Lai field was still 3,300 feet long (its original length), aircraft with full ordnance could be launched only by using JATO, and then only with reduced fuel loads. After launch, attack aircraft had to be refueled in flight from KC-130 tankers. One tanker was kept constantly on 15-minute alert status to handle emergencies.

The desire to thrust expeditionary airfields into Vietnam was a reasonable one. But it created a ripple effect in requirements—and each ripple might have offered some lucrative targets if the enemy had been able to challenge the air superiority which gave a large measure of sanctuary to US and South Vietnamese forces. Innovation was clearly not inherently a bad thing, but it was certainly not inherently a good one, either. It depended upon pertinence to the situation. And pertinence could be sought only in the midst of a competition of ideas driven by predispositions and clouded by illusions of scientific neutrality.

NOTES

1. Memorandum by Robert H. Johnson to Walt Rostow, 8 August 1961, Vietnam folder, 8/61, National Security File, Countries File, Kennedy Papers; William H. Godel, progress report, Vietnam Combat Development and Test Center, ARPA, September 1961, Vietnam (9/61), National Security File, Countries File, Kennedy Papers; memorandum by William J. Jorden to Maxwell Taylor, 27 September 1961, Southeast Asia General folder, 10/6/61–10/10/61, National Security File, Regional File, Kennedy Papers.

2. Senate, Committee on Armed Services and Subcommittee on Department of Defense, Committee on Appropriations, *Hearings, Military Procurement Authorizations for Fiscal Year 1967*, testimony of Secretary of Defense Robert McNamara, 89th Cong., 2d sess., 23 February 1966, 162–63.

3. Jack S. Ballard, *Development and Employment of Fixed-Wing Gunships, 1962–1972* (Washington, D.C.: Office of Air Force History, 1982), 1–3. Ballard specifically indicates that the importance of fixed-wing gunships grew because a guerrilla war prevailed—that is, the value of the gunships increased to the extent that one saw the war as an encounter with fleeting guerrillas conducting a complicated insurgency. In other versions of what sort of war Vietnam's was, the gunships might not seem as valuable.

4. Ibid., 3–4.

5. Ibid., 4–10.

6. Dr Thomas G. Belden, interview with LeMay, 29 March 1972.

7. Ballard, *Fixed-Wing Gunships*, 13–14. Also see Kenneth Sams, *First Test and Combat Use of AC-47* (Hickam AFB, Hawaii: Headquarters Pacific Air Forces, Project Checo, December 1965).

8. Ballard, *Fixed-Wing Gunships*, 14–15.

9. Ibid., 20–21, 25–26.

10. Ibid., 33–34.

11. Ibid., 33.

12. Senate, Committee on Armed Services and the Subcommittee on the Department of Defense of the Appropriations Committee, *Hearings, Military Procurement Appropriations for Fiscal Year 1968*, testimony of Gen John P. McConnell, 90th Cong., 1st sess., 2 February 1967, 842. For information on gunships and air base defense, see Roger P. Fox, *Air Base Defense in the Republic of Vietnam, 1961–1973* (Washington, D.C.: Office of Air Force History, 1979).

13. Ballard, *Fixed-Wing Gunships*, 35–36. Also see Marvin Cole, *Fixed-Wing Gunships in SEA (July 1969–July 1971)* (Hickam AFB, Hawaii: Headquarters Pacific Air Forces, Directorate of Operations Analysis, 1971).

14. Ballard, *Fixed-Wing Gunships*, 94–97; Richard F. Kott, *The Role of USAF Gunships in SEASIA* (Hickam AFB, Hawaii: Headquarters Pacific Air Forces, Project Checo, 30 August 1969), 26. The Air Staff paper was issued on 5 January 1968.

15. Quoted in Ballard, *Fixed-Wing Gunships*, 179.

16. Ibid., 106–7.

17. Ibid., 204–5. The AC-119 was subsequently described in Ballard's official history volume as the "main interdiction force in Cambodia" at the start of the 1970s.

18. Ballard, *Fixed-Wing Gunships*, 110–11; message, Joint Chiefs of Staff to CINCPAC, subject: The Use of Propeller and Jet Aircraft in Laos, 201740Z December 1967.

19. Ballard, *Fixed-Wing Gunships*, 142.

20. Ibid., 61–62.

21. Alan L. Gropman, *Airpower and the Airlift Evacuation of Kham Duc* (Maxwell AFB, Ala.: Airpower Research Institute, Air University, 1979), 7–8.

22. Gen William W. Momyer, USAF (Ret), *Air Power in Three Wars* (n.p., 1978), 332.

23. Ballard, *Fixed-Wing Gunships*, 67–69.

24. Ibid., 239.

25. Message quoted in Ballard, *Fixed-Wing Gunships*, 169.

26. Ibid., 171.

27. Henry Zeybel, "Truck Count," *Air University Review* 34, no. 2 (January-February 1983): 36–45.

28. See, for example, the elaborate tables on the performance of gunships in Kott, *The Role of USAF Gunships in SEASIA*. Also see cost-effectiveness data prepared by the staff of Secretary of the Air Force Brown such as memorandum, Hugh E. Witt to Assistant Secretary Robert H. Charles, subject: "Estimated Cost to Destroy/Damage a Truck in Laos," 2 May 1968.

29. William A. Buckingham, Jr., *Operation Ranch Hand, The Air Force and Herbicides in Southeast Asia, 1961–1971* (Washington, D.C.: Office of Air Force History, 1982), 6–8. Although the main text here relies on Buckingham, other studies are of interest for various reasons. The Cornell University Air War Study group included the effects of bombing (such as cratering) in a comprehensive judgment on the environmental impact of US efforts in Vietnam. See Ralph Littauer and Norman Uphoff, eds., *The Air War in Indochina*, rev. ed. (Boston: Beacon Press, 1972). Also see the critique by T. Whiteside, *Defoliation* (New York: Ballantine Books, 1970); the criticism of B. Weisberg, ed., *Ecocide in Indochina* (San Francisco: Canfield Press, 1970); and Stockholm International Peace Research Institute (SIPRI), *Ecological Consequences of the Second Indochina War* (Stockholm: Almqvist and Wiksell, 1976).

30. Buckingham, *Operation Ranch Hand,* 13–15.

31. Ibid., 16–22.

32. Ibid., 45.

33. Ibid., 46.

34. Ibid., 67.

35. Ibid., 100–102.

36. Concerning ground-spraying operations for railroad security, see COMUSMACV to RUHLHQ/CINCPAC, 18 January 1964, Vietnam Cables, vol. 2 (12/63–1/64), cable 18, Vietnam Country File, National Security File, Johnson Papers.

37. Buckingham, *Operation Ranch Hand,* 116–19. Also see Pacific Command (PACOM), scientific advisory group, "Crop Destruction Operations in RVN During CY 1967" (1967); and John F. Trierweiler, "Vegetation Control in Southeast Asia" (Kirtland AFB, N.Mex.: US Air Force Weapons Laboratory, 1968).

38. Senate, Committee on Armed Services and Subcommittee on the Department of Defense, Committee on Appropriations, *Hearings, Military Procurement Authorizations for Fiscal Year 1967,* testimony of Secretary Harold Brown and Gen John P. McConnell, 89th Cong., 2d sess., 30 March 1966, 945–46.

39. Buckingham, *Operation Ranch Hand,* 145–46; Report, AMEMBASSY Saigon, Report of the Herbicide Policy Review Committee, 28 May 1968.

40. Among the contemporary efforts to evaluate defoliation was Congressional Research Service, "Impact of the Vietnam War" (Washington, D.C.: Government Printing Office, 1971), prepared for the Senate Committee on Foreign Relations, especially page 10 ff. Also see Congressional Research Service, "Agent Orange: Veterans' Complaints Concerning Exposure to Herbicides in South Vietnam" (Washington, D.C.: Library of Congress, 1980); and Maj Alvin L. Young, "Agent Orange at the Crossroads of Science and Social Concern," Research Report (Maxwell AFB, Ala.: Air Command and Staff College, May 1981). An unflattering commentary is J. Lewallen, *Ecology of Devastation: Indochina* (Baltimore: Penguin Books, 1971). Also see W. B. House et al., "Assessment of Ecological effects of extensive or repeated use of herbicides" (Kansas City, Mo.: Midwest Research Institute, 1967).

41. Robert Frank Futrell, *The Advisory Years* (Washington, D.C.: Office of Air Force History, 1981), 24–25.

42. Report, Gen Albert G. Hewitt to secretary of defense, 6 April 1954.

43. History, Directorate of Plans, US Air Force, January–June 1954, study, Directorate of Plans, 19 April 1954, 90–92.

44. Gen William C. Westmoreland, *A Soldier Reports* (Garden City, N.Y.: Doubleday & Co., Inc., 1976), 137.

45. U. S. Grant Sharp, *Strategy for Defeat, Vietnam in Retrospect* (San Rafael, Calif.: Presidio Press, 1978), 87–88.

46. Ibid. Even the Arc Light bombings, for which considerable success could be claimed and in which considerable security could be enjoyed by B-52 crews, were not without their hazards. The first Arc Light strike on 18 June 1965 was marred by the loss of two B-52s when they collided in midair in their refueling area. Although there were five refueling tracks, all were at the same altitude; and the 20-nautical mile separation of the tracks proved inadequate. Later, provision was made to fly a triangular pattern just before entering the refueling area to correct for timing discrepancies; but such was not the case on 18 June 1965. Charles K. Hopkins, *SAC Tanker Operations in the Southeast Asia War* (Offutt AFB, Nebr.: Office of the Historian, Headquarters Strategic Air Command, 1979), 14.

47. Bernard William Rogers, *Cedar Falls–Junction City: A Turning Point* (Washington, D.C.: Department of the Army, 1974), 78.

48. Bernard C. Nalty, *Air Power and the Fight for Khe Sanh* (Washington, D.C.: Office of Air Force History, 1973), 116. Westmoreland, *A Solider Reports,* 340. Tactical air strikes at Khe Sanh were brought in as close as 400 yards.

49. Nalty, *Air Power and the Fight for Khe Sanh,* 66–67.

50. Ibid., 116.

51. See Moyers S. Shore II, *The Battle for Khe Sanh* (Washington, D.C.: Historical Branch, US Marine Corps, 1969).

52. Gropman, *Airpower and the Airlift Evacuation of Kham Duc,* 9. Somewhat ironically, sensors originally set out as part of the McNamara line at the DMZ were relocated around Khe Sanh during the Niagara operation preparatory to the extensive use of B-52s.

53. Ibid., 11–12.

54. Ibid., 14–15.

55. Ibid., 29.

56. Senate, Committee on Armed Services, *Hearings, Bombings in Cambodia,* testimony of Randolph Harrison, 93d Cong., 1st sess., 245.

57. Ibid., 235.

58. Ibid., 247–48.

59. Ibid., 239.

60. Senate, Committee on Armed Services, *Hearings, Bombings in Cambodia,* 93d Cong., 1st sess., 271.

61. Senate, Committee on Armed Services, *Hearings, Bombings in Cambodia,* testimony of Gerald Joseph Greven, 93d Cong., 1st sess., 279.

62. Quoted in introduction by Drew Middleton, *Air War—Vietnam* (Indianapolis: Bobbs-Merrill Co., Inc., 1978), 102.

63. Stuart A. Herrington, *Silence Was A Weapon, The Vietnam War In The Villages* (Novato, Calif.: Presidio Press, 1982), 129.

64. Ibid., 132–33.

65. J. Lewallen, *The Ecology of Devastation: Indochina* (Baltimore: Penguin Books. 1971); also see W. Haseltine and A. H. Westing, "The Wasteland: Beating Plowshares into Swords," *The New Republic* 65, 18 (1971): 13–15; and Westing, "Land War: (II) Levelling the Jungle," *Environment* 13, 9 (1971), 8–12.

66. Gen Donn A. Starry, *Armored Combat in Vietnam* (Indianapolis: Bobbs-Merrill Co., Inc., 1980), 91–94.

67. Rogers, *Cedar Falls–Junction City,* 78; Willard Pearson, *The War in the Northern Provinces, 1966–1968* (Washington, D.C.: Department of the Army, 1975).

68. Starry, *Armored Combat in Vietnam,* 147–49.

69. Ibid., 156.

70. Ibid., 160.

71. Westmoreland, *A Soldier Reports,* 200.

72. Ibid., 127.

73. Senate, Preparedness Investigating Subcommittee of the Committee, *Hearings, Air War against North Vietnam,* 90th Cong., 1st sess., 28–29 August 1967, 416.

151

74. Lt Gen Harry O. W. Kinnard, USA, interviewed by Col Glenn Smith and Col August Cianciolo, 31 March 1977, US Army Military History Institute, Oral History Series, The History of Army Aviation, 35.

75. Westmoreland, *A Soldier Reports*, 148.

76. Senate, Committee on Armed Services and Subcommittees on Defense Appropriations of the Appropriations Committee, *Hearings, Military Procurement Authorizations for Fiscal Year 1967*, testimony of Gen Wallace M. Greene, Jr., 89th Cong., 2d sess., 24 March 1966, 670–71.

PART THREE

REFLECTIONS AND CONCLUSIONS

The lessons of Vietnam are hostages of our reluctance to be self-conscious and reflective about the American part in the war—a part beyond the commitment and use of US forces, encompassing specifically how American preferences altered the war itself. Whatever may be learned by studying Vietnam can come only after we sense the varying reasons why the Vietnam conflict has become so elusive. Different observers have attempted to pin it down, give it concreteness, and force it to hold a specific shape. Yet the apparent meaning of each concrete event seems always open to challenge from some competing interpreter. Is there no way of determining the real Vietnam, or at least the sufficiently relevant one? Or does the ultimately pertinent reality about Vietnam lie in the painfully subtle and intangible aspects of human relationships between obvious foes and among apparent friends?

The lessons explicitly pertaining to the use of air power, except in the more restricted aspects of operations, are likely to remain embedded in ambiguities of Vietnam until the larger picture is given clarity. Yet here, too, the presuppostions that different observers bring to assessing air power affect their judgments as significantly as do the properties of air forces themselves. The relationship of air power to ground warfare—taking each of these terms somewhat abstractly—is a dialogue between ''is'' and ''ought,'' between what assets exist and varying notions of what to do with them, and between readings of capabilities and dreams of accomplishment. In the end, relevant criteria for the lessons to be drawn from Vietnam may lie neither in Southeast Asia nor among the late enemy but rather among the American people and their leaders.

CHAPTER 7

Air Power and the Ambivalence of Vietnam

No large organization . . . can fool people outside without also fooling itself.

Bernard Brodie

The battle is not between them and you, but between you and yourselves.

Alexander Solzhenitsyn

The desire to see the Vietnam War in a coherent way has driven us to view it, for the most part, in its largest scale and in its most statistically dramatic aspects. Study thus far has emphasized the large-unit, ground-force commitment and the strategic bombing program over the North; the complexity and diversity of what might well be called the "interrelated wars in Southeast Asia" have tended to receive less attention. Those who are professionally capable of evaluating the specifics of the diverse elements of the conflict frequently seem disinclined to do so. Yet in this complexity and diversity, something worthwhile may yet be salvaged from the American enterprise in Southeast Asia. Otherwise, the practical potential of air power is likely to remain clouded by the ambivalence of Vietnam as it enters historic memory. The following reflections are intended as probes into the complexity of Vietnam in search of its underlying dynamic.

The starting point for all appraisals of the Vietnam War on the tactical and operational level—the realm of means and instruments—must be that it was fundamentally a failure in conception and vision on the strategic level. More than assigning blame, this indictment underscores that tactical engagements, hardware, and the like can be assessed in some useful ways apart from the strategic scenario into which they were ostensibly placed. Each may be assessed in narrowly technical terms—and usefully so. But it is neither logically nor reasonably permissible to assume that measures which were successful in narrowly technical terms could have been successful on the broader strategic scene. Nor can one assume that such measures could not have been recombined with strategically positive effect. It is the difference between brickmaking and architecture. Thus, assessment of the Vietnam conflict may finally combine positive endorsements of some technical and tactical measures with broader cautions and criticisms in strategic matters.

Lessons concerning air power and its effects on the fighting in Vietnam are largely embedded in less-discriminant lessons about the conduct of the war in general. They are thus influenced by the particular vision of the war one adopts. Still, whether analyzing methods in the narrower or the broader realm, one needs to

155

avoid confusing efficiency with effectiveness. By maintaining appropriate discrimination, we may retrieve some useful building blocks for the future. In assessing a hypothetical airdrop of men and supplies in a largely hostile area, for example, failure to achieve the overall "winning" of the war does not impeach the ability to conduct the drop itself. Although the operation must not be judged solely by the technical standard of doing what was ordered, the existence of such capabilities invites asking how they may be exploited in the future. The issue is not to put a retrospective stamp of approval on operations in Vietnam. But even if specific missions did not amount to strategic success, similar measures could still prove useful in other times and places, especially when used according to other conceptual frameworks.

In the case of the Southeast Asian conflict, several specific observations are possible. First, Americans—whether military officers, government officials, or the public—were not only affected *by* the war; they *affected* the war, altering and influencing its characteristics and its course. What Americans believed—and specifically what they believed about air power both in theory and in practice—became a very important player in the war. Despite both altruistic concerns and national interests, Americans could not shed their own provincialisms, predispositions, and biases; and because they were relatively unconscious of them as potential liabilities, they had all the more effect. A hallmark of this fault was the often expressed fear that the United States might "lose Vietnam." As a North Vietnamese journalist once told an antiwar American journalist, "Don't worry. Vietnam isn't yours to lose."[1] The United States did not "lose Vietnam." It lost a war *in* Vietnam; and it lost something of itself in the process. The risks and dangers generated by America's own ways of thinking and behaving will all but inevitably become an element in a future conflict, especially if those ways are left to the unconscious.

Embedded ways of thinking guided the armed forces. The services' customary interest in doctrine showed their self-consciousness in such largely ideological issues and often surpassed that of civilian authorities and agencies. These differing ways of thinking made for an unpleasantly durable rivalry among the military services in Vietnam. The often repeated hope, reflected in doctrine, that interservice differences would pale into insignificance once a war began was not justified by the experience in Southeast Asia. Rivalries caused problems throughout the war. Their potential impact on a future war must not be ignored. Nor can they be dismissed by hoping a "more suitable" war scenario will be followed in the future—one in which the magnitude of the war *would* suppress rivalry or else one whose characteristics would convince even the unbeliever of the truth of one's own doctrine. The cooperation in World War II came largely because civilian authorities set clear priorities and a consistent strategy. Moreover, civilian authorities did not hesitate to suppress interservice conflict when it threatened operational success. Yet despite the gravity of World War II and the degree of cooperation achieved in it, service interests continually surfaced. Vietnam shows how much more difficult things can be when civilian authorities fail to give unswerving direction and, perhaps even worse, when there is no agreement on the nature of the war itself.

The corollary of this observation is that even when there are clear problems with it, a particular practice may prove difficult to change. In Vietnam, practices embraced by one service but dismissed by another could linger without adjustment or resolution. The debate was perhaps too often confined to externally certifiable, countable information. So "more of the same" could be a solution as promising as a change in tactics or strategy. In essence, however, a change of mind must precede a change in practice. And in Vietnam, it seemed hard to think the unthinkable—not Herman Kahn's unthinkable nuclear options, but the awesome prospect of changing doctrine during a confusing war. Technological changes seemed always open for consideration; the core of doctrine was harder to touch. This is hardly surprising in such a subtle and ambiguous war, but it still contributed to making prosecution of the war an experience in doctrinal damage control. "The lessons [of Vietnam] are to ask the right questions," Roger Hilsman said a decade after the Paris agreement on US withdrawal.[2] But which were the right questions about doctrine, and which conditions in Vietnam could spark a genuine reexamination of doctrinal precepts?

Technical proficiency, operational effectiveness and technological capabilities do not suffice in war. Without a strategic vision that turns out to be the right one (or *a* right one), these become phantom victories leading to a final spectacle of defeat or stalemate. Still, concrete accomplishments may be separated from their misuse in past conflict; and more encouraging observations become possible. In the conduct of the ground war, for example, diverse capabilities of air power at times made it a great asset, raising the expectations of ground commanders as to what they could safely attempt. The B-52 Arc Light strikes are a dramatic example, but fixed-wing gunships were also important. The role of rotary-wing aircraft in providing fire support was significant, although different in kind from that provided by fixed-wing aircraft. In addition, mobility was much enhanced; and US commanders have sought to exploit this characteristic at least since World War I.

In counterinsurgency and advisory efforts, air power provided worthwhile assets. The events of 1975 and the outcome of the war are not the test of effectiveness for air assets in advisory and counterinsurgency efforts. Where one could move, how one could supply, what intelligence could be gathered, who could be withdrawn— these and other questions received speedier and more numerous positive responses because of air power. But this sanguine view does not negate the need for a clear general strategy for employing air power assets in any future conflict. The need for unified governance of the counterinsurgency efforts was often recognized, and calls for better management appear in the record. But the greatest opportunity for producing permanent results had to reside with local authorities; and throughout the war, a balance between local responsibility and general governance proved to be hard to strike.

Still, the Vietnam conflict leaves unanswered whether the United States can successfully cooperate in a counterinsurgency war. Nor is it clear that the United

States can conduct one alone. Even the most articulate advocates of the counterinsurgency option failed to make sufficiently concrete what the enterprise required. They could more easily write words such as "harass the enemy and keep him on the move" than send trained men to do so in a politically confusing and physically demanding environment. Similarly, they could talk of "revolutionary development" and "rural reconstruction" more easily than they could effect practical reforms. Politico-military models could be conceived, but their relationship to the existing realities remained ambiguous. Lacking a persuasive concrete explanation of what was to be done and why it would give results, those who backed counterinsurgency risked seeing its potential lost in a sea of vagueness and a fog of generality. And, ironically, those who would claim that counterinsurgency failed in Southeast Asia deny with increasing frequency that the war there was ever truly an insurgency at all.[3] By that logic, however, counterinsurgency could not possibly have been proved wrong. So, in the end, Vietnam does not conclusively demonstrate whether air power was proved useful in a broad counterinsurgency program. One can only cite examples in which tasks were executed well, leaving the achievements of coherent and uncompromising commitment to counterinsurgency a matter of induction and extrapolation. But the specific tasks and operations successfully undertaken in Vietnam cannot be dismissed as trivial because the war turned out badly.

As with hardware and tactics, so with conceptualization and execution. To expect things to do what they have not been designed to do is a risky business. This applies to institutions as well as to machines; and to human beings as well, unless they have been fundamentally "retooled" for a change of tasks and mind. Otherwise, circumstantial familiarity with new tasks cannot ensure that people will perceive them as presenting new and special demands. Thus, although military and nonmilitary means of seeking a desirable resolution to a conflict must be in tandem, they need not be administered as if they bore no differences. Instead, there is much to say for assigning clear responsibility for the execution of military measures to military personnel and for assigning nonmilitary tasks to appropriate civilian agents even when they must interact effectively to accomplish a broader common objective.

Even in a counterinsurgency, for example, the need for positive economic and social change does not make the military specifically responsible to attain that goal. The armed forces may more reasonably assume such responsibilities when there is a scarcity of organized agents of any sort, as in some new nations, and when the military thus have much more skill and training than others. In some cases, the role of the military in the political development of new nations may actually frustrate the effort to extend security and reform, particularly where the army's task is to enforce the legitimacy of an authoritarian regime which fears change and resists reform. But even when the military show restraint in hope of winning new support for the government, the armed forces may lack the mission and resources to build social institutions or physical infrastructure which contribute to social justice and the image of the government. Someone must do this essential task, but perhaps not the military. It is courting catastrophe to lapse, even unintentionally, into a false assumption that the linkage of military problems with political, economic, and social ones makes them virtually interchangeable.[4]

For the most part, those lessons of Vietnam that win some agreement form a category of behaviors to be repeated or avoided. Notable is concern over the potential vulnerability of highly sophisticated aircraft to relatively less advanced weapons in the hands of hostile ground forces, or the importance of standoff capability with smart ordnance. Pressed far enough, even to the risk of *reductio ad absurdum,* this concern threatens the traditional meaning and likelihood of air superiority. The concept of winning and holding air superiority has been cardinal in Air Force thinking. It has been taken as prerequisite to efficient imposition of force against the enemy, including force exerted on the ground. Yet Vietnam has provoked worries over the balance of defensive environment against offensive penetration, and over the practical utility of air superiority in certain kinds of wars. Vietnam also illustrates how theater air superiority depends on political decisions about where the limits of the theater will be set. For example, some North Vietnamese aircraft were moved into China during periods when US forces were expected to attack, but to stop short of the Chinese border. This raises the prospect that air superiority itself may not be held absolutely in lower levels of conflict, especially if enemy resources from outside the theater can be thrown in at a later date.

Although not intrinsically a new problem, the prospect of lacking air superiority is a chilling one. Referring to the skies over Korea in the early 1950s, Ninth Air Force Commander Gen Hoyt S. Vandenberg noted that local air superiority had gone back and forth between the United Nations forces and the Communist air forces. Pointedly, he observed: "Air superiority is a fleeting thing . . . until either the factories that produce the aircraft or the oil and/or the airfields and the airplanes are eliminated. Anyone with a small force can get local air superiority at times." At the same time, 12th Army Group Commander Gen Omar N. Bradley observed that air superiority only applied to a certain area for a certain time: "You gain it over one area, and lose it over another one."[5] In the aftermath of Vietnam, the question lingers as to the cost of attaining superiority or to its value once attained, especially if it was limited and transient.

In addition, the tentativeness of air superiority complicates long-standing US interest in offsetting shortages in numbers by using qualitatively superior technology. Attrition has long been a justifiable source of concern to US military and civilian leaders, and few allegations have more bite than that the United States degenerated into attrition warfare in Southeast Asia. Apart from whether that characterization is accurate, the question emerges whether technology can really prevent a lapse into attrition. If attrition is a false strategy, it is at least a strategy— that is, a pattern of ideas. If it is false, then perhaps the truth rests in a different pattern of ideas rather than instill more inventions to compensate for limited thinking.

Uncomfortable as the foregoing may be to contemplate, the pace and especially the characteristics of techological change may well necessitate it. Relying on technology to offset perceived scarcities in manpower originated when the technology sufficient to do so was relatively inexpensive. This rule no longer prevails. Even considering the high cost of training men and women for complicated tasks, the cost of technological substitutes often seems daunting. Clearly, the loss of one's armed manpower cannot be sustained indefinitely without concern. Yet the loss of one's higher technology may be as costly and as lethal in a parallel, though not identical, way. These changing circumstances beg that we ask if the old formula remains valid.

In part, such reexamination must judge whether technological innovation and versatility validate the formula. Many observers have complained that Americans do not prepare well for future wars and that we try to refight the last one. Yet some efforts at technical and tactical innovation in Vietnam were impressive. To be sure, some—if judged by the most immediate and practical criteria—worked better than others, and one must consider further the usefulness of any of them in the broader strategic picture. But whatever the final assessment, there is at least some comfort in the fact that adaptations proved possible at all. Some capabilities with a conventional ring to them, such as airlift, were brought to unconventional precision, sophistication, and reliability. Less-conventional efforts, such as defoliation, brought new methods to traditional goals such as area security around a base. Subsequent problems related to the use of chemical defoliants raise concern over possible long-term effects, but the experiment still reminds us that naturally imposed barriers can be easier to see and fight than those created within one's own mind and within the enemy's. And when the evaluation ascends to total cost and general strategic benefit, the need to consider technology's limits becomes clearer.

In the final analysis, it may be necessary to distinguish between the actuality of Vietnam, its workable lessons, its evident effects, and a more mythic package of lessons of Vietnam. A rough parallel was suggested by Sen Howard Baker's distinction between Watergate and the lessons of Watergate.[6] The real excess of Watergate generated countermeasures that created their own problems, and the countermeasures may themselves have produced even more vexing problems. Similarly, one may wonder whether purported lessons of Vietnam are the best inheritance we may take from the war—whether, instead, the more commonly identified lessons are falsely specific and too restrictive. One may fairly ask: What basic guiding principle has the Vietnam experience changed? What basic guiding principles did Vietnam defy? Here may lie some transferable guidance and some lessons; but they are not likely to prove enduring if they are bound up in technical detail or overpowered by our unwillingness to consider the worst. What follow are excursions into some of Vietnam's deeply troubling implications.

War as an Event and as a Process

Cultural historians have tended to locate the distinctiveness of American culture in its emphasis on process as a source of identity rather than on concrete details such as race, ethnicity, and the like. One speaks freely of an American way of life, while a comparable term is hard to find in most other cultures. Yet this emphasis on process—on an unending and evolving interweaving of many variables—has not characterized how the American people comprehend war, its conduct, and its requirements. It is less that Americans have a predisposition for short wars than that they are inclined to see war as inherently short, persistently distinct from peace, and, in essence, a cataclysmic event. If war lasts too long compared to the perceived issue at stake and the resources thrown into the fray, then the US public, officials, and military are more likely to suspect incompetence than to reexamine basic assumptions about the character of war and its place in the process of world affairs. Peace thus becomes the comprehensive and customary temporal condition, like cleaning up and rebuilding after an earthquake; war is the earthquake.[7]

So, although war is obviously a process, Americans have sought to hurry it along so as to make it look and feel more like an event. For all of the importance of campaign arrows moving across the maps of North Africa, Europe, and the Pacific in the successful operations during World War II, even that war has become retrospectively accessible in the public memory through key dramatic incidents—Pearl Harbor, D-day, Hiroshima. That the Germans were defeated "at Stalingrad" obscures somewhat that they were already in the process of defeat while still on the offensive. It obscures, too, that the great confrontation at Stalingrad was not followed by a total German collapse but by something closer to an intensifying erosion. So, too, Vietnam is grasped more in terms of incidents such as the assassination of Diem, the attack on the USS *Maddox,* or the Tet offensive of 1968. Even Tet is itself a sequence of events widely dispersed in place and extended over time—an event or a moment only by comparison with the far longer duration of the conflict as a whole. But the day-to-day grind on the ground and in the air becomes relatively incomprehensible precisely because it came to seem routine and normal—and because Americans simply fail to regard war and its conduct as customary or routine.[8]

The seeming peculiarity of war may have sharpened the tendency to confuse military with political assessments and to lose concreteness as to how, step by step, military undertakings would contribute to general resolution of a conflict. For, in the end, the character of war itself—both war generally and Vietnam specifically—was in dispute. If it was hard to envision a workable relationship among US efforts, so too there was difficulty in discerning the balance of political and military efforts set by the enemy. The plan for using US forces should reasonably have responded to the local circumstances in which they were to be employed; yet the most significant of those circumstances, including the character and scope of the war itself, proved elusive.

161

The many debates over the evolving nature of the Vietnam conflict reflect this contingency of performance upon vision. For example, in a memorandum for Deputy Secretary of Defense Roswell Gilpatric on 10 May 1961, Brig Gen Edward Lansdale, USAF, said the problem in Vietnam was a clear insurgency and urged that the armed forces contribute through psychological warfare and civic action. With the insurgents seen as an essentially indigenous force (even though supplied partly from outside South Vietnam), the ARVN and provincial forces thus needed training different from that suited to large-unit combined-arms action. So, too, the United States, as Saigon's ally, should assess how measures it might take to protect its forces would affect South Vietnamese politics. Lansdale warned, for example, that stationing US forces only at US bases in Thailand and elsewhere outside Vietnam would imply that the US commitment was aimed only at protecting its own resources. How forces might be deployed and used was thus affected by how the war was envisioned.[9]

Even when the war was seen as an insurgency, officials differed on what was needed to defeat it. This came to the surface in an exchange of memoranda in 1961 involving counterinsurgency specialist Robert Komer and State Department counsel George McGhee. In a draft paper, Komer emphasized the twin tasks of the military in counterguerrilla action as "organizing, equipping and training forces for the specialized task of applying force selectively to small and elusive bands" and taking protective measures well before serious problems arose. The desirability of such goals was clear, but accomplishing them seemed moot at best to policy planning staff members at state. In a brilliant twist turned by the mere placement of a hyphen, state's planners charged that US officials had speculated too freely on what was possible in low-intensity conflict situations. They had, it was said, "confused a limited war-capability with a limited-war capability." State's planners questioned whether small and elusive bands really could be tracked and neutralized. Experts at state also wondered, even if borders could be sealed, exactly what counterguerrilla action would be needed for a mere mop-up job. They cited the time needed to put down the relatively confined insurgency in Malaya (more than a decade) as cause to doubt Vietnam's future. As for a deterrent effect from injecting US forces into South Vietnam in large numbers, state's planners saw "not much reason for supposing the Communists would think our troops would be much more successful against guerrilla operations in South Viet-Nam than French troops were in North Viet-Nam." Although counterguerrilla actions required high discrimination, they wondered how foreign troops could show it "except by the direction in which they shoot." Ironically, McGeorge Bundy dismissed McGhee as a poor planner and cast doubt over state's concerns.[10] Whatever his abilities, however, McGhee showed great doubt that Americans could shape the war to suit their preferences.

Detectably irritated, Komer chided the policy planners at state and claimed that they had misunderstood. The insertion of what Komer called token US forces was only meant to signal our intentions to the other fellow and thus avoid committing larger numbers by deterring a really serious fracas. In any case, Komer noted, his own draft was not meant as a formal proposal but as a means of generating ideas and focusing thoughts. Yet state had not missed Komer's intention at all, nor his vision of what the conflict was like. State questioned his judgment that committing either a token force or even a much larger one would prove effective. Komer claimed that a token force would serve as a plate-glass window whose shattering would reveal North Vietnamese aggression to the world and thus justify a larger involvement by US or other allied forces. It seemed to be a Southeast Asian, sublimited warfare variant of the Central European trip-wire concept. The planners at state had not missed Komer's point; they doubted its merit.[11] Sending signals to a fight might have made sense if the fighting were not already under way, but it was. And precisely how would a US force—token or main—have to be deployed for the "window" to be more than a transparent bluff? To the extent that the problems within South Vietnam were local in origin rather than imported from the North, who was to say whether the plate glass was broken from one side or the other? And was this even a relevant question?

The interpretation of just what kind of war the one in Vietnam actually was went on. By the first quarter of 1964, it had reached the point where William Bundy asserted that "the Viet Cong operation has been a North Vietnamese show from the beginning" and played down any sense of Vietcong autonomy. This view of the war justified an increase in US efforts against Hanoi and its forces and also cast doubt retroactively on the whole counterinsurgency effort until that moment. At the same time, the US mission in Saigon warned that the ability of the United States to influence the actions of the South Vietnamese regime was so limited as to make "final success probably dependent more on developments external to Vietnam than on our counterinsurgency efforts here." Genuine counterinsurgency had obviously taken mortal blows; and the basic thrust in fighting the war had to be altered to suit the changing vision of the conflict.[12]

CIA reports on the regime that had replaced President Ngo Dinh Diem (the Military Revolutionary Committee) fueled doubt that Saigon could suppress the Vietcong. Reporting on discussions held in Saigon, CIA Director John A. McCone saw "more reason to doubt the future of the effort under the present programs" than to have hope. McCone's recital of deficiencies—too few border crossings by Saigon's operatives, too little harassing sabotage of the North Vietnamese, and related actions—suggested that counterinsurgency had meant all along more than countering the insurgents on one's own terrain. It also meant to hit the enemy on his terrain, imposing damage and taking measures much like his own. But the inexperience and weakness of the new regime in Saigon made it unlikely that such tasks could be undertaken, thus adding to the reconception of the war.[13]

Yet, in a sense, Vietnam had not yet been accepted as a real war at all. It was a situation, a crisis (notwithstanding at least seven years of US involvement by the time of John Kennedy's assassination in 1963), and a counterinsurgency. As a war, it was undeclared. It was, in a deeper sense, unrecognized as one, lacking some readily detectable start and lacking the emotional conciseness to make it comprehensible as an event. It was a process, receding into an obscure past and having no clear future other than the likelihood of its own continuation. And as a process, it had invited Walt Rostow to speculate, as early as 1961, that the victory which the United States sought would see no ticker-tape parades and would have no climactic battles, nor great American celebrations of victory. The US role was to be part of a revolutionary process that would make a Communist alternative to the existing regime especially unattractive, while helping the local government to extend security to its own population. The fighting might never be called off; it might simply subside and disappear in the indefinite future.[14] So Vietnam was a process of struggle, but not exactly a conventionally discrete military event. And what Saigon's armed strength needed, as a result, was a balance between paramilitary forces for internal security and regular units. Officials in state, defense, AID, the JCS, and the CIA agreed by 1964 that too little attention had gone to the former. "The 'hold' aspect of clear-and-hold has not been very successfully applied to date," Washington officials from state, defense, and AID cabled the embassy in Saigon. Yet, if William Bundy was right in seeing the Vietcong as mere pawns of Hanoi, then why was Saigon wrong in emphasizing main-force units which might deal with the larger operating units that were supposedly expected from either the Vietcong or North Vietnam? Reasonable answers to such a question were possible, but they were as unstable as the characterizations of the war themselves.[15]

The enemy's engagement of South Vietnamese forces with large units in sustained combat was correctly perceived, by General Westmoreland and others, as significant. Yet, in some ways, this too was either misconstrued or at least open to competing interpretations. Coming upon increasing Vietcong efforts to gain control in the countryside during 1964, the attack by the Vietcong's 9th Division with two regiments at Binh Gia did represent a shift in the protracted war against Saigon to the stage of mobile warfare. As Westmoreland suggested, the leadership in Hanoi (especially Vo Nguyen Giap) saw the action as "the beginning of the final phase of the war." Yet such a term, suggesting the climax and the prospect for obvious victory which Rostow had discounted years earlier, was misleading. Nothing in the thinking and writing about protracted war had ever precluded the return to opportunistic attacks and guerrilla activity, if mobile warfare proved premature. Nor did the ascent to mobile warfare deprive the enemy of using lower intensity options simultaneously, although not necessarily in the same place. If Binh Gia was the start of the final phase, could not a similar assessment have been made of Dien Bien Phu? The setbacks which Ho and Giap suffered at the Geneva Conference of 1954 hardly ended the process of conflict. Indeed, events gave more credence to the thought that to frustrate one final phase was merely to induce a new one when prospects were more opportune. That mobile warfare with main-force units was in the offing proved to be an accurate assessment. That it must be final and decisive in reasonably short order could have been no more than hopeful speculation.[16]

Although the advent of some new vision of the Vietnam conflict did not eradicate the memory of all that had preceded it, it altered the relative importance that could be accorded to the various undertakings of the US military and the relative worth of those undertakings. Seeing the Vietnam problem as more of a real war as it entered the presumably final stage let some US officials view continued US involvement as *more* likely of success than it had been in a time of insurgency. The approximations of 10 to 1 superiority in manpower deemed necessary to overcome insurgents were awesome. But more conventional engagements could surely be turned successfully with advantages far lower than that; and, in any case, firepower could offset local enemy superiority in many circumstances. Moreover, if only some relatively limited forms of air power had seemed specifically beneficial in Vietnam until then, the more visible and more highly prized resources—such as jet fighters and bombers—soon had a point of entry. For those who regarded these forms of air power as the real fighting edge of the Air Force and the sea forces, the war as a distinct event seemed about to begin. And Secretary Robert S. McNamara, justifying increased US troop deployments to Vietnam and the use of B-52 strikes against ''VC in their havens,'' lapsed into calling Saigon to renew its rural reconstruction effort *''following* destruction of VC main force units''* (emphasis added). Although McNamara's remark can be interpreted to mean *immediately* after a main force was destroyed in a specific province, it also exemplified rhetorically the ambiguity about the whole war. Counterinsurgency and rural redevelopment were by no means abandoned, but they had to compete with the more definable and hence more attractive prospect of a potentially decisive event. [17]

But in some quarters, the war after 1965 seemed no more satisfactory than what had come before it. Arguments over target lists, rules of engagement, route packages, or districts reserved for combat by various branches of the armed forces, and tactical air control—all suggested differences over the character of the war, and only derivatively over how to fight it. Thus it should have surprised no one that the Christmas bombing of Hanoi in Operation Linebacker II came to be regarded as the 11-day war, particularly among some strategic bombing enthusiasts. For such persons, the stages of the Vietnam conflict before December 1972 thus paled into unimportance and insignificance; and Linebacker II was the contemporary equivalent of the Battle of New Orleans—an event of ambiguous pertinence to the war, but an indispensable mythic force for reasserting long-held beliefs. [18]

The difficulty in determining what sort of war was occurring in Vietnam—of firming up its contours and sharpening its dimensions—was reflected in the later efforts to define it as history. Historians could not achieve a consensus on whether the war began with the French, with their departure in 1954, with the increasing US support of Diem in 1956 and the displacement of the elections called for under the Geneva accords, with the intensifying of local guerrilla action in South Vietnam in 1959, with the increase in US personnel in 1961, or with troop commitments in 1965. If specific events were to serve as guides, perhaps the Gulf of Tonkin incident provided one such significant moment, or the start of Rolling Thunder. And when did the war end? For some, the end meant the removal of US combat personnel; and 1973 served as a convenient date. For others, the end meant the collapse of the Thieu government in Saigon in 1975. For still others, for whom war was defined in terms of doctrinal and operational norms, other dates had more allure. For some of these, the war in Vietnam was, in essence, the air war that was undertaken in December 1973; all other efforts did not constitute true air power, since the assets employed were not organized according to true and traditional air power theory and doctrine. In such a view, air assets used in support of counterinsurgency had amounted to little but fumbling in the jungle. Under such an extreme view, the war had not really been attempted until very late in the game. Yet this beginning point was years after the American public had already concluded that the war had been going on altogether too long. And even as there are those who would see a traditionally conceived air war as the appropriate standard for Vietnam, so too are there those who would, in the words of an Army civilian historian Vincent H. Demma, "magnify the importance of the war as a large-unit, traditional conflict," thus underestimating the role of squadrons and platoons. This resulted partly from records being concentrated at the upper levels of command, giving a view from the top down. "But the Vietnam War was a war of smaller units and the individual soldier," Demma suggested in 1983. Those inclined to see the activities of small units as little more than reconnaissance and skirmishing might wonder if this was war at all.[19]

What air power in particular could do within the war in Southeast Asia necessarily hung in the balance of judgment over the meaning of war itself. Confusion came for one of many reasons. Perhaps it was the reluctance to define any combat as war in an era when war might include nuclear weapons. Or perhaps it was the lingering misconception that waging war without committing all one's resources was somehow a novel concoction of the modern age. Or perhaps it was something else. But the confusion over what war was and what it entailed put all planning in jeopardy, invited frustration in every undertaking, and gave no sufficient and shared standard for choosing among alternatives proposed by the military or by civilians. Absent a shared explanatory logic for the war's origins, contours, and dynamics, it lost discrete identity. Intellectually and emotionally unmanageable as an event, the Vietnam conflict became a tapestry of overlapping, competing, and contingent processes.

Limited War and Limited Commitment

In the aftermath of Hiroshima and Nagasaki, speculations about the next war centered on a massive commitment by the major powers to a World War III that promised even more ruin than had been visited in the conflict just completed. Much prediction in the United States suggested that the next war would be relatively brief, extraordinarily violent, and geographically extensive.[20] And as the cold war developed, high officials in the Truman administration projected that it would lead inevitably either toward a full-scale shooting war or else to a peaceful accommodation between the United States and the Soviet Union.[21] Against this emerging anticipation of full-scale and possibly nuclear war as the norm, any lesser level of conflict took on the aspect of peculiar and exotic restraint. In this context, the term limited war seemed a novelty of the nuclear age, as well as something of a self-contradiction. After a great world war that Eisenhower had called a crusade and that had unconditional surrender as its proclaimed objective,[22] limited war struck many as an absorbing eccentricity—critically important yet seemingly free of historic constraints.

The Vietnam War, like the Korean conflict, obviously fell into this subnuclear category. Despite the concern and interest expressed by governments around the world over action taken in Southeast Asia, the Vietnam War never attained anything like the level of international participation seen in World War II, or even in Korea. A limited war it was; but what were its limits? What did the very term limits really mean when applied to Vietnam and, more broadly, to warfare after Hiroshima? What overtones and undercurrents surrounded the concept of limited war, and how did these matters of perception affect the design of the war and the use of resources to prosecute it? Although full answers to these questions may never be within grasp, asking them is essential to gain more than a mechanistic sense of the sources of American conduct during the Vietnam War.

In actual practice, all wars have limits of some kind. The question is one of degree; and, rarely, the degree can be so intense as to constitute a difference in kind. Yet those cases are the distinct exception. Even the much mentioned unconditional surrender pursued in World War II proved to be only an approximation of Allied objectives, as the quiet guarantee of the personal security of the Japanese emperor illustrated; and, in any case, the grand objective was attained by the calculated use of measured resources. Particularly on the US side, the manipulation of human and material assets to achieve the greatest effect while doing the least damage to one's own society showed itself in such measures as the 90-division gamble through which US combat units were kept limited in number.[23] Thus, even if the object of the war can be called unlimited, the means for its prosecution cannot be. In addition, the avoidance of poison gas by both sides testifies to at least some shred of restraint in an exceptionally devastating and violent conflict. If some modicum of limitation may be found within the very war which fixed in America's and the world's mentality the notion of unrestrained violence as the norm in war, so do much greater limits show themselves in other conflicts. In some, civilians were at least less vulnerable, if not immune. In others, the maneuver of small professional forces nearly substituted for combat engagement. But the erasure from memory of this long history of warfare waged at every band along a spectrum of conflict cheated post–World War II Americans of the relevant context in which to appreciate what was happening to them and to understand at least somewhat better the implications of what they were doing.

The first essential is to ask for whom the war is a limited one and whether the parties to the war differ in their perceptions of the conflict. It is a painful irony that the Korean War should have popularized the term limited war, since it could hardly have seemed a half-hearted or restrained effort to the Koreans.[24] For the Koreans, either north or south of the line of partition, the conflict was a civil war pursued with passionate intensity. And the definition of a Korean state as well as the determination of Korean national identity were caught up among the stakes in the outcome. Although it is clearly desirable for any nation to take counsel of its own interests when determining its commitment to a war, it seems equally desirable— but far less common—to defer to the indigenous combatants when forming the primary construct for understanding the war. It may be necessary to see a conflict such as that in Korea essentially in a regional or global context to justify US involvement, but it is imperative to understand the local dynamics of the war if one wants to win battles and make them add up to the achievement of one's own goals.

The proposition that any government should appreciate the motivations and perceptions harbored by its adversaries seems nearly self-evident. Yet it has slipped out of favor, in practice if not rhetorically, during the cold war years and afterward—a casualty not only of simplistic anticommunism but also of academic abstraction. For all the brilliance and imagination that Raymond Aron showed in *The Century of Total War* (1954), for example, even he emphasized the contingency of local problems upon ever larger contexts of conflict.[25] Although this approach can be attributed to his emphasis on political more than military conceptualization, the effect was still to short-circuit the essential complementary question: How must the global confrontation be adjusted to accommodate imperatives inherent in local problems? Aron termed the cold war itself a limited war, not as to the stakes but as to the means employed by the belligerents. Yet here, too, the source of limits lay in the apprehensions of Washington and Moscow. Was it not conceivable that limits could be imposed by a less-powerful player on the global scene, even to the point where a party totally lacking global interests and aspirations might govern the terms of actual combat engagement? Here, also, the retrospective interpretation of the Korean War provided a damaging legacy. Critics of United Nations prosecution of the war alleged exaggerated concern over the possible behavior of China and the Soviet Union while various defenders suggested that the concern was not exaggerated. In a sense, both were beside the point. The first essential was not to know what the Soviet government had in mind but what Kim Il-sung wanted, then to identify the aspirations of Rhee, and only subsequently to mesh them with the goals of the United States and the United Nations.

Vietnam showed a diversity of limits—a diversity in conception of the war's scope and character—that significantly surpassed that in Korea. For a US serviceman in Southeast Asia, it was a one-year limited liability to danger and combat—limited in time, in role, in clarity of purpose, and often in commitment. For US-supported peoples such as the Montagnards, it meant a limited and contingent involvement with the regime in Saigon. For Australian troops, it represented an expression of cooperation with its old Pacific ally, the United States. For various factions in Saigon, the limits and the commitments ranged all across the board. In the end, it was Ho Chi Minh who refused to perceive the conflict as a limited war; and, in the end, perhaps only his judgment of the issue mattered.

Differences of perception about a war's limits are born of differences between the means and the objectives of conflict. This distinction, at least, has been at the bedrock of limited-war theory since World War II. Not surprisingly, the limitations under this construction are driven by assessments of national interest—sometimes disdainfully called political considerations—rather than by a more restrictively technical set of military calculations. Still, as long as the use of military forces is intended to be more than a mere display, a difficult interplay between the demands of political vision and those of operational craftsmanship almost necessarily develops. The size and character of forces committed may be established according to judgments of national interest. Yet it is simultaneously a technical question, more than a political one, whether the forces thus formed can operate successfully to the desired end. Historical experience offers few examples where either alternative has prevailed to the exclusion of the other; but striking an operationally successful balance is far from easy. At the same time, the perceptions of political planners and military operators can diverge to the extent that a specific involvement, once initiated, becomes ambivalent. Although intensely committed to victory in the cold war, the political leader may still regard a specific case immediately at issue as negotiable—even as an expendable means to an unswerving end. Those commissioned to undertake the specific intervention are far less prone to see the issue ambiguously.

The entry of the United States into a more direct role in the anti-Communist effort in Southeast Asia after the Geneva Conference of 1954 provoked an evaluation of US interests, commitment, and material contributions that illustrates the contingent quality of limits in a war. In the immediate aftermath of the conference, the Joint Chiefs estimated the force levels that South Vietnam would need to meet its foreseeable challenges, specifying an army of 234,000 men and an air force of 5,000 men with five aircraft squadrons as essential. The Office of the Chief of Naval Operations cautiously mentioned a figure of 1,400 naval personnel, increasing gradually to 3,000. These recommendations had hardly been made when the State Department, notwithstanding Secretary Dulles' reputation for anti-Communist ardor, lodged strenuous objections on 4 August 1954.[26] State called the JCS force levels excessive. More broadly, state desired to prepare a firm position on the forces that the United States regarded as the "minimum level to assure the internal security of Indochina." This action reflected a desire to set a maximum level for United States government support early and to keep the "maximum" low. As an administration pledged to avoid repeating Korea-type involvements, the Eisenhower team fully intended to encourage the maximum indigenous security forces through a minimum commitment of US personnel and resources.

The JCS responded promptly, dramatically scaling down from its previously stated essential minimum. The total was now a more modest 88,000 in all—a figure compatible with those suggested to Secretary Dulles by Gen J. Lawton Collins, former Army chief of staff and special United States representative in Vietnam with the rank of ambassador. The new JCS figures may thus have satisfied an institutional imperative to catch up with the military advice which the civilian authorities were soliciting outside the framework of JCS or, for that matter, outside the Department of Defense. But they did not satisfy President Diem, nor is it reasonable that they should have. The figures proposed by Collins and by the revised JCS plan meant a reduction in the South Vietnamese armed forces from the then current level of 170,000 down to less than 90,000. Moreover, this was to occur in the face of a present guerrilla threat and the possibility of outside attacks. Somewhat ironically, this reduction came at the same time that the common wisdom drawn from the British counterinsurgency effort in Malaya was suggesting the need for a government-to-insurgent ratio anywhere between 12 to 1 and 25 to 1.[27] It would be difficult to see in the force size set for South Vietnam anything other than the supremacy of US concerns about its own commitments and costs over the demands of the local conflict and its character. Limits to the involvement and to the war in Southeast Asia as it gradually developed came from internal US considerations, as well as from events on the scene; and their evolutionary quality made them especially difficult to envision clearly or firmly.

The appropriateness of the operational limits given to armed forces in a war, then, depends on the accuracy with which the problem and one's stake in the outcome are envisioned. To be sure, as George Herring has suggested, "assessing the ultimate costs of intervention at an early stage" is critical if one is to judge fairly the worth of the stakes against the aggregate cost of gambling for them."[28] Yet this is far easier said than done, especially because one's own involvement contributes to the continuous restructuring of the war itself. In an unpublished memoir, William Bundy reflected on his own problems, while deputy assistant secretary of defense, in grasping the Southeast Asian conflict as a whole—an awareness that came to him when he visited Vietnam in the fall of 1963 with Robert McNamara and Maxwell Taylor. "I became aware for the first time," he said, "how immensely diverse the war was in itself," leaving in question the adequacy of policies and perceptions developed during the preceding two and a half years of the Kennedy administration's stewardship of the US involvement. "I was left," Bundy added, "as I think Bob McNamara was, with a lasting skepticism of the ability of any man, however honest, to interpret accurately what was going on. It was just too diffuse, and too much that was critical took place below the surface."[29] How one was to assess the final cost of intervention, even from Bundy's vantage some nine years after Dulles and the Joint Chiefs of Staff attempted to stabilize the commitment, was especially unclear if no one could even get an accurate reading of the present conditions. How one could wisely employ the instruments of war without a clear picture of the war itself was similarly elusive. The problem in Southeast Asia was not that the war was fought within limits as much as it was the inability to determine firm criteria by which to stabilize them.

As Harry Summers has suggested, it is imperative to distinguish between the use of limited means in war and the compromising of one's commitment. Limiting violence is not the same as being limited in commitment.[30] Yet here, too, problems arose in Vietnam, as they might elsewhere. Expressions of full commitment by the Saigon government or by the administration in Washington could not ensure that both sides meant the same thing either by "full" or by "commitment." Even assuming that professions uttered by both sides were sincere, the terms were subject to interpretation, receding into the diffusion which puzzled William Bundy. Commitment can survive uncertainties when trust in the other side is strong. But if trust is weak when uncertainties are many, the commitment to one's ally may weaken sufficiently so that the real obligation is transferred, knowingly or not, to persistence in the military means themselves shorn of the premises that had fathered them. And if trust in what we are thinking fails, perhaps it, too, can be replaced by a greater fervor in whatever we currently happen to be doing.

The convolutions and complexities of military organization, pursuit of funding, distribution of roles and missions, and relative eminence of competing doctrines tend to be normal phenomena of the US forces in peacetime. But when Americans have agreed that they were at war with an external power, problems have often diminished or even at times dissipated. However, the Vietnam War lacked that fundamental agreement. Disillusionment and discontent prevailed in various civilian quarters; comparable problems existed within the military. Lacking a shared sense of the specific urgency of a war in process, or an agreed notion of what sort of war it was, it may have become inevitable for each party to reconceive the war in more limited terms—suited to the doctrinal familiarities of one's own subsection of the military, comfortable to one's own conditioned inclinations, and ultimately devoted to saving one's own institution from damage more than prosecuting the ill-defined and ambiguous larger war. The measure of success could thus become the degree to which one's own institution had weathered the vagaries of operations in Southeast Asia rather than what the effects of those operations had been in resolving the broader and deeper problems of that region. Although it clearly was not peace, it was not quite a war either—but something in-between.

Complexity and Simplicity

One of the classic formulations concerning war and its purpose has characterized war as the continuation of politics by other means. Yet, seen another way, the purpose of war (or at least its effect) is to transform a situation of intangible complexity into one of comparatively less complexity and subtlety.[31] At least in the short term and even though a new complexity must finally emerge, a war truly fails when it does not generate some measure of simplification. Moreover, this principle obtains overridingly in the political dimension; and it is not compromised by the appearance of exceptional complexity in military operations and technology, even when this actually intensifies during the course of the war. The relative stability of a political simplification, in this view of things, thus serves as a reference point against which other things may be determined. Without such a reduction from complexity, the risk of being left, to all appearances, with nothing but variables becomes deadly. With nothing but variables to go by, both purpose and coherence suffer.

The specific form of simplification accorded to the political complexities assumes relevance since the apparent importance, meaning, and value of military operations change according to the common and overriding considerations used to give direction to a war. Because of this link to specific military behavior, the simplification process needs to be concrete, even if it is not overly detailed. In the historical example of the US war with Mexico, the Polk administration had a standard against which to judge specific military performance—would it result in the reduction of the Mexican army? President James K. Polk had determined this concrete measure to be the key to bringing about negotiations that would result in the territorial transfers which were his political goals. At the same time, matters became clouded when disagreement arose as to how much territory was needed to achieve the desired political objectives. Whatever the difficulties experienced in the war, the concreteness and tangibility of the general military goal provided a means by which President Polk could guide himself while evaluating results. By the same token, political controversy sharpened precisely when the political goals to be reaped from military success temporarily lost that concreteness.

The Vietnam War lacked any concrete, comprehensible, and stable goal that could serve as such a common and overriding consideration. The objectives of the war fluctuated; when they were given expression, the rhetoric was often ambiguous. The US government voiced interest in a self-determined and relatively free society (or one which might have a potential for future freedom); yet specific administrations in South Vietnam became expendable, and regimes founded without popular support and without reference to democratic process gained recognition and aid. Variations and nuances of goals that ranged from the defeat of Hanoi's aspirations to unify Vietnam, through staving off collapse of one or another of the successive regimes in Saigon, to extricating US personnel from North and South Vietnam belied any stability in strategic intentions, especially of a political nature. Moreover, they jeopardized the development of a comprehensive strategy for prosecuting the war as a military enterprise.

One would be hard-pressed to find a war in which "common and overriding considerations"—the objectives of the war—were so lacking in concreteness and specificity. In major American wars such as the War for Independence, the Civil War, and World Wars I and II, the confusions and subtleties of the political discourse prior to the war yielded to a process of simplification upon entry into actual hostilities.[32] As to Vietnam, the political complications grew and multiplied.

Even in such wars as the US war with Mexico and the Spanish-American War, which were undertaken against significant vocal and organized opposition within the United States, there were counterbalancing, clarity, and continuity in the positions of the wars' key proponents. Such clarity and continuity were lacking in the Vietnam War.

Perhaps more than coincidentally, Vietnam was also the one US war that was presided over and tended to ("prosecuted" hardly seems to apply) by a series of presidential administrations with appreciably different political priorities, both at home and abroad. Even the Korean War was substantially determined before Eisenhower's installation as president, even allowing for his possible influence in the timing and final character of the armistice agreement. Vietnam was nobody's war in particular, fought according to no one party's particular conception or plan, and executed with no one authority assuming unqualified responsibility and accountability except for occasional excursions in rhetoric and metaphor. That South Vietnam must fall "not on our watch" thus serves as an apt, if regrettable, final cynicism.

The war that Vietnam in some ways most resembles politically, as an illustration of the ties between complex thought and confused action, is the War of 1812. The complexity of political aspirations, material interests, and potential liabilities helped to confuse the military operations undertaken to achieve them. As that war began, theoretically related but autonomous military campaigns launched by the United States foundered in an ocean of political confusion, including debate over the proper scope of presidential authority to command troops and to wage war. Only gradually, as defeat mounted upon defeat and after successful British punitive attack on various US targets, such as the burning of the capital city of Washington, did a political simplification emerge that sufficed to displace the complications of the war's origins. In the end, the mere fact of fighting the British made it a mythic second war for independence and gave the conflict something like coherent importance, meaning, and value. Admittedly, it was a process that did violence to the historic origins of the war itself, ran roughshod over genuine political and partisan differences, and was accomplished, in any case, only by the skin of our teeth. Yet the actual fighting gave a necessary, if brief, functional clarity to the enterprise. It even provided the basis for a subsequent mythology about the war that served to give it meaning in retrospect. Moreover, it gave a clearly visible object for military effort—the defeat of British forces and their forced withdrawal from US territory. To the early complexity of the War of 1812, Vietnam became similar. To its later simplification, it never did.

In the end, war is the reality of force; and the realities of political, economic, and social problems do not precisely match it. Even as military solutions cannot be said to resolve political problems in a fundamental sense, neither do political and other measures necessarily meet military difficulties and dangers. In the end, it may sometimes prove more useful to construe military measures not as attempted solutions to political problems but as an alternative to political discourse altogether.

173

In Vietnam, the process of simplification in search of clear purpose failed. At the same time, the combat operations of US and allied forces became increasingly diverse, complicated, and often intricate—largely to accomplish stopgap measures or to achieve short-term goals. As an official Air Force history has noted, for example, "U.S. air operations, supplemented more and more by those of the VNAF and RLAF, had grown infinitely complex with a great number and variety of missions, munitions, aircraft, and tactics."[33] This increase in the complexity of the fighting happened against a confusing and constantly evolving political context. It is not uncommon for operational complexity to develop during a war; but this tendency, when coupled with a diffusion of political objectives, can prove burdensome and lethal.

The course of behavior in Vietnam thus reflects nuances of intention distinctly different from those of other American wars. For, in Vietnam, what seemed to matter most was to manage the crisis and the war—a concept that may have contributed more to its longevity than to its resolution. Management contradicted urgency. What Jonathan Miller has said of the human body probably applies to social endeavors such as war as well: "Urgency reduces behavior to a simplicity which is comparable with that of our primitive ancestors."[34] By implication, that which does not become simple, at least in the realm of perceived problems and appropriate response, has not been interpreted as urgent. At best the mechanism of response breaks down so that an increasingly urgent situation generates reactions which seem questionable precisely because they are increasingly subtle. Moreover, as Miller observes, the issue is "not merely a question of simplification, but of the principles by which the simplification has been achieved."[35] Just as the most effective medicine has often derived from "the tactful reproduction of the living system's own . . . wisdom,"[36] so may the most effective remedies in urgent politico-military situations call upon the most basic approaches.

Simplicity is an established principle of war, but its practice is elusive. All seemingly simple actions may be analyzed and described with great complexity. The fallacy lies in confusing the manner of analysis performed after the fact, or the gaming done before it, with the appropriate manner of pursuing the act itself. Getting US prisoners out of Hanoi was urgent to a US president; preserving the principle of the unity of air power was urgent to the Air Force; and demonstrating the worth of armor and airmobility was urgent for the Army. But for whom, other than Hanoi, was comprehensive victory achieved by force in Vietnam the urgent issue beyond equal?[37]

And as the war in general lacked that impression of coherence born of simplicity, so did the use of air power within the war suffer from complexity of purpose and competition spawned by alternative visions of how air forces could be organized and employed. Nor was there any firm basis on which to declare one service's or one command's views as unjustified by the demands of the war, since the seeming requirements of the conflict remained in flux. That Vietnam saw spasmodic efforts should cause little surprise, and that direct participants lacked a full understanding of events is hardly peculiar. These qualities are born of war itself. The absence of a simplifying myth was what was distinctive and quite possibly far more devastating than any specific material failure.

Managing War and Waging Diplomacy

Many benefits were expected from military action, but the actual material damage and physical effect of combat operations did not receive either earliest or greatest priority. This damaged the coherence of the American effort in Vietnam. Although critics said that Lyndon Johnson misconstrued Vietnam and sought to force a military solution on a political problem, a more accurate view is that he applied political tests to everything. Yet he lacked assurance that the actions he authorized produced the concrete military results from which political and psychological impact was expected. Even more, to the extent that merely performing a military mission was supposed to be politically significant even apart from its material effects, military operations were transformed into abstractions. Therein lay a genuine problem. The complaint, often made by the military, that Vietnam was handled "too politically" is at best too vague. All wars are handled politically in some respects, as the reasoning over use of the atomic bomb and the selection of Hiroshima and Nagasaki as targets remind us. The danger flows from equating military and political considerations, from inferring political impact from military undertakings whose concrete effects are no more than putative, and from slighting the operational distinctions between crisis management and warfighting. The problems the United States encountered in Vietnam were nurtured by the imposition of managerial instincts upon warfare at the same time that an inclination to use force in diplomacy was in the ascendant.

The confusion of Vietnam revolved, ultimately, around a core of altered preconceptions about military capabilities and the character of war, although these surely worked reciprocally with such detrimental forces as interservice rivalry. Within that core of novel beliefs were the presumption of a need for ever closer civilian control, the transformation in what was accepted as a "normal" war such that violence on the scale of Korea was construed as "limited" and implicitly abnormal, and the related suspicion that historically rooted notions about military strategy and tactics had been made obsolete by nuclear and other modern technology. One of the most noted of limited war theorists, Robert Osgood, described war as "an upper extremity of a whole scale of international conflict" and asserted that "no definition can determine precisely at what point on the scale conflict becomes 'war'."[38] In a stinging critique, Stephen Peter Rosen pointed to a consequence of this approach: "War, as such, did not deserve study, Osgood thought, because war was like peace, only more so." What appeared to be simple common sense was overturned; and the understandable proposition that war must serve political policy was transformed to suggest that war, since it lacked definitive boundaries, also lacked what Clausewitz called its own "grammar."[39] A cliché suggests that there is an inexorable tendency to envision the next war largely in terms of the last one. Yet, in the years after Hiroshima and Nagasaki, a shared vision of the next war became difficult to stabilize; and, with it, the likelihood of common commitment to the war effort diminished. How much chance of common effort was there if parties could not agree to what war was and when it was happening?

The instinct toward having close civilian involvement in the design, oversight, and execution of military action in Vietnam and elsewhere owed much to a widespread sense that special demands were imposed by the circumstances of the post–World War II world. Although civilian authority over the military has always been a zealously guarded national tradition, the more active international role of the United States in an era when aviation and nuclear technology had expanded military potential led to a degree of concern over governance of the armed forces that encouraged new kinds of control.[40] Aberrational measures such as the peacetime draft came to be regarded as normal, and the definition of a small or modestly sized peacetime force gradually enlarged relative to previous historical experience. Meanwhile, conflict retained the global connotations that were fresh from World War II and which were strengthened by the intensifying hostility between the United States and the USSR. Particular cases became components in a worldwide struggle, and the importance of each case escalated because it was tied to global stakes, entailing such risks as ideological extinction and physical destruction. This combination of a sweeping apprehension of worldwide danger and traditional American instincts about civil-military relations ultimately supported a series of managerial aspirations that, in turn, would affect when, why, and how the United States would wage war.

On the one hand, nuclear weapons invited a reexamination of distinctions between combatants and noncombatants, eventually spawning a profusion of strategic notions about the potential usefulness of targeting installations traditionally regarded as civilian. At the same time, since the military and civilian threads were thus seamlessly interwoven, special means were taken to guarantee the traditional primacy of the civilians over the military. If the military were not to exert control over the civilians in a world in which military and civilian spheres were inextricably intertwined, then the military could not exert control over the military sphere either—certainly not without adequate civilian supervision. Such an approach to the management of force was seen as justified by the hideous exigencies of the nuclear age in which, as the logic went, one false step could swiftly escalate into the incineration of the earth and the extinction of humankind.

For all its many excesses, the Vietnam War encourages reconsideration of this overriding proposition of the post–World War II era. For one thing, perhaps escalation is not inevitable simply because it is conceivable. Excesses of a subordinate may not necessarily frustrate the general policy and political options of superior civilian authorities, as the unauthorized air strikes by Gen John Lavelle indicate. So, too, even questionable undertakings do not necessarily induce further escalation, even if they themselves are regarded as extensions of war, as the secret bombing of Cambodia under President Nixon suggests. Whatever the merits or even the enormities of any such cases, the consequences to the immediate and final political denouements in Southeast Asia seem limited—perhaps even negligible. Even greater freedom of action may be possible as long as the ultimate nuclear gamble is not being played, and perhaps genuine authority can be delegated to those to whom significant responsibilities are assigned. Reexamination of this issue would seem especially justified by the likelihood that future wars will fall far short of the worst-case scenarios of nuclear exchange or full-scale conventional force commitment, possibly calling for dispersed simultaneous action and appreciable autonomy of operation. In these respects, Vietnam suggests that error in the field need not equal doom for the world and that the damage caused by reducing centralized control must now be gauged against the damage caused by exerting it.[41]

Even if one sees delegating authority as more problematic, the experience in Southeast Asia richly illustrates the pitfalls of rejecting the "grammar" of war in favor of the political idiom. Actions do not have automatic political meanings— their specific political significance often, perhaps always, arises from the special circumstances in which they take place. To this extent culturally determined then, political effects and the military procedures for attaining them must be viewed from the vantage of the party to be affected. In Vietnam, for example, what might the enemy have done if he had possessed the military power available to the United States. Such a hypothetical scenario, which could be explored at least through inference, might have discouraged the United States from pursuing a program of measured and graduated response in which military undertakings were intended primarily as political displays. Instead of conveying a sense of resolve, such responses may have hinted at the opposite, suggesting that the US government lacked heart for the war and that Hanoi should probe the limits of US commitment. In the end, this conclusion neared the truth more closely than did the US government's belief that Hanoi would yield to graduated pressure.

This does not mean that the United States must rush to use maximum force in a future conflict. Nor does it require acting as we believe would typify our enemy. But it does mean that the United States should avoid projecting its own reactions to pressure onto an adversary. Things look different depending on context. A lobster is a staple of the sea in Maine, a delicacy inland, and an unsettlingly large scorpion to a traditionalist Navajo. Things derive much of what they are—derive their effective identity—from their contexts and from human expectations.[42]

It is possible, then, that precisely *how* one makes war is, in essence, what delivers the message of political intent as much as the concrete actions undertaken. The *how* in the use of force, after all, changes its impact. Since force is itself relative, it derives its real meaning and possible value from the context in which it is applied. Optimized projections of the capabilities of one's forces must defer to real-world assessments of their limits. So, too, in managing the armed forces, real operational requirements might be given greater priority than they have had against the theorizing and abstraction that have intensified in the post–World War II era. The political and the military are intertwined in the United States, and the military sphere serves the political. But neither control over the military nor control exerted by the military can be an appropriate terminal objective or central fixation. The issue is performance, and its criteria lie in specific contexts. Military force in general and US military institutions in particular constitute one such context; and they cry for attention since they traditionally foster the expertise in how, technically, force can be applied. Yet, in Vietnam, this arrangement was not always so. For example, ingenuity was shown in adapting weapons and tactics to new, varied, and sometimes unexpected political purposes. Yet there was also much to be said against it militarily, and the delay in achieving over-optimistic military goals raised political doubts and difficulties of its own.

Although war is an effort to impose one's will on an opponent, the military aspects of the confrontation necessarily entail much adaptation to conditions that are not under one's own control, including environmental and cultural factors and extending to the enemy's mentality and way of war. So, as Rosen has pointed out, the ''general problem of limited war is not only the *diplomatic* one of how to signal our resolve to our enemy, but the *military* one of how to adapt, quickly and successfully, to the peculiar and unfamiliar *battlefield* conditions in which our forces are fighting'' (Rosen's emphasis).[43] Diplomatic success is unlikely to occur unless military success preconditions it, partly because resolve cannot survive repeated failure, but also because the absence of success in combat is likely to strengthen the political hand of one's enemy. This point sharpens the irony of Walt Rostow's complaint to Defense Secretary McNamara in November 1964 that ''too much thought is being given to the actual damage we do in the North, not enough to the signal we wish to send''—this after years during which what the Joint Chiefs called a protracted series of messages had been the primary consideration.[44] By behaving true to form, the US government could do little but reinforce the impression that had previously persuaded the regime in Hanoi to continue its effort against the Saigon government despite the involvement of Washington. At the same time, the failure to distinguish more clearly between military and political dimensions largely precluded the delegation of authority to operators in the field, or at the very least circumscribed it in ways that could prove debilitating.

This discrepancy between political conceptualization and military performance showed itself often, as in the search for a coherent and effective bombing policy for the various regions of Southeast Asia. Divergent purposes coexisted uneasily. Among them were changing the sentiment in Hanoi to reduce support for the Vietcong, actually interdicting the flow of supplies from north to south, and diminishing the effectiveness of North Vietnamese army main-force units. How to perform military operations had to depend on what purposes were sought and what means were available, yet these latter suffered from instability and imprecision. The focus on the specific results of using force was not sharp at the highest policy-formation levels, where concern for intentions, attitude, and will increasingly guided assessment. Unfortunately for the purposes of those who conceived it, the reliance on bombing to produce a change in enemy attitude that would benefit ground combat conditions in South Vietnam foundered. Not only was the use of more raids and more tonnage uncertain but picking targets was also an act of war as politics. On 2 April 1965 as President Johnson was contemplating a gradual increase in bombing of the North simultaneous with substantial increases in US ground forces, CIA Director John McCone predicted, with considerable accuracy, where this course could lead:

> I have reported that the strikes to date have not caused a change in the North Vietnamese policy of directing Viet Cong insurgency, infiltrating cadres and supplying material. If anything, the strikes to date have hardened their attitude.
>
> With the passage of each day and week we can expect increasing pressure to stop the bombing will come from various elements of the American public, from the press, the United Nations and world opinion. Therefore time will run against us in this operation and I think the North Vietnamese are counting on this.
>
> What we are doing is starting on a track which involves ground operations which in all probability will have limited effectiveness against guerrillas, although admittedly will restrain some Viet Cong advances. However, we can expect requirements for an ever-increasing commitment of US personnel without materially improving the chances of victory.
>
> In effect, we will find ourselves mired down in combat in the jungle in a military effort that we cannot win and from which we will have extreme difficulty extracting ourselves.[45]

McCone's comments showed the danger of seeking too much political result from military operations. When military actions are viewed as political gestures, their specific military effects may come to seem unimportant. If the mere execution of a gesture seemed to be the criterion for its effectiveness, long-term effects spawning confusion in the war and controversy at home could be overlooked until it was too late.

And so when it came time to determine the proper use of air power to support the ground war in Vietnam, there was no satisfactory framework through which to build a genuine common effort. Instead, there were divergent views and preferences, tied to differing doctrinal positions, themselves rooted in alternative interpretations of history and varying visions of war. Meanwhile, the chances of turning military action into political victory would not automatically brighten as the burdens of the war accumulated. Increases in the cost of the war may have underscored the need for better strategy. But they could not ensure that a new strategy would be adopted. Clearly, the loss of life mattered, as did suffering wounds and permanent disabilities. Loss of aircraft and materiel mattered, as did the related impact on government expenditures and their inflationary pressure on the domestic economy. But the benefits of activities in Vietnam remained a realm of hypothesis and speculation, projected at the grand psychopolitical level. Benefits were intangible even when adorned with maps showing zones supposedly under Saigon's control according to percentage of influence. Yet the crucial intermediate material objectives received less weighty consideration, suffering from inaccuracy even when they were given attention. And when concrete and distinctly military effects did receive notice, their worth could scarcely be calculated effectively since criteria continued to change. Without stable objectives and pertinent criteria, cost-benefit assessments became listings of manifest costs and unpersuasive claims of unproven benefit.[46]

Between Rigidity and Vacillation

In the quest for clarity in Vietnam, one might have supposed that military doctrine would serve as a worthy guide. Yet military doctrine itself was fragmented among the services and within each force. Even though a list of principles of warfare can be agreed upon, the meaning given to them often remains in dispute. Without a firm and overriding concrete objective in a specific conflict, standards for choosing among doctrinal alternatives become especially hard to discern. In Vietnam, this left the US armed services in perpetual competition, each all but inevitably driven to an unqualified faith in its own views.

Doctrine should synthesize the lessons of experience. But when doctrine becomes impervious to experience, it degenerates into dogma and courts disaster. Yet doctrine that changes with the slightest shift of the wind is at best irrelevant and at worst ruinous. The challenge is to find the special place between rigidity and vacillation where doctrine guides one through experience without warping it to suit preconceptions. As the variables given importance during the conflict in Southeast Asia became more numerous, that special place became obscured; and a fair mix of pertinent external standards against which to gauge the continuing appropriateness of existing doctrine became excessively difficult to determine. Absent some coherent and tangible set of external referents with which doctrine might be seen as reciprocal, doctrine itself could be cut loose from experience to temporarily exert a merely dogmatic claim to faith and loyal practice.[47]

Under pressure from other military agencies and from civilian authorities, each service was pressed to use its assets in ways for which they had not been conceived. This may have heartened those who feared rigidity within the military. But it also meant a splintering of strength—either because of diffusion of the potential of air power or because of the widening gulf between doctrine and the overall war policy. Not having prepared for something quite like Vietnam, it became easier for the services to see virtually any military measure as the wrong thing to do.

Determining the right thing to do necessarily includes a cultural component as well as technical ones. Doctrine, strategy, and practice are all affected by this broadly ideological factor, no matter how unconsciously it works its effects. Few characteristics attributed to air power are actually properties inherent in it in any absolute sense. Choices about what aircraft and weapons to build determine what is inherent in hardware. But what about how the hardware is used? Beyond the "ability to do something in the air," implying some platform that gives the combatant at least a limited "sustained" presence above the ground, agreement on what air power is rapidly deteriorates. What inherent property of air power determines the priority to be accorded strategic bombing, close air support, airlift, and other functions? What inherent characteristic even dictates "unity of command and control," especially over actual day-to-day operations? Such determinations reflect interpretations of experience, ingrained expectations, and accommodations to outside pressure. The uses of air power thus do not flow from an absolute or an abstraction but from cultural and political understandings of the potential of air power.

One's own way of war thus does much to shape the employment of air power, and no assessment of air power can truly be neutral and isolated from political and cultural factors. What air power consists of in any practical sense—what forces are in being, what technologies are developed—is driven by whatever may be embedded in the thinking of a nation or its leaders. But weaponry itself is no abstraction, nor is it the result of some scientific neutrality. Those who believed that the machine gun would reduce death on the battlefield by reducing the number of men required to generate a fixed amount of firepower did not mistake the machine gun's inherent mechanical properties. They erred in judging the mentality of those who brought the machine gun into their tactical and strategic planning. Giulio Douhet did not err with respect to the inherent properties of air power when he predicted that a bombing assault on cities would cause a rapid change in the enemy's policy. He mistook the character of the populace in the mass nation-state, their capacity to absorb punishment, and their leaders' persistence in letting them do so. In the much more recent past, similarly, human determinants have persisted in the face of seemingly antagonistic technical ones. Technical considerations produce options; human choice determines specifically what will be done.

These considerations elevate doctrine to a level of pressing importance—specifically, the establishment of real agreement among the services on doctrinal issues of common interest. Memoranda and letters that actually paper over disagreements do little to prepare the services to cooperate effectively in the event of war. Even in wars where the stakes were manifestly great, as in World War II, doctrinal disagreements have continued, inspiring the various strategic alternatives presented. Thus, the absence of doctrinal consensus or compromise may continue even in the face of clear and present danger. On the other hand, fragmented and competing views have so complicated military activities since World War II that minimizing the negative impact seems justified. Fragmented vision and apparent overemphasis on service interests led former Deputy Secretary of Defense Roswell Gilpatric to suggest, in March 1964, that the Joint Chiefs of Staff be removed from the chain of military command. "Too often," he wrote in an article for the *New York Times*, "in critical conflict situations, the president and his other policy advisers are confronted with a fractured military position reflecting divergent service positions rather than differing military judgments."[48] Gilpatric believed that the advice offered by the JCS lacked range and depth, partly because competition among the services trivialized whatever the JCS could agree to. Gilpatric discussed a new approach in which military advice would come from personnel of the president's own choosing on a case-by-case basis. Such was a symptomatic reaction to competition among the services on doctrine and strategy. Gilpatric's kind of proposal gave a narrowly institutional reason for the services to reduce the problems in the existing system. Even more, there was also a war at stake, however disdainfully one was inclined to view it. Whose doctrinal and strategic views ought to prevail could presumably be tested in Vietnam. But Vietnam still sometimes became the arena for a shoot-out between the services rather than for a wholehearted experiment in cooperation.

In the Vietnam War, doctrinal differences did not mean absolute failure in conducting the war. However, they definitely added to confusion and tensions, added to costs (possibly in lives as well as dollars), and lengthened the war thereby playing into the general strategic approach of the enemy. Doctrines matter. And they matter enough to demand resolution in peacetime if their wartime impact is to be lessened.

Agreement on doctrine—on the guiding thought for the war's conduct—could not be achieved either before or during the Vietnam conflict unless civilian authorities clearly indicated what kinds of fighting they would seriously consider, shared that vision with the military services, and insisted upon dedicated effort on their part to prepare for the possibilities sanctioned by policymakers. But since the general vision of the war remained unstable, the employment of air power eluded assessment on a common ground. In mid-1964, for example, when Maxwell Taylor favored air operations against infiltration routes, Secretary McNamara was reported in strong and consistent opposition. In a memorandum to the president on 13 August 1964, McGeorge Bundy implied that Taylor's interest in various proposals stemmed from their likely political or psychological effects. One example was the authorization of DeSoto patrols. South Vietnamese commandos would run raids against the North, and US ships would monitor the North Vietnamese response by means of electronic equipment on board. But Bundy was not altogether fair to Taylor, who gave much attention to the practical benefit of military actions. If the determinant of the proper course of action were to be psychological impact on North Vietnam, one set of standards might apply. But if the goal were to impact on the war in South Vietnam and near border areas, then a different kind of criterion might come forward.[49]

Nuances of difference in justifying various uses of air power suggested inconsistency beneath the surface. In his 1968 report, General Westmoreland claimed that the ''objective of the air strikes [against North Vietnamese targets] was to cause the government of North Vietnam to cease its support and direction of the insurgencies in South Vietnam and Laos.''[50] At the same time, Walt Rostow spoke of the effort as a kind of tax imposed on the North Vietnamese, which might make Hanoi see the war's costs but would not directly end its activities in the South.

Army Chief of Staff Harold Johnson told the Preparedness Investigating Subcommittee of the Senate Committee on Armed Services that the material benefits of bombing the North would come primarily in strengthening the morale of ground combat units in the South, both US and ARVN.[51] He further estimated that nearly 100,000 North Vietnamese were engaged full time in coping with the effects of the bombing, with another 370,000 to 500,000 involved on a part-time basis.[52] Thus, three important personalities described the primary thrust of the air war in the North in ways that were not mutually exclusive but were substantially different. Not only was there disagreement on what effects the air war might have, but also over what it was authorized for and intended to do.

Although some problems resulted from asking air forces to do the wrong thing, other problems came from insufficient preparation to do the right ones. Since no purely technical standard can determine right and wrong military behavior, judgment depends on what the war was conceived to do. To the extent that any military doctrine adequately deals with both the technical and the political requirements, it too may be construed as right in the sense that it helps to accomplish steps to the desired end. But if doctrine mistakes the balance between the technical military culture and the evolving political culture, it risks seeming irrelevant. Absolute doctrine can be rejected absolutely. It is true that in times of challenge people commonly recommit themselves to their own special institutional culture.[53] Yet, in a war such as Vietnam, challenges came to various institutions in different ways. For one, the pressing importance given certain issues by Air Force leaders was not fully appreciated by some of their civilian superiors. Without a comparable sense of urgency, civilian leaders could sometimes view insistence upon certain traditional concerns as simply self-serving and pigheaded.

Even for those who would agree that "air power shapes the character of modern warfare," there is much to determine in what that statement means concretely. On one extreme, it may mean that air power—or perhaps, even more, the ability to act without being interfered with from the air—is indispensable for operations across the full spectrum of conflict. On the other extreme, however, it may suggest that air power can actually govern the character of specific wars. Unless delivery of ordnance through the air exhaustively constitutes the war itself, as might be envisioned theoretically in a thermonuclear spasm war, the mechanism of governance through which air power could do this is hard to pinpoint. Air power has distinctly expanded the range of what is possible; but it has by no means settled the question of which of these things are necessary, useful, or desirable. That answer begs for doctrine which integrates technical military considerations with the real world political context in the best and highest sense of the term.

Long-standing traditions among air power enthusiasts have emphasized the importance of command of the air or air superiority coupled with an autonomous bombing offensive. The bet has often been rhetorically hedged. But this approach has an implicit psychological dimension as well as an immediate military one. Ever since Douhet, there has been an undercurrent of hope to change the enemy's policy, apart from fully incapacitating that enemy. This tends to mean waging war at relatively higher levels of technology. War against a society with a well-developed infrastructure thus seems reasonable. But it is less clear what effect air power will have at progressively less sophisticated levels. In the specific case of Vietnam, air power—and doctrines for using it—played against both infrastructural sophistication and enemy will. But assessing infrastructure and will was a matter of political judgment, complicated by psychological dimensions, as well as technical ones. At its worst, the inability to pindown the psychological factor tended to enhance the prominence of the technical side—in delivering an attack on an enemy target, there was at least the knowledge that it had been done, even if its effects were unclear. Just as some critics saw Vietnam as a problem without a solution, exponents who gave extreme interpretation to the potential of air power to change the course and outcome of the war risked turning air power into a solution without a relevant problem.[54]

That an autonomous air operation was in fact the relevant solution, however, has been restated, and the lineage of ideas born in the 1920s has been preserved. Most representative is the interpretation of Linebacker II operations over Hanoi in December 1972 as "the decisive factor leading to the peace agreement of 15 January 1973." Henry Kissinger's comment that Linebacker II probably encouraged the North Vietnamese to agree to terms strengthened this interpretation of the bombing.[55] As Gen William Momyer has argued, "the concentrated application of airpower produced the disruption, shock, and disorganization that can be realized only by compressing the attack and striking at the heart with virtually no restraints on military targets which influence the enemy's will to fight."[56] In a limited sense, even this leaves unclear how to determine which targets are best seen as military and which genuinely influence the enemy's will. The one uncompromising stance is for a *concentrated* attack—in other words, a technical military statement as to the appropriate mode of conducting a strategic operation. In an even broader sense, however, the question of whether Linebacker II actually produced the effects claimed for it is far from closed. As Gareth Porter has suggested, internal considerations in North Vietnam affected the Hanoi government's behavior; and a single-causal explanation of the peace agreement falters.[57] Beyond that, Daniel S. Papp has raised questions about the substance of what was agreed to, concluding that the difference in the terms discussed before and after the Christmas bombing was not commensurate with the magnitude of the operation. In this view, though not an absolute bust, Linebacker II was a remarkably large bang for what it actually contributed to the outcome at Paris.[58]

In essence, recurrent expressions of faith in autonomous or strategic air action imply a particular interpretation of the notion that air power has inherent flexibility, one suggesting that the forces capable of deterring or waging war at a high level will enable one to deter or wage war at lower levels. Air power may have the potential to affect all warfare. But is it a unitary air power that does this or is it a system of rather specific subsets? To say that air power has inherent flexibility cannot mean that any one manifestation of air power has great flexibility; and the efforts to build more diversity into a single aircraft by adding hardware to multiply its missions are often criticized as fundamentally wrongheaded and counterproductive.[59] Perhaps air power can affect all things—but not all at once, and not by the same means.

Vietnam should encourage some measure of reflection rather than an abrupt reaffirmation of preexisting doctrinal notions. For one can point to difficulties in the war whose origins were, in the end, doctrinal rather than political and which came largely from internal dynamics within the air power community rather than from outside. One well-known problem was the deficiency in conventional ordnance available for use in the Vietnam War—a circumstance related to which military threats had been given priority and how wars had been expected to be fought. The needs that appeared in Vietnam had often lacked persuasive attraction before the 1960s, and technical shortcomings were not surprising.

One of the cautions suggested by Vietnam, then, is to distinguish between preparing for wars that are likely to occur and concentrating on the most dangerous possible war. The impact of such a war would clearly be great, but its likelihood is widely regarded as low. Obviously, such a responsibility demands attention. But a nation can be nibbled away, too. Air assets vary in effect. The defense of Khe Sanh implied that air power could be used in diverse ways in a single location and, most of all, that air power could be saved from a doomed submission to an escalatory imperative. In other cases, including the Son Tay raid, various forms of air power showed their worth as tools, whatever the shortcomings of the raid as executed; and the raid testified, too, that air power could be used with efficiency at a deliberately contained level of violence and force. The inexorable need to do something specifically within Vietnam, sooner or later, required thinking about how air power could be tailored to limited-conflict scenarios. There is little cause to expect otherwise in the future.

At the same time, the conduct of warfare may be the student of doctrine but not its slave. We need to know if in Vietnam technical and doctrinal issues approached preeminence as the object of war even more than as its means. And, in the aftermath, what lessons are to be made of past events when services continue to hold diverse views on the broad issues? In this process of putting a meaning on past events, the isolation of some specific definition for the war has been crucial— whether it is an 11-day war of Linebacker II or a conventional warfare encounter between North Vietnam and the United States. Will it be possible to achieve clarity in understanding the war? Will it be possible to separate what happened in Vietnam from preconceptions of what ought to have happened, as the pursuit of clarity requires?

The Illusion of Neutrality

The war in Vietnam and the use of air power within it were driven substantially by various assumptions sometimes so deeply ingrained in Americans that they were all but unaware of their presence. As Bruce Miroff has suggested of the Kennedy administration, the "wizards of fact" and " 'tough-minded' operationalists" were amply augmented by "ideologists and theoreticians," including Walt Rostow and Maxwell Taylor. Neither Kennedy nor his advisers would have accepted the denomination; but, as Miroff adds, "*their* abstractions were couched in a 'hard' social science language," and at the same time they were sufficiently close to conventional wisdom in the United States that they "escaped the pragmatic censure which so often fell upon the Administration's critics." It was, Miroff suggests, less that the US officials were either genuinely scientific or pragmatic than that they were able to seem so to themselves and to others.[60] Even more, however, one must question whether their wizardry extended over actual facts or only over pretenders. Challenges against the administration's expertise often centered on how they used supposed historical facts, as in Secretary of State Dean Rusk's frequent linkage of 1960s antiwar activism with 1930s appeasement of Hitler. Ho may not have been the best friend of US interests, but Ho was not Hitler, and Rusk knew it. "I am not the village idiot," he is said to have exclaimed in irritation.[61] Still, advancing such comparisons encouraged doubt over which facts were pertinent—and which facts were really facts at all.

Not every bit of information is a fact; that is, an accomplished event which is formally knowable. So it is possible to develop a considerable base of data whose pertinence is unstable. Even if they are construed as bits of information, moreover, data need not constitute intelligence in any usable sense. Intelligence depends on the vision of how those data should be organized—on the human preconceptions, ideologies, and concerns that are too easily and quite falsely dismissed as mere bias. In fact, this vision is the naturally generated human software without which the supposed facts give nothing but parody of scientific methods. As Miroff has warned, however, "while the measurable and the tangible were avidly gathered up by Kennedy and his associates, the underlying, unquantifiable social reality continually eluded their grasp." Political commentator James Reston once attempted to engage Kennedy in discussion of his vision or design for the broad future of American society. "He looked at me," Reston recalled, "as if I were a dreaming child. . . . It was only when I turned the question to immediate, tangible problems that he seized the point and rolled off a torrent of statistics."[62] As anthropologist Earnest Albert Hooten pointed out decades ago, however, "the existence of intangibles must not be denied because a rudimentary science cannot measure them. . . . A single well-considered opinion may be worth a whole array of trivial facts."[63] Absent vision, facts are necessarily cheapened and trivialized; for their meaning depends upon relationships. And familiarity with data is thus not equal to understanding. McNamara was awesome in his command of facts, as, apparently, was Kennedy. But this skill did not enable the defense secretary to act effectively because the talent did not guarantee that he comprehended truly the situation in Southeast Asia—or in the United States.

In Vietnam, behavior was the hostage of vision, but the line between vision and illusion was thin. The need was for a vision that encompassed the available aspects of the problem at hand—the evident facts of the matter. The illusion stemmed from an assumption that facts were ideologically, politically, and ethically neutral. The persistence of Hanoi and its resilience as well, owed nothing to irrational defiance of facts and owed everything to consistency, born of ideological self-consciousness and enabling the North Vietnamese to give retrospective meaning to all that was happening. Unlike Washington, Hanoi thus largely avoided what commentators in another area of inquiry have called "the anguish of defeat that shatters the spirit rather than the physical pain that destroys the flesh."[64] The pain which *they* suffered was made to make sense for them.

If, as Drew Middleton has cautioned, "no power ever learns from another's defeat," one may still hope that it is possible to learn from one's own trials and failings.[65] In the process, these lessons can include many practical and specific remedies to ailments that revealed themselves in Southeast Asia. Yet many of these more limited prescriptions have already been written. To repeat them incessantly may lead to doubt that Vietnam continues to matter as it is succeeded by more recent events and their challenges. Ultimately, the potential of air power for impact on ground combat can neither be fully known nor fully realized without also knowing the impact of American mentality about the uses of air power, whether in Vietnam or elsewhere. In the end, then, the enduring pertinence of the Vietnam conflict rests not in what it says about Asia, nor in what it prescribes about combat technique and preparedness, but in what it says about ourselves.

NOTES

1. Judith Coburn, "Losing Vietnam," *Mother Jones* 8, no. 9 (November 1983): 21.

2. Roger Hilsman, interview on the "Today" program, National Broadcasting Corporation, 2 November 1983.

3. Among the most heralded interpretations of the Vietnam experience which tends to adopt this view is Harry Summers, *On Strategy: The Vietnam War in Context* (Carlisle Barracks, Pa.: Strategic Studies Insititute, US Army War College, 1981).

4. The paragraph draws on Morris Janowitz, *The Military in the Political Development of New Nations* (Chicago: University of Chicago Press, 1964). Janowitz points out that the early role of the armed forces in South Vietnam was just to show that the newly declared state had genuine national sovereignty, simply by having armed forces suited to a sovereign state.

5. Quoted in Robert Frank Futrell, *Ideas, Concepts, Doctrine: A History of Basic Thinking in the United States Air Force 1907–1964* (Maxwell AFB, Ala.: Air University, 1971), 166.

6. Richard Reeves, "Why Howard Baker Is Leaving the Senate," *Parade*, 7 August 1983, 10.

7. Although the emphasis on American identity as process is to be found widely in the literature of the nation's culture, see especially John Kouwenhoven, *The Arts in Modern American Civilization* (New York: Norton, 1967). The emphasis on war as an abrupt upheaval may be found in Frederic C. Jaher, *Doubters and Dissenters: Cataclysmic Thought in America, 1885–1918* (London: Free Press of Glencoe, 1964).

The phrase "American way of life" is customarily assumed to mean essentially the way of conducting national and private business during peace. The notion of an explicitly American way of war, as a subset of the more general American way of life, is much more the preserve of creative historians and political scientists. See especially Russell F. Weigley, *The American Way of War: A History of United States Military Strategy and Policy* (New York: Macmillan Publishing Co., Inc., 1973).

8. In fact, Americans have been at war frequently and, sometimes, for considerable periods (as during the Indian wars or in the action against *insurrectos* and Moros in the Philippines); and war can be found somewhere on earth at virtually any time. The issue here, then, is not a matter of fact but the way of perceiving events, which affects what one is likely to wish to do about them.

9. Memorandum, by Brig Gen Edward Lansdale to Deputy Secretary Gilpatric, 10 May 1961; memorandum by Lansdale to McGeorge Bundy, 12 May 1961; Robert W. Komer, "A Doctrine of Deterrence for SEA—The Conceptual Framework," Southeast Asia folder, 1/20/61–5/31/61, Regional Security File, Kennedy Papers.

10. Memorandum by George C. McGhee to Walt Rostow, 28 July 1961; and draft paper, "Security in Southeast Asia," 27 July 1961, Southeast Asia General folder, 7/25/61–7/28/61, National Security File, Kennedy Papers; memorandum, by McGeorge Bundy to the president, 4 April 1961, Bundy folder, 2/61–4/61, Staff Memoranda File, President's Office File, Kennedy Papers.

11. McGhee to Rostow memo, "Security in Southeast Asia."

12. Memorandum by William P. Bundy to Sullivan, McNaughton, and Yarmolinsky, 2 March 1964, Vietnam Memos, vol. 4 (2/64–3/64), Memo 94, Vietnam Country File, Johnson Papers; cable from N.E.S. to Harriman and Hilsman, 18 February 1964, Vietnam Cables, vol. 4 (2/64–3/64), Cable 5, Vietnam Country File, National Security File, Johnson Papers.

13. John McCone, "Highlights of Discussions in Saigon, 18–20 December 1963," 21 December 1963, Vietnam Memos, vol. 2 (12/63–1/64), Memo 141, Vietnam Country File, National Security File, Johnson Papers.

14. Walt Rostow, "Guerrilla Warfare in the Underdeveloped Areas," speech at US Army Special Warfare School, Fort Bragg, North Carolina, 28 June 1961, Army 1961 folder, Departments and Agencies Files, President's Office Files, Kennedy Papers.

15. Joint State-Defense-AID cable to the American embassy, Saigon, 23 March 1964, Vietnam Cables, vol. 6 (3/64), Cable 105, Vietnam Country File, National Security File, Johnson Papers.

16. Gen William C. Westmoreland, *Report on the War in Vietnam as of 30 June 1968*, sec. 2, Report on Operations in South Vietnam January 1964–June 1968 (Washington, D. C.: Government Printing Office, 1968), 89–91, 95, 97.

17. Memorandum by Robert S. McNamara to the president, 20 July 1965, McGeorge Bundy Memos to President, vol. 12 (July 1965), Memo 38, Aides Files, National Security Files, Johnson Papers.

18. Among articles concerning Linebacker II, see John L. Frisbee, "Not with a Whimper, but a Bang," *Air Force Magazine* 56 (March 1973): 5–6; John C. Meyer, "The Eleven Day Air Campaign," *Air Force Policy Letter for Commanders,* no. 6 (June 1973): 22–25; James R. McCarthy and George B. Allison, *Linebacker II: A View from the Rock* (Washington, D.C.: US Air Force [Southeast Asia Monograph Series], 1979).

19. Karen J. Winkler, "Documenting Vietnam Presents Problems for Archivists and Researchers," *The Chronicle of Higher Education* 27, no. 8 (19 October 1983): 5 and 11.

20. The need to be ready for a war because of its brevity and its gravity is suggested in Henry H. Arnold, "Science and Air Power," *Air Affairs* 1, no. 2:184-95. Also pertinent are Arnold, "Air Power from Peace," *National Geographic* 89 (February 1946): 137–93; Carl Spaatz, "Air Power in the Atomic Age," *Collier's* 116 (8 December 1945): 11–12.

21. An important illustration of thinking among Truman's advisers is George Elsey, manuscript memorandum, April 1948, Western Union folder, Papers of George Elsey (Harry S. Truman Library).

22. See Dwight D. Eisenhower, *Crusade in Europe* (Garden City, N.Y.: Doubleday & Co., Inc., 1948).

23. See Maurice Matloff, "The 90-Division Gamble," in Kent Roberts Greenfield, ed., *Command Decisions* (Washington, D.C.: US Army Office of Military History, 1960).

24. An obvious example is David Rees, *Korea: The Limited War* (New York: St. Martin's Press, 1964).

25. Raymond Aron, *The Century of Total War* (Boston: Beacon Press, 1954).

26. Edwin Bickford Hooper, Dean C. Allard, and Oscar P. Fitzgerald, *The United States Navy in the Vietnam Conflict,* vol. 1, *The Setting of the Stage to 1959* (Washington, D.C.: Department of the Navy, 1976), 311.

27. Ibid., 312.

28. George Herring, *America's Longest War* (New York: John Wiley, 1979), 270.

29. "Untold Story of the Road to War in Vietnam," *U.S. News and World Report,* 10 October 1983, 1VN-24VN. The quotation is on 16VN.

30. Summers, *On Strategy,* points to the distinction, emphasizing the need to retain clarity of purpose and strength of commitment.

31. The term "intangible complexity" comes from Homer Lea, *The Valor of Ignorance* (New York: Macmillan Publishing Co., Inc., 1909).

32. The Confederacy may be an exception to this process of simplification in the Civil War, largely because the specific political objective of separation tied to the concept of states' rights undermined the potential for a simplifying centralization. However, it is not pertinent here to explore the specific ways in which simplification was achieved in the various wars mentioned.

33. Jack S. Ballard, *Development and Employment of Fixed-Wing Gunships, 1962–1972* (Washington, D.C.: Office of Air Force History, 1982), 256.

34. Jonathan Miller, *The Body Human* (New York: Random House, 1978), 111.

35. Ibid., 99.

36. Ibid., 103.

37. Vietnamese Premier Pham Van Dong is reported to have said: "Waging a war is simple, but running a country is difficult." Quoted in Lee Lescaze, "Journey into an American Nightmare," *Wall Street Journal,* 17 October 1983, 28. Perhaps, to the extent that Americans in the 1960s perceived "nation-building" and "running a country" as means of waging a war (albeit largely a counterinsurgency), they thus made war less simple and more difficult—inappropriately so. As Henry Kissinger suggested toward the end of a fact-finding tour in Central America in 1983, there may very well be problems that cannot be solved by political and economic measures and, also, that can be alleviated by reforms only after certain military preconditions have been achieved.

38. Robert Osgood, *Limited War Revisited* (Boulder, Colo.: Westview Press, 1979), 20. One of the persistent problems in dealing with so-called limited wars is the difference of commitment and intensity depending on the combatants' point of view. The Korean conflict was taken as a limited war by Americans, but not by the Koreans. A similar difficulty exists in assessing Vietnam; it points to the necessity of escaping from US–centered criteria when seeking to comprehend the objective conditions of a conflict.

39. Stephen Peter Rosen, "Vietnam and the American Theory of Limited War," *International Security* 7, no. 2 (Fall 1982): 85.

40. The process of reorganization and efforts toward so-called unification of the armed forces after 1945 reflect the concerns which were largely generated by the new characteristics of modern warfare. See, for example, Paul Y. Hammond, *Organizing for Defense: The American Military Establishment in the Twentieth Century* (Princeton, N.J.: Princeton University Press, 1961).

41. Contemporary periodical coverage of the controversy over General Lavelle's exceeding his orders are: "The Lavelle Case," *Time* 100 (15 September 1972): 20; "Lavelle's Back Flips," *Newsweek* 80 (2 October 1972): 45; "Lavelle's Private War: Unauthorized Bombing Raids," *Time* 99 (26 June 1972): 14; Ward Just, "General Lavelle's Private War," *New Statesman* 84 (22 September 1972): 376; "USAF Closes the Lavelle Case," *Air Force Magazine* 55 (December 1972): 20. The present argument is not to condone General Lavelle's alleged breach of proper authority but only to observe that its consequences were not militarily cataclysmic.

42. It is perhaps ironic that Americans who had so recently heard slogans such as "better dead than Red" and speeches calling on them to "pay any price" and "bear any burden" should have even unintentionally excluded this intensity of motivation when attempting to forecast Hanoi's response to US action in Southeast Asia.

43. Rosen, "Vietnam and the American Theory of Limited War," 83.

44. Ibid., 91.

45. Quoted in U. S. Grant Sharp, *Strategy for Defeat*, 74–75.

46. This principle holds true despite the efforts of Rand and others which suggested that bombing by B-52s discouraged insurgents. For one thing, the assessment of impact on guerrillas came at a time when some US officials denied that the conflict in Vietnam was essentially an insurgency, suggesting that the reference points continued to be in flux. For those who were skeptical of the importance of the guerrillas in the general war effort, an assurance that the B-52s discouraged guerrillas perhaps should have seemed a somewhat technical conclusion with uncertain application to the conflict in progress.

47. The logic here is simple. Recall the notion, "I don't know anything about art, but I know what I like." Without knowing the relevant variables in art in a general sense, one has only one's own unconsciously formed prejudgments as to the nature of what is good in specific forms of art. Challenged by an authority in the field or by differences of viewpoint, as well as by well-organized arguments for a different point of view, the instinctual viewer who "knows what he likes" is thus encouraged to rely deliberately and consciously on the prejudgments which have become his personal tradition or "doctrine." In military matters as in art or anything else, only a doctrine which remains consistent with general terms of argument also shared by adherents of different doctrines has a chance of finding the safe ground between rigidity (born of ignorance) and vacillation (born of the lack of pertinent criteria). It is perhaps instructive and surely interesting that Clausewitz wrote art criticism, fully aware of the tension between the instinctual and analytical realms.

48. Roswell L. Gilpatric, "An Expert Looks at the Joint Chiefs," *New York Times Magazine*, 29 March 1964, 11, 71–72.

49. Memorandum by McGeorge Bundy to the president, 13 August 1964, McGeorge Bundy, Meetings on Southeast Asia, vol. 1, Memo 4, Aides Files, National Security Files, Johnson Papers.

50. Westmoreland, *Report on the War in Vietnam*, 16.

51. Senate, Preparedness Investigating Subcommittee, Committee on Armed Services, *Hearings, Air War Against North Vietnam*, 90th Cong., 1st sess., 28–29 August 1967, 387.

52. Ibid., 425.

53. Warren I. Susman, ed., *Culture and Commitment* (New York: George Braziller, 1973).

54. It is interesting, in retrospect, to compare the recommendations of some of strategic air power's strongest proponents with some of what happened subsequently during the Vietnam War. In 1964, after his retirement as commander of SAC, Gen Thomas Power postulated the benefits of warning the Communists in North Vietnam to cease supporting the guerrillas in the South. "If the Communists had failed to heed our warning and continued to support the rebels," he added, "we would have gone through with the threatened attack" on a carefully chosen installation. "And if this act of 'persuasive deterrence' had not sufficed, we would have threatened the destruction of another critical target and, if necessary, would have destroyed it also." This approach was expected to end the war "within a few days and with a minimum of force." Thomas S. Power, *Design for Survival* (New York: Coward–McCann, Inc., 1964), 224–25. Although one could debate the choice of targets, the basically progressive or escalatory prospect posed by General Power was not without similarity to President Johnson's advisers' envisioning of Hanoi's important installations as hostages to American bombing.

55. Kissinger's remarks appear in the US State Department's *Bulletin* 68, no. 750 (8 January 1973): 33–41.

56. William W. Momyer, *Air Power in Three Wars* (n. p. 1978), 243.

57. See, for example, Gareth Porter, *A Peace Denied: The United States, Vietnam, and the Paris Agreement* (Bloomington: Indiana University Press, 1976).

58. See Daniel S. Papp, *Vietnam: The View from Moscow, Peking, Washington* (Jefferson, N.C.: McFarland & Co., Inc., 1981).

59. The tactical fighter experimental (TFX) project, which yielded the F-111, is a widely mentioned case. The core of the problem was attempting to develop a single craft to serve the purposes of the several services. The McNamara team in the Defense Department was attracted by the hope of cost reductions if essentially the same aircraft could be used by more than one service, as a larger total purchase would result in lower unit cost. But at the heart of managing this problem was the role of civilian experts—the "whiz kids" as they were known by friends and detractors alike. Should the services have modifications and compromises in equipment imposed on them by civilians who often lacked any personal military experience? Still, even this controversial process produced an aircraft which had substantial versatility and an interesting range of possible uses. Various reports and studies suggest merits in the aircraft and its use. See, for example, Harris J. Taylor, "The F-111 in Southeast Asia" (unpublished professional study no. 4248, Air War College, Air University, 1971); Jock P. Patterson, "The F-111 in Combat" (unpublished research study, Air War College, Air University, 1977); Wayne Thomas, "Whispering Death: The F-111 in Southeast Asia," *Air Force Magazine* 56 (February 1973): 22–27; John Francis, Jr., "The F-111: A Pilot's View," *Air Force Magazine* 54 (April 1971): 30–39; "The F-111 Shows Bombing Support Strength in Indochina," *Aviation Week and Space Technology* 98 (30 April 1973): 88–89.

60. Bruce Miroff, *Pragmatic Illusions, The Presidential Politics of John Kennedy* (New York: David McKay Co., Inc., 1976), 5.

61. Marvin Kalb and Elie Abel, *Roots of Involvement* (New York: Norton, 1971), 111.

62. Miroff, *Pragmatic Illusions, 4*, 8.

63. Earnest Albert Hooten, *Why Men Behave like Apes and Vice Versa, or Body and Behavior* (Princeton, N.J.: Princeton University Press, 1941), 13, 161.

64. David M. Robb and J. J. Garrison, *Art in the Western World* (New York: Harper & Row, 1935).

65. Drew Middleton, *Crossroads of Modern Warfare* (Garden City, N.Y.: Doubleday & Co., Inc., 1983), 234.

Index

Fechet, Maj Gen James E.: 9
Felt, Adm Harry D.: 33, 59
Firepower, reliance on: 4
Fixed-wing gunships (see Aerial fire support):
70, 85, 108, 125, 131, 142
Flexible response: 15
Forrestal, Michael V.: 59, 60, 62, 63, 109

G

Gavin, Lt Gen James M.: 16
Gilpatric, Roswell: 16, 52, 54, 135, 162, 181,
182
Goodhand, Brig Gen O. Glenn: 29, 91
Greene, Gen Wallace M., Jr.: 82, 148
Guevara, Ernesto "Che": 69

H

Hanoi (government of the Democratic Republic
of Vietnam): 2, 59, 62, 63, 64, 103, 106,
164, 165, 169, 172, 177, 178, 182, 184
Harkins, Gen Paul D.: 34, 35, 59, 136
Helicopters: 36–37, 76–78, 84, 92–93, 112,
114ff, 116
Herrington, Stuart A.: 92
HH-3: 115–17
HH-43: 115, 116
HH-53: 115, 116
Hilsman, Roger: 157
Ho Chi Minh Trail: 73, 103, 128, 135
Hopwood, Maj Gen Lloyd P.: 16
Howze, Lt Gen Hamilton: 31, 32
Hughes, Sen Harold: 88
Humphrey, Hubert H. (US vice-president): 86

I

Interdiction: 105, 106, 128, 131, 145ff
Interservice rivalry: 1–2, 6, 27ff, 32, 36, 82,
156, 175

J

Johnson, Gen Harold K.: 31, 39, 147, 183
Johnson, Lyndon B. (US president): 1–2, 61,
62, 74, 78, 86, 90, 141, 148, 175, 179
Johnson, Robert H.: 58
Johnson, U. Alexis: 134
Joint Chiefs of Staff (JCS): 33, 55, 57, 62, 87,
88, 129, 134, 164, 169, 170, 178, 181, 182
Jorden, William J.: 124

K

KC-130: 84
Kennedy, John F. (US president): 2, 18, 21, 69,
90, 123, 134, 135, 163
Kennedy, Robert F.: 52, 53
Kham Duc: 85, 141–42
Khe Sanh: 4, 42, 70, 77–83, 141, 142, 143,
148, 185
Khmer Rouge: 104
Kinnard, Brig Gen Douglas: 119
Kinnard, Lt Gen Harry W.O.: 31, 76, 77, 147
Kissinger, Henry A. (Sec State): 15, 184
Komer, Robert: 52, 162, 163
Korean War: 5, 12, 14, 22, 29, 46, 159, 167,
168, 173

L

Laird, Melvin (Sec Def): 129
Lansdale, Maj Gen Edward: 54, 162
Laos: 18, 28, 51, 53, 57, 59, 63, 73, 88, 89,
104, 105, 109, 112, 128, 131, 136, 147
Lavelle, Gen John D.: 88, 176
LeMay, Gen Curtis E.: 19, 21, 31, 35–36, 53,
55, 126
Lemnitzer, Gen Lyman: 55, 56
Lemos, Rear Adm W. E.: 86–87
Lon Nol, Gen: 104
Lovett, Robert D. (Sec Def): 30
Luftwaffe: 12

M

MacArthur, Gen Douglas: 37, 40
McChristian, Maj Gen Joseph A.: 107, 108
McCone, John A. (Dir CIA): 163, 179
McConnell, Gen John P.: 93, 127, 128, 136
McDonald, Adm Thomas D.: 54
McGhee, George: 162
McNamara, Robert S. (Sec Def): 18–19, 21, 23,
34, 53, 60, 61, 63, 124, 128, 134, 140, 146,
147, 165, 170, 178, 186
McNaughton, John T.: 64, 86
Mahan, Alfred Thayer: 7, 10
Malayan insurgency: 162, 170
Marshall, Gen George C.: 10
Massive retaliation: 15
Military Assistance Command, Vietnam
(MACV): 34, 35, 36, 73, 89, 107, 130, 135,
136, 138

Military Assistance Command Vietnam Studies and Operations Group (MACSOG): 110, 112

Mitchell, Gen William "Billy": 7–8, 11

Momyer, Gen William W.: 17, 22–23, 31, 42, 46, 74, 76, 82, 130, 140, 184

Moore, Maj Gen Joseph H.: 36

Moore, Col Orin H.: 17

Moorer, Adm Thomas H.: 87, 88

N

National Security Act of 1947: 14, 29, 88

Nitze, Paul (Sec Navy): 16, 54

Nixon, Richard M. (US president): 2, 74, 86, 112, 177

Nolting, Frederick E., Jr.: 135

Nuclear war, fear of: 14, 167, 176, 183

O

O'Donnell, Maj Gen Emmett E., Jr.: 33, 34, 135

Oden, Gen Delk: 31

Operation Attleboro: 118

Operation Cedar Falls: 81, 118, 140, 145

Operation Commando Hunt: 131

Operation Farm Gate: 35, 59, 116

Operation Linebacker I: 102

Operation Linebacker II: 22, 165, 184, 185

Operation Nathan Hale: 93

Operation Niagara I: 79

Operation Niagara II: 83

Operation Ranch Hand: 132–138

Operation Rolling Thunder: 64, 89, 101, 165

Operation Tiger Hound: 107

Operations Plan 34a: 64

OV-1: 107, 109

OV-10: 110

P

Pacific Air Forces (PACAF): 35, 40, 129, 135

Page, Brig Gen Jerry D.: 20–21

Pentomic Division: 75, 76

Powell, Brig Gen Edwin L.: 77

Project Jason: 146–47

R

Radford, Adm Arthur D.: 30

RB-57: 107

RC-47: 107

RF-4C: 107

RF-101: 101, 107

Ridgway, Maj Gen Matthew B.: 75

Rogers, Gen Bernard: 118

Rosson, Lt Gen William B.: 42, 55

Rostow, Walt W.: 50–51, 54, 58, 164, 178, 182, 186

Rusk, Dean (Sec State): 50, 53, 135, 186

Russell, Sen Richard: 148

S

SA-7: 92

Saigon (government of the Republic of Vietnam): 17, 38, 50, 92, 135, 171, 172

Schriever, Gen Bernard: 21

SH-3: 117

Seamans, Robert (Sec AF): 88, 129

Search and rescue: 70, 114ff

Seneff, Maj Gen George P.: 31, 76, 77

Seventh Air Force (USAF): 40, 43, 79, 108, 128, 131

Seversky, Alexander P. de: 10–13

Sharp, Adm U. S. Grant: 39, 61, 136

Simmons, Capt John C.: 126

Skyspot, Combat (radar): 89, 141

Smith, Maj Gen Dale O.: 16–17

Son Tay raid: 116, 185

Song Be: 77

Special Warfare Center (USAF): 55

Special Warfare Training Center (Fort Bragg): 53, 56

Starry, Gen Donn A.: 23, 145

Strategic objectives: 169, 171–75

Sullivan, William: 136

Sweeney, Gen Walter C., Jr.: 126, 127

Symington, Stuart (Sec AF): 14, 87, 88, 105

T

T-28: 60, 126

Tactical Air Control (TACC): 41, 43–44

Taylor, Gen Maxwell D.: 15, 20, 54, 61, 63, 74–75, 124, 170, 182, 186

Technological innovation: 6, 8, 12, 101ff, 106, 123–25, 146, 159, 160

Tet offensive (1968): 78, 83, 85, 130, 161

Thailand: 33, 37

Thanh Hoa Bridge: 101ff

Thieu, Nguyen Van (President, Republic of Vietnam): 166

Thurmond, Sen J. Strom: 81

Tompkins, Maj Gen Rathvon McC.: 82

Tonkin, Gulf of: 63, 165

Truman, Harry S. (US president): 14, 166
Twining, Gen Nathan F.: 16, 30, 139

U

UH-1: 115, 142
UH-2: 117

V

Van Fleet, Gen James A.: 56
Vandenberg, Gen Hoyt S.: 159
Vietcong: 5, 17, 23, 34, 50, 79, 81, 86, 92,
    103, 106, 107, 124, 127, 134, 136, 140,
    163, 165
Vietnam Air Force, Republic of: 38, 41–42, 174
Vietnamization: 112, 113

W

Weigley, Russell F.: 4
Westmoreland, Gen William C.: 36–39, 61,
    73–79, 82, 90, 91, 101, 103, 136, 139, 141,
    146, 164, 182
Weyand, Gen Frederick C.: 5
Wheeler, Gen Earle E.: 19, 59, 61, 78, 104
White, Gen Thomas D.: 18
Wild Weasels: 106
Williams, Gen Robert R.: 29, 30, 91
Wilson, Charles E. (Sec Def): 14
Woodring, Harry (Sec War): 10

Z

Zuckert, Eugene (Sec AF): 21–22